Derek Jewell has written about and broadcast on popular music for many years, notably as jazz and popular music critic of *The Sunday Times* (from 1963) and as deviser and presenter of the weekly *Sounds Interesting* show on Radio 3 (1972–79). His much-acclaimed biography, *Duke: A Portrait of Duke Ellington*, appeared in 1977, following the publication of two novels, *Sellout* and *Come In Number One, Your Time Is Up*. He has also edited and written parts of two other books, *Alamein and the Desert War*, and *Man and Motor: The 20th-Century Love Affair*. After a career in full-time journalism, he has spent the past decade in the management of newspapers, book publishing and other communications businesses.

Also by Derek Jewell in Sphere Books:

DUKE: A PORTRAIT OF DUKE ELLINGTON

The Popular Voice

A musical record of the 60s and 70s

DEREK JEWELL

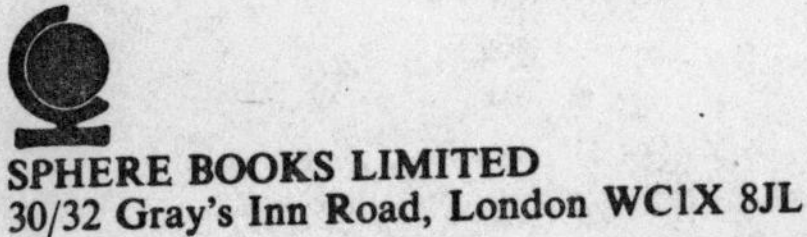

SPHERE BOOKS LIMITED
30/32 Gray's Inn Road, London WC1X 8JL

First published in Great Britain by André Deutsch Ltd 1980

Published by Sphere Books Ltd 1981

TRADE
MARK

Set in Imprint

Printed and bound in Great Britain by
Cox & Wyman Ltd, Reading

All the new groups have given it to pop music. More honesty than it ever had.

Paul McCartney, 1963

I find it difficult to know the place to draw the line where jazz begins and ends. It all depends on how it *sounds*.

Duke Ellington, 1964

I believe the best results come from doing what you know and like. I'm a jazz musician, and this is really my excuse for existence.

Ronnie Scott, 1969

When I was ten I found my guitar was a better way of communicating than words. I still feel that way.

Mike Oldfield, 1973

Let's be realistic. My children are going to see rough times. You and me, we've had the best of it.

Bing Crosby, 1976

Contents

Author's Note

Most of the articles in this book first appeared in *The Sunday Times*, and I am grateful for that newspaper's agreement to reprint them. The exceptions are the interview with Ornette Coleman, first printed in *Encounter*; the profiles of Cleo Laine (from *In Britain* magazine) and Nina Simone (from *The Times*); and the articles on Benny Goodman and the Modern Jazz Quartet, which were written for programmes at concerts presented by Robert Paterson and Harold Davison.

I have warmly to thank a host of people involved with the making of music – from artists to fellow enthusiasts – who have played a part in sustaining my writing over two decades or more. Their names are found throughout these pages, and especially in the first two chapters. I am also indebted to my editors, Faith Evans and Genevieve Clarke, and to Carole Haynes and Robert Ducas for their help in the preparation of this book. There would have been no book at all without the encouragement and care given down the years by many *Sunday Times* colleagues, including Harold Evans, Jack Lambert, Godfrey Smith, John Whitley, John Peter, Oscar Turnill and Michael Rand.

Acknowledgements

The author and publisher would like to thank the following music publishers concerned for permission to reproduce quotations from the following works: *All Things Must Pass* by George Harrison, Copyright © Harrisongs Limited; *Close to the Edge* by Jon Anderson, Copyright © 1972 Rondor Music (London) Ltd, Rondor House, 10a Parsons Green, London, SW6 4TW/Topographic Music Ltd; *I've Got a Girl in Kalamazoo* by Mack Gordon (music) and Harry Warren (words), Copyright © 1942 Bregman Vocco & Conn Inc./Chappell Music Ltd; *Jesus Christ Superstar* by Tim Rice and Andrew Lloyd Webber, Copyright © 1970 Leeds Music Ltd; *Joseph and the Amazing Technicolor Dreamcoat* by Tim Rice and Andrew Lloyd Webber, Copyright © Novello and Co. Ltd; *Lilli Marlene* by Schultze, Leip and Connor, Copyright © 1944 by Appolo Verlag (Germany)/Peter Maurice Music Co. Ltd, 138–140 Charing Cross Road, London WC2 0LD; *Nancy* by Phil Silvers (words) and James Van Heusen (music), Copyright © 1944 Barton Music Corp./Chappell Morris Ltd; *So long, Frank Lloyd Wright* by Paul Simon, Copyright © Pattern Music Ltd; *That Lovely Weekend* by Moira and Ted Heath, Copyright © 1941 Bradbury Wood Ltd/Chappell Music Ltd; *We'll Meet Again* by Ross Parker and Hughie Charles, Copyright © Dash Music Co. Ltd; *We're Gonna Hang out the Washing on the Siegfried Line* by Carr and Kennedy, Copyright © 1939/Peter Maurice Music Co. Ltd; *Whispering Grass* by Fred and Doris Fisher, Copyright © Campbell, Connolly and Co.; *Who?* by Charles Aznavour and Herbert Kretzmer, Copyright © 1964, TRO Essex Music Ltd; *You've Let Yourself Go* (Tu te laisses aller) by Charles Aznavour and Marcel Stellman, Copyright © 1960 France Music Co., Editions Star Music Co./Leeds Music Ltd.

Foreword

For popular music, the 1960s and 1970s were a golden age: the most fascinating, eventful and confusing period of the century. Old heroes were still performing superbly. New heroes arose by the hundreds. More good music was created than ever before and, conversely, more bad music. Adventure, innovation, iconoclasm and outrage were in the air. Above all, there was diversity. At no other time had so many performers offering so many different styles of music found an audience.

The breathtaking diversity of popular music in these two decades was for me the most exciting aspect of a very exciting time, and provides perhaps the most important single reason for producing this book, the contents of which were originally written at various times between 1963 and 1978 as reviews, interviews and profiles, mostly for *The Sunday Times*. Such a collection is unlikely to give a definitive and comprehensive portrait of the period. The idea, rather, is to reflect how incredibly varied popular music was in those years, and to recall the distinctive flavours of an astonishing musical era as it was taking place. I've indulged in no second-guessing, no hindsight, no wart-removing. The judgments are what they are, and so are the inconsistencies where they exist.

No moment of blinding revelation turned me into a writer on popular music – it was a therapeutic activity, a hobby, not a career. The process was gradual and, in retrospect, inevitable. I grew up in an age when music was everywhere around one – on radio, records, platforms and screens. You couldn't escape it whether you liked it or not, and to write or talk about it seemed as natural as commenting on movies or politics or books or sport. After early exposure to dance bands, jazz, blues, folk and singers like Peggy Lee and Frank Sinatra, I developed a taste for good musicals, good rock and much else besides. That broadening of taste, as popular music expanded its range, brought me more delight than doubt. Those who stuck with one style or another, who rejected 'rock' or 'jazz' or 'folk' or whatever, missed a great deal. My touchstone is Duke Ellington's characteristic remark that there are only two kinds of music: good and bad. In the 1960s and 1970s, you *had* to listen with an open mind, and to beware of sliding artists into easy pigeonholes.

What gave these decades so interesting and so eventful a character? First, and inescapably, the evolution of rock 'n' roll. Elvis Presley ignited the revolution in popular musical taste, especially among the young, in the 1950s. With the arrival of The Beatles and others, rock 'n' roll – sometimes spontaneous and vital, sometimes boring and crude – developed into a music of such various complexity under its portmanteau description 'rock', that successive generations were able to identify with one or other of its many styles. Nor was the identification only musical; rock was attitude, fashion, cult and sometimes near-religion.

Yet to talk only of rock 'n' roll's convolutions in the past twenty years would be to give a sadly limited view of the period's riches. Rock did not emerge or exist in a vacuum. It was (and is) part of the evolution of twentieth-century popular music, not somehow separate from it. It wouldn't have happened at all without blues, rhythm and blues and American country music from which it derived – and they themselves were just some of the many different popular forms which flowed from the meeting of European and African musical cultures in the United States during the nineteenth century. (It's that outflowing, a turbulent river of sound, to which I refer when I talk about our century's 'popular music'; its currents may often be distinctive, but their source is the same.) So, even when rock 'n' roll became pre-eminent in the 1960s, the older musical forms didn't die. Jazz, folk, blues, Latin-American, country-and-western, ballad singers, Broadway musicals and all the rest survived, often in distinctive sub-divisions too, commanding sizeable audiences and – more importantly – interacting with rock and with each other.

These interactions were another reason for the peculiar magnetism of the post-1960 years. Not that musical fusions in the popular field were new; they'd been happening throughout the century. Gospel training in black church choirs had influenced the vocal style of singers, like Aretha Franklin or Sarah Vaughan, who went on to perform in theatres and clubs. Blues had brushed with jazz and changed it. Popular musicians had continually stolen or adopted European 'classical' forms and melodies. But in the 1960s and 1970s, there were probably more mixed marriages in music than ever before, particularly as rock musicians became more technically skilled. Jazz-rock, as one of these hybrids was loosely called, attracted artists as diverse as Miles Davis and the young bands, Chicago, and Blood, Sweat and Tears. Sometimes the fusion happened deliberately, when jazzmen became tired of playing to small audiences and 'crossed over' into jazz-rock, funk and soul to make more money and reach more ears, doubtless encouraged by managers and record companies. Other jazz-rockers played this way simply because they'd grown up with both rock 'n' roll and jazz in the air around them, and to play an improvised sax solo over a rock beat seemed idiomatically quite natural to them.

Jazz-rock, though, was only one facet of this age of musical fusion. Rock 'n' roll became mixed in with so much more: with folk music and brass bands, with political cabaret songs and the distinctive sounds of India, with urban blues and country and western, with European classical music and space technology, with medieval ballads and Broadway shows. The terminology invented to cope with the resultant musical and cultural gallimaufry reflected the confusion of riches which marked these years. Folk rock, art rock, pomp rock, country rock, glam rock, glitter rock. Disco, punk, New Wave, heavy metal. Pop, teenybop, bubble-gum. Space music, rock opera, singer-songwriters, funk, soul. New Wave was a wry phrase. It meant the 'free jazz' of Ornette Coleman, Albert Ayler and company in the 1960s; ten years or so later it was in part a euphemism attempting to give respectability to punk, and beyond that a loose description of some artists who defied easy categorization and who sometimes had genuine talent. Labels were misleading in a period when they flourished as never before, when record companies ruthlessly carved up the market into segments and sub-segments according to class, taste, sex, age, skin colouring and much more.

The terminology of popular music is a maze. Meanings change; no authorities on usage exist; little wonder that newspapers, magazines, TV and radio employ the language of modern music so loosely. 'Rock 'n' roll' for some means the fairly crude music used for dancing or as general leisure background produced in the immediate wake of Elvis Presley; others use it to signify the very broad spectrum of youth music, some simple, some very sophisticated, covering the whole of the 1960s and 1970s. 'Jazz' means Louis Armstrong to a multitude of people who would be puzzled by the electronic excursions of Chick Corea and who would dive for the exit in two minutes if exposed to particular passages of Ornette Coleman.

Re-reading the articles in this book, I can see the terminology which I employed down the years changing, as definitions were revised and new words were invented. 'Pop' (even 'beat') was once used to describe The Beatles. Then, as their music and that of others grew more complex, more serious, more loaded with social, political, drug and mystical references, 'rock' tended to be set in contra-distinction to 'pop' by the young pundits who found their platform in journals like *Melody Maker*, *Rolling Stone* and *New Musical Express*. No one has ever satisfactorily *defined* 'rock', any more than 'jazz' has been defined satisfactorily – you suggest its properties, rather than pin it down firmly – but the word carried overtones of toughness, protest, politics, seriousness and sometimes of sophisticated and skilful musicianship compared with the frothy, easy-listening and more childish connotations of 'pop'.

Towards the end of the 1960s and thereafter, rock and pop were used as separate terms by some commentators and interchangeably by others. 'Rock' became increasingly an art form as the 1970s arrived, with elaborately produced studio albums and quasi-orchestral writing making full use of synthesizers and the growth of 'supergroups' like Led Zeppelin, Yes and Genesis. Yet 'pop' still dominated the singles charts, with artists like T-Rex or David Cassidy. Other performers – say, David Bowie or Elton John – succeeded with both albums and singles, breaking out of category. Christmas records could defy the rules for other months. A pipe band playing an old hymn tune might suddenly catch the tide of popular taste; so might a reissue of an old swing band hit. Punk rock and disco arrived in the later 1970s further to confuse the scene.

All this only begins to suggest the changes of popular fashion and the continual flux of its vocabulary. Amidst the turmoil, it was still possible for record companies to market different kinds of music to different kinds of consumers very successfully. But popular music is remarkable for the way it *can't* be expressed only in terms of commercial formulae. That's because it is both an industry and, sometimes, an art: because 'manufactured' artists can achieve major success, and so can other artists who just 'happen' with an idiosyncratic and unpremeditated style.

Popular music can also work on several levels. It can be intended purely for dancing, for entertainment or for background; but it may have purposes far more serious. That rock after the early 1960s came increasingly to deal with social and political concerns – The Beatles and Bob Dylan provided much of the impetus – was one of its most compelling characteristics. In this, it was partly a mirror of its age, reflecting revolutions of taste, wars, changing public and domestic fashions. It also helped to fashion the age, however, and popular music has always been so used – as a spur to make war or peace, make love, make happy, make mistakes, make laws, make almost anything happen.

So the sixties and seventies gave expanding dimensions to popular music's 'social' role (and bred a new kind of sociological critic too), whilst at the same time continuing a pattern which had always existed. The blues had been a social and political language for years. Woody Guthrie had been a protest singer. Billie Holiday had sung about lynchings in the South ('Strange Fruit') and Bing Crosby about the Depression ('Buddy Can You Spare A Dime'). Cole Porter had looked at prostitution ('Love For Sale'). For all of its innovations and extravagances in the past twenty years – from the unending quest for ear-splitting volume in concert halls to the mixing of sound with bizarrely hypnotic light shows – rock couldn't escape many debts to the past.

And the next twenty years? Predictions about popular music range from the pessimistically limited to the optimistically expansive. The concentration of media interest in the later 1970s on 'disco' and, in Britain especially, on 'punk' would suggest a future of increasing limitations. Discotheques had been around for many years; but the emergence of a specific genre of disco music, gushing everywhere after the movie *Saturday Night Fever*, was something quite different. More accurately, one should say genres of disco music. Its repetitious rhythms and phrasing may be a common denominator between styles, but for its multi-millions of consumers, disco spawned a mass of sub-divisions: 'pure' disco, jazz disco, funk disco, gay disco, etc. Major artists often slid in a disco-beat number on albums to ensure radio plays, especially in America, where disco stations soon won large audiences in competition with the existing specialist stations for rock, soul, country and the rest. Disco has been well done and badly done, and it's here to stay for some years yet – especially for dancing to, but perhaps decreasingly as all-purpose 'wallpaper' for all-day radio.

'Punk' rock was even less predictable. In Britain, it seemed at first (in 1976–7) to be a reaction against supergroups, against the life style of super-rich rock stars and the sophisticated technicalities of their music. It was crude, intentionally shocking, revolutionary, stripped-down, nihilistic, 'political', and was explained by some sociologists as the simple frustration of the young working-class unemployed, a derisory scream at bourgeois values. Since its birth it has changed, continued to change, has won champions and enemies of all classes, has grown both more sophisticated and more crude, has been called 'New Wave' as well as punk, and has left the rock scene in a state of flux still unresolved.

Yet the post-1977 obsession of so many commentators with disco and punk was sad, because popular music still retained its variety. Cleo Laine and Genesis, Frank Sinatra and Bette Midler, Billy Joel and Abba, Elton John and Neil Diamond, Weather Report and Mike Oldfield, Kate Bush and Barry Manilow could command huge audiences for concerts or in record shops. Jazzmen played in pubs and clubs. 'Nostalgia' acts, from Manhattan Transfer to the Pasadena Roof Orchestra, flourished. There was country or folk, ragtime or reggae, style after style competing, either expanding or fighting to hang on.

I suspect that the present abundance of popular styles is likely to continue, and I foresee that popular taste will become increasingly catholic. Of course, rock and pop remain primarily music for the young, just as jazz concerts by Woody Herman or Count Basie still draw mostly middle-aged audiences. All kinds of music have their specialist, inturned fans. But these easy assumptions are less true than they used to be.

Paul Simon, for example, could attract an audience of a very broad age span (eighteen to sixty) to concerts in the mid-1970s. So could Buddy Rich in 1979. What kind of audience will they – and Billy Joel, Joni Mitchell, David Bowie, Joan Armatrading or Weather Report – be entertaining in the mid-1980s, assuming they're still performing? Certain popular performers throughout the century have retained a following which has grown older with them, and this might well happen with rock too. Obviously, people won't be as enslaved by rock when they're forty rather than twenty, but some artists carry their followers with them. A glance at the audiences for Yes in 1978 suggested that many of their fans had moved from eighteen to twenty-eight during the band's ten-year existence. Similarly record re-issues can win new young audiences for styles of the past.

Such speculation encompasses what one music publisher described to me as the nostalgia factor. Most people have an instinctive liking for the music which was the style in their youth, which is why revivals of thirties' foxtrots or forties' Glenn Miller or fifties' Elvis always find an audience. The Beatles and Beach Boys are already 'nostalgia' music for many forty-year-olds and – discounting the people whose arteries harden so rapidly that they just stop listening to anything – those who retain their liking for good popular music will in the 1980s have a bewildering variety of 1960s and 1970s vintages to choose from. The best, whatever its style, will probably retain its currency through the next decade and beyond. It's just as certain, however, that what is regarded as adventurous today will come to be thought of as middle-of-the-road or (to use music-paper jargon) hip easy listening tomorrow. The popular music industry, like the rag trade, depends upon launching new fashions continually, and fresh waves of critics have got to reject what went before to justify their presence on the scene when they arrive. Epithets like 'progressive' will be tossed around, although I've never seen 'progress' in art as *necessarily* concomitant with quality. You don't discard Shakespeare or Dickens, Ellington or Gershwin just because natural causes have halted their 'progress'. They are what they are; great art can achieve the kind of perfection which makes 'progress' an irrelevant word.

Mostly, you'll read in this book about artists whose various approaches to perfection I've immensely enjoyed. Paradoxically, given that I'm so wary of pigeonholing, I've had to put the pieces into loose groupings to give the book a semblance of organization. But the compartments keep breaking down, especially when an article referring to two performances by dissimilar artists (say, Yes and Stan Getz) has been reprinted in full. Often, articles have been cut for this book – on grounds of length, because some detail seems now irrelevant, or because one artist is worth recalling from a column, another not. Within each chapter, the order of articles is chronological.

As no claim for comprehensiveness is made, so there's no intention either to prove one's 'rightness' or 'wrongness' in judgments on artists. If I'm delighted to have watched the development of Tim Rice and Andrew Lloyd Webber from early days (see page 36), I smile with awkward embarrassment at other judgments I've made, beginning with The Beatles in the first article of all. 'For although they are probably big (and good) enough to survive the demise of the "beat" vogue, they know how cold the wind cuts around Liverpool's Pier Head.' In retrospect that conclusion smacks of praising with faint damns.

Sometimes, although not always consciously, I've found myself suspicious of or even completely opposed to the vogues of the moment. The publicity and hype mills of the music industry often grind exceeding small talents into very large bags of self-raising flour, so that scepticism in the observer is as vital as enthusiasm. The extravagances, follies and hypocrisy of modern popular music have also at times been off-putting. In the 1960s, rock idols had a duty to tell their fans that acid would ruin them. By and large, they didn't; they left the drugs myth unchallenged, even when they weren't takers. All kinds of stars shrug off the responsibility that goes with power. They are wrong. The extremes of punk are not for me, either. The history of popular music suggests, however, that it goes through traumas from time to time, and you need to keep a sense of humour and perspective. Recalling the past helps. 'Merely a raucous and inarticulate shouting of hoarse-throated instruments, with each player trying to outdo his fellows in fantastic cacophony.' That was one Sigmund Spaeth in 1928 denying that jazz was music; and it was Ellington and Armstrong he referred to.

When in doubt, as I have often been, I've tried to be on the side of the musicians – I mean those who play most skilfully and seem to me to perform most sincerely. For all the hype, the marketing and commercialism, popular music is still primarily *music*. Maybe much of it is meant to be consumed like cornflakes; but it reaches its heights when all the other *raisons d'être* are transformed by elements of artistry which can reasonably be assessed in the same way as with any other kind of music – memorable melody, perhaps, or striking lyrics, or surprising harmony, or inspired production, or a personal performance which is exceptional in feeling, aptness or technique. I've found those elements somewhere in virtually every kind of popular music; without them, the appetite for it would have died long ago.

DEREK JEWELL
May 1979

Chapter One

Some are Special 1963-70

For everyone who listens to music, there are special artists: the ones you enjoy more, whose performances you hate to miss, whose records you play over and over again, or who in ways other than musical become entangled with your life. The people in the first two chapters of this book are of that kind for me. I have been especially fascinated by them or their music at various stages in their careers between 1963 and 1978 or, more sadly, after their deaths. Their names are not intended to be a short list of 'the greatest', although genius or high talent gives each of them that special quality, but they surely adumbrate the rich variety of music to be heard in our time.

To find Duke Ellington, Charlie Parker, The Beatles and Louis Armstrong here is perhaps not surprising. Armstrong was an early hero, Parker a shattering musical experience. Ellington became, I admit, an obsession. I went to his concerts year after year, interviewed him, was almost always delighted by the music he made and the sentences he spoke. The Beatles I was aware of before they took flight, since I worked in Liverpool for several years until 1962, and the various pieces about them reflect their arrival, their break-up and something of what happened afterwards. Other artists will be less expected. Cleo Laine and John Dankworth I had followed since the early 1950s, always astonished that Cleo hadn't become a major star until, suddenly, she did. Yes seemed to me the best of the 'orchestral' rock bands who emerged in the 1970s and the Rice-Lloyd Webber partnership the kind of happy accident which happens very rarely in a musical generation. I was lucky enough to stumble across them early, hearing their *Joseph and the Amazing Technicolor Dreamcoat* performed at a school concert in 1968. The next decade for them was to be really amazing. Other artists and other music you will find mentioned, too, when they form an interesting or integral part of an article or review – sometimes they're special (as with Stan Getz), sometimes not. There is one special institution covered as well: Ronnie Scott's Club. Where would jazz in London have been without it during the past twenty years? In world terms, even, it must have been seen by countless jazz practitioners and fans as a bright beacon in a naughty world. Within its walls, at both its sites, I have seen more magnificent musicians than in any other single place.

Beatles breaking out

15 SEPTEMBER 1963

By night they flood out into the raw mistral that rips in from Liverpool Bay; over two hundred semi-professional trios and quartets on Merseyside, trailing their electric guitars, drums, voices and amplifiers into cars and vans. From New Brighton Tower to Garston Baths the 'beat' (beat for rhythm, not beatnik) groups thump, shout, kick and tremble in pubs, clubs and church halls.

They make the hearts of promoters, customers, instrument-makers and electricity meter-men smile. This is the nursery of that loosely-named species of pop music, the 'Liverpool sound', whose star pupils, The Beatles, have just received the music industry's most tangible accolade: the *Melody Maker* awards for the top vocal group of the year and the best pop vocal record. Like half of the dozen other award winners they were not even in the mystic selling charts a year ago.

Very few of Merseyside's strivers, and the host of imitators who now rave from Looe to Leith, will finger the crock of gold which The Beatles, a quartet of intelligent, twenty-one to twenty-three-year-old Liverpudlians have discovered. Most groups are mere copyists, lacking talent or managerial expertise.

But the crock of gold – for The Beatles around £3,000 a week – still lures the seekers. Even if they miss it, *la vita*, at £40 and upwards a one-night stand, is still *dolce*; while the tonsils last.

Meanwhile the posters throughout Britain shout the names of those who are not yet as automatically on the disc-jockey's lists as The Beatles; Billy J. Kramer and the Dakotas, Gerry (Marsden) and The Pacemakers, The Searchers, and a handful of others. Their names are either palsied puns – Rory Storm and The Hurricanes, The Fourmost – or simply bizarre – The Spidermen, The Mind-Benders, The Undertakers. This is the language of the 'beat' wave which dominates popular music.

As music, it is vigorous, aggressive, uncompromising and boringly stereotyped. It is exaggeratedly rhythmic, high-pitched, thunderously-amplified, full of wild, insidious harmonies. It scalds over the listener as the screams of its devotees scald back at its performers.

There is nothing exceptionally novel about it; the 'new' music is only a minor variation on an old theme. Its roots are in the mid-fifties, when rock-and-roll devastated the ranks of soft-centred croonerdom. 'Rock' was emasculated Negro rhythm-and-blues music; today's 'beat' has, at its best, put some of the guts, rawness and home-made quality back into British rock-and-roll.

Although there is no pat explanation for Liverpool's gift of early impetus to this music in Britain, there are many clues. It is a big, in-drawn city, sustaining its own self-centred life. It has a tradition of home-brewed entertainment, based on a rash of clubs which thrive, too, in its hinterland. The opportunities for semi-pros are immense, and its outflow of entertainers (Handley, Askey, Ray, Vaughan) has always been unparalleled. It also possesses, fortunately for The Beatles, a twenty-eight-year-old alumnus of Wrekin College, Brian Epstein.

No pop singer emerges without a promoter. When Epstein, running a thriving family record-shop business, stumbled across The Beatles two years ago he had a wider vision than other local impresarios, who were too involved with a Liverpool rock-and-pop world which had been lively, prosperous and isolated for several years.

Tapes of The Beatles went to London: George Martin, of the massive EMI group, was impressed; and early this year The Beatles' second record, 'Please, Please Me', roared to No. 1 in the charts. 'Suddenly writers found a convenient peg to hang The Beatles on,' says Epstein. 'It became called the "Liverpool sound".'

Record company representatives raced to Merseyside to sign up other groups, often disappointingly. The ascending Liverpool twang became as viable in pop as in theatre and television; one embryonic London idol, it is said, decamped to Merseyside to attend to his vowels.

Epstein, who also manages The Beatles' hottest pursuers, Liverpudlians Kramer and Marsden, says he helps 'develop and guide' his charges, but in no Svengali sense. 'My role is between one extreme and the other. I doubt if anyone can create a world-beating artist out of nothing. The Beatles are not makeshift pop idols. I really do believe in them. They are great artists and great talents.' He also insists, not unfairly, that within the 'beat' school there are, despite the gaggle of imitators, differences between artists. 'The Beatles are quite individual.'

Yet they are still individualists within a well-established mainstream of younger-generation cult and fashion which began in the fifties, when the mass-producers of clothes, coiffures and canned music began to court the multi-million teenage market. The Beatles haircuts (long, fringy, French-cum-Stone Age), are copied by fans, but they spring from similar teenage styles; so does their 'gear' (boots, black sweaters, drainpipes, short jackets from which they have cleverly removed the lapels), which is also aped.

The Beatles have given personal idiosyncrasies to a cult; but they are essentially the products of their generation, not its pace-setters. And the crush-and-cry adulation they are offered follows the hysterical pattern which also encompassed Elvis Presley, Tommy Steele, Cliff Richard and the rest.

One genuine novelty, however, may make the sociologists twitter. Their talk reveals them as very much a part of that questing, confident, cool, sharp and unshockable stream which has come out of the grammar schools in the last decade.

'It's not us alone,' says Paul McCartney, one of the group's three guitarists and an Eng. Lit. specialist at Liverpool Institute till he was eighteen. 'All the new groups have given it to pop music. More honesty than it ever had. Once you could get on being a fake: sequin shirts, dyed hair, false eyelashes, no talent. Not now. All that phoney image-building. When I used to read about those pop singers who didn't smoke or drink and went for a run in the mornings I thought, what's wrong with them. Most teenagers do smoke and drink and miss their morning exercise. It's the healthy thing to do.'

The Beatles are as uninhibited and spontaneous in a recording studio as on-stage. Last week, at a St John's Wood studio, they stood around microphones, superimposing hand-clapping and spurts of words on to a played-back tape of voice-and-instrumental they'd already recorded. From time to time McCartney and John Lennon (together they write most Beatles' songs and those for others in Epstein's stable) would crowd a piano, with recording supervisor Martin, to work out a new passage in a previously unrehearsed song for the LP they were making.

'No, they don't read music,' said their Press representative. 'Certainly they need electricity. What other performance in entertainment today doesn't use amplification of some kind?'

Their talk picks up odd words from teenage slang ('fab' or 'drag'), but not obtrusively. They are also reputed to like sick humour. McCartney again: 'Well, only if it's funny. It's just that we're not *touchy* about things.'

Already the proliferating pop-journal pundits are, after scarcely nine months of the Beatle rage, worriedly asking if 'beat' is being bashed to death. 'Of course it could all fold. But it doesn't *worry* us,' claims McCartney. 'We could all start modest little businesses now. And we don't want that all-round entertainer bit.'

As they stampede around the country on the one-night stand sweat, toil and beers circuit, they save carefully, through Beatles Ltd, Northern Songs Ltd, and a good accountant. For although they are probably big (and good) enough to survive the demise of the 'beat' vogue, as Presley and the other rare big fish have survived the pop fashions, they know how cold the wind cuts around Liverpool's Pier Head. And next year, who knows?

The Duke – born 1956

23 FEBRUARY 1964

Duke Ellington, jazz music's greatest genius, will be sixty-five in April. The musicians who have worked in his orchestra down the years and who are playing more dazzlingly than ever with him in Britain now – Johnny Hodges, Cootie Williams, Harry Carney, Lawrence Brown, Russell Procope – are all deep in their fifties. It is depressing to consider that, however profoundly he may have influenced jazz and contemporary music generally, the Ellington tradition will one day simply cease to exist.

For two reasons: Ellington, first, has always written not just for an orchestra of a certain instrumentation but for a particular group of highly individual instrumentalists: continuity of personnel has been crucial to him. The second reason was given to me last week with characteristic casualness by Ellington himself, sprawling at ease in the hotel suite whose doors, while he is in town, are usually ajar to callers, where a new bottle is always being uncorked.

'You know me,' he says, by way of prelude. 'I'm a great talker. I'm always duly flattered by being asked.' The irony is gentle; the face, criss-crossed with the lines of forty years of early mornings around the globe, is relaxed; no man at the summit gives more generously of his time and wisdom.

Later comes the crunch: 'We hardly ever keep scores. We have nothing to go back to. Out of the thousands of numbers we've done, only about ten per cent of the scores remain. They disappear. People wrap their lunch in them.' Even allowing for Ellingtonian exaggeration, the thought is chilling.

'He doesn't care about this sort of thing, you know – collecting his stuff.' Billy Strayhorn, short, dapper, barefoot, the Duke's collaborator in composition for a quarter century is now speaking as Ellington disappears momentarily. If Ellington's customary indifference about his life's work *is* only a pose, it is the cleverest artifice of the age.

'Four years ago, for his birthday, we thought it would be a good idea to collect all Duke's work together and present it to him. John Saunders, he used to play trombone with us, did the work. There was no time to find more than a small part of it even in a year. It ran to several volumes. Now it's kept in a warehouse.'

Fortunately Ellington himself shows no sign yet of wanting to opt out of the big-band jungle, where only a few prize lions remain on the prowl: fortunately, too, many of the lost scores remain for the present in the heads of the orchestra. To what extent the musicians are now playing old numbers from memory, yet with the surprising freshness which gives the illusion of instant improvisation, makes a fascinating speculation.

The only pieces one can be sure are actually on the music stands are those being minted now. Ellington and Strayhorn are in the midst of composing a suite based on their Middle and Far Eastern tour last year, the evocation of things seen and people encountered which has always characterized Duke's music. 'The memory of things gone is important to a jazz musician,' he once said. Four pieces from the suite are being played at his concerts, and he promises to finish it before he leaves England.

'We decided not to write it while we were out there. We thought we'd be too strongly influenced by the exact melodies of Eastern music. So we waited till we got back, let it settle a little. It's coming now, but I've no idea how long it will be. We've so *many* ideas after seeing all those old cities. The Taj Mahal – all those lizards on the roof – they're there to protect you from the insects. But when you first look up and see them, all you can think is "Man, there are lizards on the roof?"'

Coincidentally, Ellington's mind is moving strongly towards the theatre. Last summer he was responsible for the complete writing and staging of *My People*, a twenty-four-scene exercise performed by dancers, singers and a sixteen-piece orchestra of Ellington *alumni* in Chicago, to mark the anniversary of Emancipation. Nearly ten thousand people a day saw it during its three-week run; now Ellington is kicking around ideas for more musicals.

Like his only other show, *Jump for Joy*, a revue produced in 1941, *My People* contains a strong element of social criticism and satire, not exactly the first trait you think of as Ellingtonian. Yet – 'I've been in this civil rights thing for years. But just to go out screaming about it on the stage doesn't make a show. It's all right for some cat on a soapbox, but in the theatre you've got to find some way of saying it without saying it . . . At the end of *My People* we've got the lines, "What colour is virtue, what colour is love?" You know?'

He breaks off and sings a passage, then plunges into prediction about jazz. He is sanguine, delighting in the massive numbers of musicians better equipped to write and play it, the increasing maturity of the audience for it. But he refuses to categorize jazz. 'I find it difficult to know the place to draw the line where jazz begins and ends. It all depends on how it *sounds*.

'Take rock 'n' roll, even. Perhaps Ella, she says "I'm gonna make a rock record" and you'll wind up with a real *jam*. Isn't that jazz? Now you take a symphony – something by Britten – and put it in the hands of some old cat with no finesse and you got the worst noise you ever heard.

'Jazz,' says Ellington – and the definition is as good as any for the undefinable – 'is a matter of having fun through freedom of expression.'

His own music is as difficult to pin down in words. Almost everything one can say about it is now a cliché, including the observation that he remains completely modern in spirit. When I mention James P. Johnson and Willie 'The Lion' Smith, his early mentors, he says: 'That's dangerous ground. I was born in 1956 at the Newport Festival.'

Beatles breaking down

22 JANUARY 1967

Paul McCartney, twenty-four, of independent means, sits in a heavy green chair in his drawing room at tea time in St John's Wood. The television screen flickers – 'Jackanory', without the sound. A record of Britten's *Gloriana* is playing quietly. A massive coal fire crackles. An Old English sheepdog called Martha breathes heavily. Beyond the room the house is silent and empty. The couple ('Sheffield and Stafford, not Spanish') have a day off.

'I'm spending a lot of time alone in the house. Just doing things or thinking. I've a year to find out what I want to do. It's very self-indulgent.'

Since The Beatles last year opted out of being an entertainment phenomenon – regular records, regular tours – and joined the leisured classes, they have been doing something like this, alone. For John Lennon, twenty-six, a film and a book; for George Harrison, twenty-six, an obsession with Indian music; for Ringo Starr, twenty-three, home life and talk of acting.

The thirty-minute score for the new and warmly received Boulting Brothers' film, *The Family Way*, due for general release in a month's time, is the earliest tangible sign of McCartney's independence. The film's situation – based on a Bill Naughton play about young married love unconsummated in Bolton – must have made the idea of McCartney as composer irresistible to a movie producer.

This is the first time he has moved from song-writing to more formal composition, and it also marks a breakaway from the usual Lennon-McCartney musical partnership which has covered around a hundred songs. But the important figure of George Martin, the producer who has worked with The Beatles on all their hit records, remains. The music is composed by McCartney, 'supervised and arranged by George Martin'.

'He is the interpreter,' says McCartney. 'I play themes and chords on piano or guitar. He gets it down on paper. I talk about the idea I have for instrumentation. Then he works out the arrangement. I tried to learn music once with a fellow who's a great teacher. But it got too much like homework. I have some block about seeing it in little black dots on paper. It's like braille to me.'

McCartney says he is embarrassed at talking with professional session musicians because he lacks a formal musical education. 'I'd like to talk more with them, but they'll ask how you want it – *legato, fortissimo* or what. All I can say is "You just *feel* it". But things worked out better on *The Family Way*. I spent a lot of time with the strings.'

The music is interesting. The main theme is tender, simple, easily picked up, reflecting McCartney's passion for the romantic, melodic line, as in 'Yesterday' or 'Michelle'. But elsewhere there is a throwback to his Northern past in the brass-band sound which fits the film's setting so aptly. There are euphoniums, tubas, cornets as well as strings, guitars and organ.

'I like the sound of brass bands. I heard a lot of them when I was young because my dad liked them. He used to play trumpet and double on piano till his teeth gave out. His band had different names. Like one night, they were The Masked Players. They all had Woolworth's masks, but it was so hot the glue melted and they went mad trying to get them off. Never again The Masked Players.'

McCartney on growing up: 'We've all of us grown up in a way that hasn't turned into a manly way. It's a childish way. That's why we make mistakes. We've not grown up within the machine. We've been able to live very independent lives.

'Now we're ready to go our own ways. We'll work together only if we miss each other. Then it'll be hobby work. It's good for us to go it alone.'

McCartney's house is nineteenth-century and very spacious. 'I never saw it before I bought it. Now I'm beginning to enjoy it.' The carpeting is mostly chocolate or dark grey, with several Persian rugs. The heavy Victorian suite in the main sitting room, with apricot velvet curtains at the French windows, cost him £20 at a shop in Old Brompton Road. He buys a lot of old furniture and pieces there, piles them in a basement room, and works at restoring or changing them – scraping, glueing, painting.

There are three bathrooms, with expensive Italian tiling and floor-level tubs. There is a music room which contains a large Paolozzi piece called *Solo* – a figure in chrome on gun-metal, reminiscent of robots and pin-tables. In the dining room is a clock with an eighteen-inch dial, from the Great Exhibition in 1851. There are electric press-button curtains in his bedroom, an Indian peacock tapestry in one of the spare rooms, and a tambura (the Indian drone instrument) in the sitting room, as well as a cabinet full of old sheet music like 'Little Dolly Daydream', 'The Pride of Idaho' (*with banjo accompaniment*).

One bare upstairs room is a chaos of overturned chairs, trophies, statuettes, gold discs – some still unpacked – and relics of Beatlemania like Tokyo-made shirts printed with McCartney's head. 'What do you do with all this? You can set it up like a museum or just let it lie. People will find something wrong either way.'

Tony Barrow, Beatles' press officer for many years: 'Paul is now leading a very organized life. The other three don't know what they are doing. They wait for others to tell them. But Paul always knows – you ring him up and he will say, "No, not Thursday, I am dining at eight. Not Friday, because I have got to see a man about a painting. But Saturday's okay." It isn't that he's changed. But out of all of them he has developed the most.'

During his retreat, McCartney has been on safari in Africa, has put together a film he shot in France, and has grown a moustache which gives him the sad look some French comedians have. The moustache: 'It's part of breaking up The Beatles. I no longer believe in the image. I'm no longer one of the four mop-tops.'

The film: 'Just look at that,' he says, as the camera crawls at close range across the face of a piece of corrugated iron, which changes in colour and in texture. 'It's like flying over the Sahara desert.'

McCartney's film is a collection of random images: a tree, a wall, a broken pot, crosses in a graveyard, coloured streamers of lights, jumbled together with random superimposition of other images, including a fizzing red spot which turns out to be the ignition light of his car. It has affinities with *Fantasia* (his favourite background music for it is Stockhausen's *Kontakte*) and cine-club entries in the avant-garde section.

'I'd like to make longer films. Perhaps that's the way I'll go. This is why I'm trying.'

The past seems very dead for McCartney. 'The only record I ever like of ours is the latest record. You get repelled by what's gone before because there are so many things wrong. "She loves You", for example, I hate.'

He puts on the solitary tune yet recorded for a new Beatles album. It's basically Lennon's, is called 'Strawberry Fields For Ever' – after a Liverpool approved school for girls – and one repeated phrase runs: 'Nothing is real, nothing to get hung up about.'

What McCartney is worth in cash is always being worked out. A million, or more or less, it makes little difference. 'Two years ago I was worried about money. Now I'm surprised to find that I'm rich yet I'm not miserable. I've noticed, even over the last five years, how people are clinging more and more to material things. I'm sad because Britain is going the American way in this. I know we four would be scruffy, dirty and obscene to the Americans if we didn't have money.'

It's been said that both Lennon and McCartney, being shrewd and intelligent men, have guilt complexes about their wealth, their influence on the young, their appearance of non-involvement in politics and sociology.

McCartney: 'How can you be specific in politics? Everybody is trying to do the same thing – get power. The idea of people fighting *en masse* over land is so maniac, so chaotic, that in the end everyone must be intelligent enough to see the madness of it.

'I'm desperate about what is happening in Vietnam. But what happens if you identify with either side? You lose the power to sway people.

'What could we do? Well, I suppose that at a Royal Command Performance we could announce a number and then tell people exactly what we thought about Vietnam. But then we'd be thought to be lunatics.

'The only way I can see is to talk to people straight, at a personal level, and say look, I'm not a nut, and this is what I believe. If you keep saying it maybe people will see you're not a nut.

'All this pull together now for England is great till you know what the people who run things really think of you, the plebs. Just like Parliament now. "We've got to rule you," they're saying, "so let's get on with it. We don't want *you* seeing *us* on TV." Isn't that ridiculous?'

McCartney has no ambition to be a writer ('I couldn't write more than a couple of words without being embarrassed. For me it's too flowery') or a conventional film-score composer. 'It's too regimented, fitting music into small slots. There's no freedom.

'So in the end I don't know what I'll do. I'll have a go at anything. Something will turn up.'

Bird lives

29 JANUARY 1967*

The evening of 4 March 1955, Charlie Parker, called 'Bird' or 'Yardbird', was to play at Birdland, the New York jazz club named after him. Behind him lay a history of nervous breakdowns, drink and drug problems, three broken marriages, the death of an idolized daughter, suicide attempts, desperate unreliability, and the most beautiful and original music played by any single jazz musician. It was the latest of the last chances he was always being given.

When he was announced by Charles Mingus, a fellow musician, Parker did not at first come to the stand. Finally he did and began arguing, loudly, with the pianist, Bud Powell. They played at last, briefly, and not very successfully. Then Parker walked off. Later he returned, but did not play much. When Powell left the stand, Parker shouted the pianist's name into the microphone, over and over. 'Please don't associate me with any of this,' Mingus told the audience. 'These are sick people.'

The afternoon of 9 March, Parker arrived at the hotel suite of Baroness Pannonica de Koenigswarter, who had befriended him and many other jazz

*Originally one of a *Sunday Times* magazine series, 'The Lost Heroes'.

musicians. He began to vomit blood and a doctor who was called wanted him to go to hospital. Parker refused.

On the evening of 12 March, Parker said he wanted to watch the Tommy Dorsey show. The Baroness and her daughter wrapped him in a chair with pillows and blankets. Parker was watching some jugglers playing with bricks. When they dropped the lot, he laughed, uproariously. Then he choked, rose from his chair, fell back, and was dead within seconds. He was thirty-four. They buried him in Kansas City, where he had been born.

The doctor who had been attending him gave the cause of death as a heart attack and advanced cirrhosis of the liver. He also had stomach ulcers. Later the autopsy report called it lobar pneumonia. It could have been called almost anything. Parker had been destroying his powerful body for years, like a man intent upon death. He had become addicted to drugs very early, some say at twelve, some at fifteen. He ate massively, drank gargantuanly, had a vast sexual appetite. He slept little.

At sixteen he looked thirty-eight; when he died he looked sixty. As soon as his death became known, chalked notices appeared on fences and walls in New York: 'Bird Lives'. He is the greatest single continuing musical influence in the history of jazz.

He is impossible to explain, except in terms of his music. This was the only coherent element of his life. He changed the face of jazz utterly – from a diatonic into a chromatic music, employing (to speak technically) such heresies to the traditionalist hard core as the Flattened Fifth. To speak untechnically, what he did was to surprise and often outrage his listeners by producing unexpected notes in phrase after phrase. He and other experimenters, like Dizzy Gillespie, who created in the 1940s this new mode of jazz called bop, brought jazz into line with the chromatic advances already made in more formal music by Debussy, Stravinsky, Ravel, Bartok.

Parker was the greatest modern jazzman because of his melodic gift and his sense of form, his ravishingly beautiful saxophone tone and his originality. Thousands of lesser men have copied his solos.

Musically, here is hero material. But personally? He had, certainly, the customary heroic circumstance of the artist who dies too young, self-destroyed. More important, though, to the process of deification was that shift in social values during the 1950s which created image-phrases like the 'beat generation'. Parker was the ideal hipster hero – neurotic, amoral, anarchistic, arrogant, gentle, hedonistic, kind.

This can be shocking or very boring. To some sad people Parker is symbol rather than musician. They are the ones who wore berets and dark glasses in the forties because Bird and Dizzy did. He has helped sustain a creed of social revolt, like James Dean.

But such nonsense does not touch the question *why* Parker destroyed himself. 'Everyone treated him like a bum, so he obliged by acting like it,' one companion said. This is possible.

The crushing humiliations he suffered because his music was disliked by so many for so long are as sickening as those he endured because he was black. Jo Jones, a great drummer with Count Basie, once stood up while Parker was playing in a jam session and, very deliberately, hurled a cymbal the length of the hall. Parker left, shattered.

Is it easier because you are black, because you look at armies of harsh uncomprehending faces, because oppression, despair, disgust and hopelessness crowd in, to become a junkie or a lush? Doubtless it is. Yet how inadequate that sounds as an explanation of Parker. The truth is still private and enigmatic. One man says Parker was mean about money, another (Art Blakey) that Parker gave him $2000 during a bad spell. One man says he was bitingly scornful to inferior musicians, another that he never put another player down. Strangely he liked Rudy Vallee, rock 'n' roll groups, Tommy Dorsey. At home he played Stravinsky, Hindemith, Bartok and Bach all the time. Of Heifetz he said: 'He's the only man that screams. He's got the greatest beat.'

There is the chilling evidence of a psychiatric report from Belle Vue Hospital in New York. 'A hostile, evasive personality with manifestations of primitive and sexual fantasies associated with hostility and gross evidence of paranoid thinking.' There is the evidence of thousands of men and women who warmed to him, despite everything. Among these is Annie Ross, who lived with the Parker household for several months in the early fifties.

'Bird was beautiful. He would have moments of great anger and moments of great tenderness. He was like a child, furious about the injustices he felt had been done to him in business dealing, frustrated because he hadn't the adulation of a larger public. Ultimately you knew he would destroy himself.'

Parker seemed to know it too. Baldly he once said: 'Any musician who says he is playing better either on tea, the needle or when he is juiced is a plain, straight liar.' Yet he couldn't kick his habits.

He died broke. His estate, over which there has been endless bickering, may have been pushed into six figures by royalties.

Ellington: 'impatient inside'

12 FEBRUARY 1967

I find it impossible, whatever the proprieties, to write solely of Duke Ellington's *music*; as if what you hear can be divorced from its creator, put into a test-tube, and laboratory-analysed. Ellington is his music is his orchestra is Ellington.

No musician this century has possessed his unswerving singleness of purpose. 'My only interest in life,' he said around two one morning last week, which is a good Ellingtonian hour for dinner, 'is to write something I'll hear tomorrow night. I'm impatient inside.' That single-mindedness has led to the composition of thousands of songs, suites and musicals; to the punishing treadmill of all-year touring round the world; to performances with his own orchestra, with symphonies, choirs and tap-dancers. He has superhuman stamina.

Last Sunday, when he opened his present British tour at Portsmouth, he sat on stage at the piano twenty minutes before the curtain rose, committing something new to paper. Rex Stewart tells a wonderful story of Ellington tearing up a piece he had written and flushing it down the lavatory. 'If it's good, I'll remember it,' he told the curious Stewart. 'If it's bad, well, I want to forget it and I would prefer that no one catches on to how lousy I can write.'

It is important that all this be said again; that we realize how tremendous a genius is once more in our midst. The quality, quantity and diversity of his writing is in itself staggering. Inseparable from it is his leadership of an orchestra of superlative musicians for more than forty years. He does not write music *for* an orchestra: he uses his orchestra like a pen, knowing each nuance of every man, to write music. Unique music. This dual, yet unified achievement makes the contribution of most other twentieth-century musicians seem minor.

Ellington's present visit is the most richly variegated he has ever made. The concerts by his orchestra alone are swollen with new material and with considerably changed versions of recent major works, like the stunningly beautiful *La Plus Belle Africaine*. He and the whole orchestra are so much better than ever that were it any other group of middle-aged gentlemen you would talk about a burgeoning Indian summer.

What will happen at next Sunday's Albert Hall concert with the Ellington orchestra and the LPO? He will play 'Single Petal of a Rose' (from his unpublished *Queen's Suite*) and a score of other opuses. Doubtless he will by his definition ('swing is the ultimate of compatability') make even the LPO swing. It would be an absurd self-denial to miss, this week, any chance of hearing a man who, atop Everest, is now eyeing the moon.

Swinging with the LPO

26 FEBRUARY 1967

There was at least one period during last week's barrier-breaking Albert Hall concert when, by his own definition of swing as 'the ultimate in compatability', or simply in terms of a regular rhythm infectious and elastic, Duke Ellington had the London Philharmonic Orchestra swinging.

It came near the end of his new work, *The Golden Broom and the Green Apple*. Ellington, conducting the LPO with stabbing, unadorned gestures, broke off to clap his hands in time with a tumbling passage for flute, oboe and cello. The mood caught. The LPO brass began to whoop, propelled by nine basses playing pizzicato, and the orchestra's young drummer swooped into a passage of four-bar breaks – the familiar call-and-response pattern of jazz. It has probably never happened to the LPO before, and won't again until Ellington returns.

As an occasion, the concert was an overwhelming success, received with great enthusiasm, running on for close to three hours. Whenever Ellington's orchestra played with the LPO – in *Tone Parallel to Harlem*, in the long medley of his classic songs (from 'Sophisticated Lady' to 'Solitude') – there was little sense of unease or incoherence at the fusion, despite the occasional aura of under-rehearsal which was the only reservation to be made about the quality of the concert.

The whole affair, indeed, illustrated Ellington's contention that categories in music are increasingly meaningless. There is now a broad mainstream of modern music, in which swim musicians whose tastes, training and practice encompass the traditions and devices of all music, classical or jazz or whatever. Leonard Bernstein is one, and he has plainly learned from Ellington. Categories have broken down, and it is now an interesting judgment, but no longer a conclusive one, to say that one prefers *Harlem* in the version for Ellington's band only, instead of in its band-plus-symphony orchestra guise. It was, devotees sometimes forget, originally written for the NBC Symphony during Toscanini's reign.

Sergeant Pepper: the freedom to change

4 JUNE 1967

The Beatles could, secure in the untouchability of their indestructible image, have shut up shop long ago. Instead, they are using their unique freedom in the pop world to raise the levels of their idiom and enlarge its vocabulary in most exciting ways.

The new LP *Sergeant Pepper's Lonely Hearts Club Band* (Parlophone) is remarkable. Listening to its strange cadences, its sitar passages, its almost atonal propensities the learned critic might easily assume derivations ranging from English seventeenth-century music to Richard Strauss. It is true that George Harrison has been to India to study with Ravi Shankar and that I have heard Britten's *Gloriana* playing in Paul McCartney's drawing room. But the influences are likelier to be music hall artists of the last twenty-five years, and the images which Lennon and McCartney retain of their Liverpool childhood – of places, priests, old women, young girls.

'Eleanor Rigby', on the *Revolver* LP, reflected the latter background. The very moving and beautiful 'She's Leaving Home' illustrates it on *Pepper*. As for the music hall aspect, The Beatles have the trait which artists from Marie Lloyd to George Formby possessed of telling a story wryly or humorously, often with the cocky bounce of the melody belying the sadness of the lyric.

Pepper is a tremendous advance even in the increasingly adventurous progress of The Beatles. Some of the words are splendid urban poetry – almost metaphysical in 'Lucy in the Sky with Diamonds'. The tone is humorous, sympathetic, sceptical and often self-mocking. Musically it is always stimulating. There won't, though, be much dancing done to *Pepper*. The Beatles are now producing performances, not music for frugging to. Will the kids follow?

A springboard called 'Joseph'

19 MAY 1968

'Give us food' the brothers said,
'Dieting is for the birds.'
Joseph gave them all they wanted,
Second helpings, even thirds . . .

Even on paper the happy bounce of lyrics like these comes through. They are exactly right for singing by several hundred boys' voices. With two organs, guitars, drums and a large orchestra, the effect is irresistible.

The quicksilver vitality of *Joseph and His Amazing Technicolor Dreamcoat*, the new pop oratorio heard at Central Hall, Westminster, last Sunday, is attractive indeed. On this evidence, the pop idiom – beat rhythms and Bacharachian melodies – is most enjoyably capable of being used in extended form.

Musically, *Joseph* is not all gold. It needs more light and shade. A very beautiful melody, 'Close Every Door To Me', is one of the few points when the hectic pace slows down. The snap and crackle of the rest of the work tends to be too insistent, masking the impact of the words which, unlike many in pop, are important.

But such reservations seem pedantic when matched against *Joseph*'s infectious overall character. Throughout its twenty-minute duration it bristles with wonderfully singable tunes. It entertains. It communicates instantly, as all good pop should communicate. And it is a considerable piece of barrier-breaking by its creators, two men in their early twenties – Tim Rice, the lyricist, and Andrew Lloyd Webber, who wrote the music.

The performers were the choir and orchestra of Colet Court, the St Paul's junior school, with three solo singers and a pop group called The Mixed Bag. It was an adventurous experiment for a school, yet Alan Doggett, who conducted, produced a crisp, exciting and undraggy performance which emphasized the rich expansiveness of pop rather than the limitations of its frontiers.

A sort of pop Forsyte Saga

24 NOVEMBER 1968

Of course the new Beatles double LP, containing thirty fresh-minted pieces, is toweringly the best thing in pop since *Sergeant Pepper*. Their sounds, for those open in ear and mind, should long ago have established their supremacy.

What major popular artist does not now sing the Lennon–McCartney classics – 'Yesterday', 'Michelle', 'Eleanor Rigby' and the rest – which rank with anything produced in this century's popular music? At so fast a clip, they will by thirty-five have achieved enough in quantity as well as quality to surpass Cole Porter or Berlin or Rodgers. Maybe, like Gershwin, they will have made an opera. Strong narrative flows from them along with the melodies.

They have misses, but there aren't many on *The Beatles* (PMC 7067/8, 73s 6d), the unvarnished title of the album. It is a world map of contemporary music, drawn with unique flair and colouring. Musically, there is beauty, horror, surprise, chaos, order. And that *is* the world; and that is what The Beatles are on about. Created by, creating for, their age.

Superficially, the two records sound like a return to basics. The rock flavour is powerful, but now done with intuitive skills in orchestration and choice of instrumentation. Such, too, is the illusion of spontaneity and dynamic use of voices as instruments, it's almost jazz reclothed.

The content is vastly varied. They echo the music hall ('Martha My Dear') and take off the Beach Boys ('Back in the USSR'). They knock the world ('Piggies' – a Harrison song) and lament it ('While My Guitar Gently Weeps'). They still write beautiful songs about girls ('Julia'), move into blues ('Yer Blues') and country-and-western ('Don't Pass Me By') and folk ('Mother Nature's Son') and electronic impressionism ('Revolution 9'). They are shiningly simple ('Long, Long, Long') and as obscure as any metaphysical poet ('Happiness is a Warm Gun'). And they transform and recreate each genre they touch.

Original and encyclopaedic musically, then, but what of the evocative words? Have they not told us not to search for coherence in their philosophy? They are Liverpudlians, and their style is a cocky Liverpudlian two-fingers-to-the-world one moment, with glimmers of moral remorse the next. So the searchers after significance stay tempted.

Avid PhDs will one day gloom over couplets like 'a soap impression of his wife he ate/and donated to the National Trust', footnoting the text as densely as Beowulf. In 'Glass Onion', Lennon sings 'I told you about the strawberry fields . . .' Cross-references to themselves abound. The plot thickens. They are making a sort of pop *Forsyte Saga*, bursting with fools on hills, lady madonnas and walruses.

The Beatles are big boys now, though. They'll need ultimately to come clean. They may not yet be philosophers, but they shouldn't invite equation with the regiment of Liverpudlian funny men either.

Duke at seventy

27 APRIL 1969

'He's a genius, sure,' the Ellington trombonist Joe Nanton once said, 'but Jesus how he eats.' And then there have been Constant Lambert and Percy Grainger and Stokowski and Stravinsky variously saying that he is one of the greatest modern composers or the only great living American composer or whatever. There is another Ellington who says 'Duke, he makes me feel sleepy, like rain on a roof'. There is Edward Kennedy Ellington himself: 'I don't write jazz, I write Negro folk music.'

The man is like quicksilver, hard to grasp, living as he wishes behind his many masks, warm and easy, yet gently eluding his pursuers. Too much talk, he says 'stinks up the place'. He half-rationalizes his aversions. 'I'm not old enough to be historical and I'm too young to be biographical. Biographies are like tombstones. Who wants one?'

He will hate being reminded he is seventy, for he likes to say 'I was born in 1956, at the Newport Festival' – a reference to a triumphant reassertion of his place in American music. Yet seventy he is, still leading the world's finest jazz orchestra virtually fifty-two weeks a year on the non-stop grind of one-night stands and world tours, still composing at flood-peak: the musical miracle of our century. To say that he is also its greatest living musician is, of course, a matter of judgment and taste; but the incidental evidence is strong.

Ellington has, first, and despite his dislike of musical categories, worked in what is arguably the only new (at the least, one of the few new) art forms our century has produced: jazz. He has been a bandleader for more than fifty years, and for over forty years has led a large jazz orchestra which has maintained a totally unique and recognizable character, and whose nucleus has more or less remained constant – Harry Carney, Johnny Hodges, Lawrence Brown, Cootie Williams and others.

For that orchestra, Ellington has written all his music, much of it in collaboration with Billy Strayhorn, who from 1939 until his death in 1967 was the Duke's *alter ego*, uncannily and telepathically in tune with his friend's musical ideas, complementing them and enriching them. Though many musicians can perform 'Sophisticated Lady', or even a major tone poem like 'Black, Brown and Beige', only the Ellington orchestra can play his melodic twists and harmonic conceits as they should be played, for Ellington conceives everything in terms of the personal style of each of his men and the collective sound they make.

He is, of course, a magnificent pianist: sparse, oblique, surprising – and an influence on scores of pianists, most notably Thelonious Monk. But his real instrument, as Strayhorn and many others have pointed out, is his orchestra. He is comfortably off, but has probably lost money at times keeping the orchestra going and could have earned far more by becoming a concert hall or movie studio composer. He knows it: 'If I didn't like the way the band played I wouldn't pay so much for the pleasure of listening to it and of writing for it.'

In quantitative terms, Ellington's (or Ellington's/Strayhorn's) output is incredible. Maybe two thousand pieces ranging from great pop songs of the Kern or Cole Porter kind ('Solitude', 'Satin Doll', 'Don't Get Around Much Any More') to major suites and tone poems numbering twenty or more. Symphonies might not suit him, but oratorios do, and opera could. Maybe it's 4,000 or 5,000 things he has written – no one knows. The chilling truth is that perhaps ninety per cent of it has not been preserved in manuscript: it is in the heads of his musicians, consciously or sub-consciously, and already they are growing old.

He has been compared with Delius and Debussy, Mozart and Bach – the latter most appropriately in some ways, remembering how important improvisation was both to Bach's art and to jazz. Of all the thousands of words written on this subject, those of Constant Lambert (in the early 1930s, long before Duke had really got moving) may serve as a symbol. 'I know of nothing in Ravel so dexterous in treatment as the varied solos in the middle of the ebullient *Hot and Bothered* and nothing in Stravinsky more dynamic than the final section.'

Consider also the circumstances in which this unparalleled torrent of composition has taken place. Not for Ellington the quiet retreat, emotion recollected in tranquillity. His drawing board has been the overnight railroad coach, glass walls of recording studios, dim-lit darkened buses, backs of hotel menus – or the telephone. He and Strayhorn would often work by phone, singing snatches of tunes to each other, occasionally and astonishingly finding that they had already written the same notes, though they might be a few thousand miles apart. Ellington never seems to sleep or take a holiday. He is an iron man.

To jazz alone, if one must talk in categories, he has given the 'growl' brass sound and 'jungle' noises, has confirmed the role of the tenor saxophone (first through Ben Webster) and revolutionized the role of the double-bass (through Jimmy Blanton) as well as treating the music orchestrally, with a wealth of complex harmonies, melodies, rhythms and tone colours. His colouring is fantastic, considering he uses only the conventional instrumentation of jazz: percussion, trumpets, trombones, saxes, clarinets. 'Strings?' he said. 'Positively no! What could I do with strings that hasn't been done wonderfully for hundreds of years?'

He has played for parties and proms, jitterbugs and intellectuals, in concert halls and cafés. Lack of pretentiousness has been his hallmark. When told that over-serious fans had questioned his performing for jive dancing in ballrooms, he replied: 'If they'd been told it was a Balkan folk dance, they'd think it was wonderful.'

This man is many things: snappy dresser, gourmet and gourmand, health-worrier and hypochondriac – a dose of vitamins daily. He is delighted by beautiful girls and beautifully correct in addressing them, loyal to friends who deserve it and those who don't, fanatical about family ties, a city-lover (grass reminds him of graves; he won't wear green) and tolerant beyond reason of human folly.

He is cool at all times – which a very low pulse rate helps to explain. He and his musicians – Lawrence Brown, trombonist, expresses a desire to be a doctor or funeral director – defy all the hoary myths about 'typical' jazzmen. Duke says he's never felt the need of dope: 'I never smoked anything which hadn't got printing on it.'

He has humour. Explaining the 'Lady Mac' joke in 'Such Sweet Thunder' he said he believed Lady Macbeth had a little ragtime in her soul. His musicians down the years have adored him, proudly and correctly believing their music to be twenty-five years ahead of its time. He is deeply religious, reading the Bible daily, and in the 1960s placing more store by his Sacred Concerts than anything else. 'I had three educations – the street corner, going to school, and the Bible. The Bible is the most important. It taught me to look at a man's insides instead of the outside of his suit.'

He has not marched or waved banners, but has pursued civil rights his own way. 'Screaming about it on stage doesn't make a show. It's all right for some cat on a soapbox, but in the theatre you've got to find some way of saying it without saying it. At the end of *My People* we've got the song "What Colour Is Virtue, What Colour Is Love?" You know?'

Going his own way, making music to please himself, music always intensely personal. A subtle man, Ellington. He'll do anything to pursue the single-minded aim which has pleasured and enhanced our living: to write his music and to have the band *he* wants sitting there and playing it every day of every year. We need him till he's at least a hundred.

Ten years of Ronnie Scott's Club

14 SEPTEMBER 1969

For every few thousand who have been there, there must be a few hundred thousand who know what it is. Ronnie Scott's Club is to jazz as Stratford to Shakespeare. There is a further twist even to this proposition, for the club's world-wide reputation is based on what is, after all, an Afro-American art form. That Scott's should have become arguably the world's most important centre of continuous jazz performance is roughly comparable with the concept of Wembly Stadium blossoming into the home of World Series baseball.

As anniversaries go, of course, ten years doesn't sound much. In the timescale of jazz clubs, though, that span could fairly be translated as more like a century. The rock music vogue of the 1960s has decimated jazz clubs even in America, even famous ones like Birdland. Jazz, despite the occasional Norman Granz or Miles Davis, isn't really a money-maker. For most musicians, the playing of jazz is an economic, though often a compulsive, luxury. Duke Ellington is fond of saying that he must love his orchestra, otherwise he wouldn't pay so much for the pleasure of hearing it play.

Scott and his partner Pete King, both veterans of the touring bands of the 1940s and 1950s, have been unstinting patrons of their chosen art form if you measure patronage in terms of total dedication or stress, mental and physical, as well as in £ s d. It has taken a ten-year pattern of sixteen-hour days in the club, a running battle with the forces of musical ignorance, and raw-nerve handling of erratic virtuosi to achieve the position where to have played at Ronnie's is an accolade internationally, where the mere existence of the place has been a powerful factor in drawing an army of great American musicians to live in Europe.

To list the jazz artists who have appeared there would be a rough draft for a musical encyclopaedia. In the past twelve months alone, the several hundred names would include Stan Getz and Ben Webster, Buddy Rich and John Dankworth, Benny Carter and Maynard Ferguson – as well as the great classical guitarist John Williams, stilling the arena with Bach and Ibeniz. In the next two months an army headed by Miles Davis, Sarah Vaughan, Thelonious Monk, Teddy Wilson and Lionel Hampton will have passed through.

Nothing of all this seemed likely when the club was born in Gerrard Street, on the fringes of Soho, in 1959. You walked to it down steep narrow steps, a tight and smoky padded temple overwhelmed by the jungle of strip and clip joints. 'We never thought of being in business ten years hence,' says

King. 'We just wanted a place where Ronnie and other Britons could play in the right atmosphere.'

The atmosphere was soon established: a cross between a small concert hall and a welcoming back-room. 'Like a workshop,' the then house pianist, Stan Tracey, said. 'You take off your coat and get on with it.' The play-British policy was less successful, and in those early days Scott was rather bitter about the lack of support for local talent. 'A slight bit of twist to the mouth, that's Ronnie,' said one jazzman. Yet the nights when few people came, the insistence upon the right artistic policy – music to be listened to not talked through, some refreshment, and no dancing – was to lead to the first major contribution by Scott's to the arts in this country. The club was forced to fight the long-standing Musicians' Union ban on American jazzmen playing in British clubs. It won. The crowds began to come for American stars, the foundation for the *international* jazz centre above all others was laid – and, indirectly, British musicians got an established base in which to work.

'Only Ronnie would have had the faith to stick with his gamble,' says the BBC jazz producer, Steve Allen. 'He made it possible for British jazz musicians to walk as tall as the Americans. He killed our inferiority complex.'

The Gerrard Street days have come to possess a legendary quality since Scott's moved to its present vast and comfortable home in Frith Street. The club had a rare intimacy at the old place, though the new one is better suited to widen the audience for jazz and to present big bands like Woody Herman's without afflicting the listeners with permanently dented eardrums.

The early 1960s were the time when Sonny Rollins began his first set virtually in the street, blowing his way towards the bandstand ('just testing the acoustics, man') while Tracey sat wondering what was happening; the time when raw life-seekers from out of town might come to the door to inquire if anyone had some 'tea', not knowing that the feet of anyone producing drugs in the club wouldn't touch the ground on their way to the pavement outside. Even today, Pete King takes laconic pleasure in pronouncing: 'We run a tight door.'

These were the days when bankruptcy was a possibility most Mondays, especially the week when no one came to the first week of Stan Getz, for whose plump fee the management had hocked their all. The week-end reviews, upon which King admits the club relies tremendously, saved the day. All the time, too, the club poppled with the unexpected. One evening Roland Kirk, the blind American multi-instrumentalist, challenged critic and pianist Steve Race to sit in with him after Race had called Kirk 'the Charlie Cairoli of jazz' in a review.

'I laid down a slow introduction to "These Foolish Things", following

Kirk's foot-tapping,' Race recalled, 'but when he came in it was at double tempo. I could see it was going to be a mean kind of session.' It was – and when Race returned to his seat, Kirk kept up the fire through the mike. 'Well, what do you think, man?' Race: 'I think Ronnie needs a new piano.' Kirk: 'Ronnie can't afford a new piano, you know that.' Race: 'The money he's just charged me for a glass of wine, he can afford a new piano.'

This quirky, sardonic quality is typical of the club even in its new home, disguising the immense debt which music owes to Scott and King – the setting of standards, the arena for performance, the presentation of the cream of this century's only original musical art form to an ever-widening audience of all ages. Now that the club has another cockpit upstairs, it has also encouraged the new confluence between jazz and literate pop by presenting rock-blues groups.

No one encourages lack of portentousness more than Scott, now a greying forty-two, very relaxed, but still tautly thin. I remember him long ago describing a luncheon with Robert Graves in Majorca, where he often plays at a jazz club in which Graves has an interest. 'Graves went on about jazz being the only real religion these days. It was all a bit beyond me.'

Scott seems still to carry the memories of thin nights in Gerrard Street with him. He will tell any audience which responds to an artist with modified rapture: 'You are to be congratulated on your self-restraint.' Pause. 'What have you been drinking? Concrete?'

Then the address will really begin. 'It's good to see you here, though. It's good to see *someone* here. Last night there were so few people we thought our cashier had died. The band was playing "Tea For One". And the bouncers were throwing them *in*.' That's a natural lead-in to the jokes ('If God had meant us to fly he would have given us air-line tickets'), which are as sardonically Jewish as the tune he wrote called 'Some Of My Best Friends Are Blues'. He is as notorious for his tune titles (another 'I'm Sick and Tired Of Waking Up Feeling Tired and Sick') as he is for his unsuccessful punting. 'Show me a runaway horse and I'll stop him just by putting money on him.'

Perhaps that's the formula for running an art form successfully: pretend you're doing no such thing. Certainly with Scott, the smokescreen has disguised for too long the fact that he and King are impresarios of superb judgment and uncompromising faith, that Scott himself is a major tenor saxophonist in an age of too many gimmicky pygmies and that he can write on music like an angel.

King has a quite straightforward explanation for the club's survival and success: 'If you put on good things, you're there.' As for Scott, nothing better depicts the man than the words which he spoke to me in the club's early days. 'I believe the best results come from doing what you know and like. I'm a jazz musician, and this is really my excuse for existence.'

Transformation act

5 APRIL 1970

As a singer, Cleo Laine is one queen of a musician. 'Lush Life', by Billy Strayhorn, with the melancholy alcoholic pun in its title, is a very good song. Her precise interpretation of its agonized melody makes it seem the greatest ever written.

She transforms most popular music in this way, song after song, meticulously chosen, sung with persuasive idiosyncrasy. You perhaps think she is a touch too baroque when she collides with 'On a Clear Day', changing tempo and key and tone continually in a running skirmish with her accompanying quintet. Then she strips Richard Rodgers' 'It Might As Well Be Spring' down to the bone, treating it gravely, stark as plainsong.

No other singer in the world could have coped so awesomely with the range of material she performed in her *Spring Collection* at the Queen Elizabeth Hall on Friday, an occasion which must become annual if it continues to inspire songwriters to compose for her, and her husband, John Dankworth, to create such striking settings.

Gershwin and Bach, Ellington and Charles Ives, Hugo Wolf and Kern were among the composers represented. Lyrics came from sources as diverse as T. S. Eliot and Spike Milligan, with a stunning new narrative from Fran Landesman, called *This Must Be Earth*, beautifully set by Richard Rodney Bennett, who took over for three songs from Miss Laine's inspiring pianist, Laurie Holloway.

In all this, she is convincing proof of what the Dankworths' Wavendon Allmusic Plan is about: a demonstration that music is one, that we are foolish to stuff artists into exclusive pigeonholes.

Miss Laine's triumphant evening owed much to her natural endowments, especially the remarkable range of her voice in both tone and pitch – creamy-rich low down and crystal-sharp three octaves above. Her diction, determinedly English in words like 'charnce', is flawless, and the sense of dramatic surprise is always there. Above all, she is surrounded with a relaxation and joy which totally disguises the effort underpinning her fantastic technique.

Annie Ross, who in the early 1950s was creating a jazz sensation with 'Twisted', her neurotic lyrics set to a tenor sax improvisation by Wardell Gray, at the same time as Miss Laine was starting out on the ballroom circuit with Dankworth's first big band, is having a happy renaissance at Ronnie Scott's Club.

She still sings 'Twisted'. She has new songs, too, but the set I heard last week was largely a wondrous evocation of the post-war jazz age – all those warm and witty vocal transcriptions of solos played by bands like Basie and Louis Jordan, with a dash of bossa nova and red-hot momma. It's rare silver, and it can be dug this week too.

Last will and testament

10 MAY 1970

'I hope we passed the audition,' says John Lennon at the close of *Let It Be* (Apple), the LP from The Beatles issued on Friday, recorded more than a year ago and, in the light of recent events, perhaps the last to contain a significant quantity of new good songs.

As an epitaph his words have a quality of authentic Beatles irony. And everything else about the album is just right for a last will and testament, from the blackly funereal packaging to the music itself, which sums up so much of what the Beatles as artists have been – unmatchably brilliant at their best, careless and self-indulgent at their least. They sound as if they were still working as a group, not as individuals, and that's important too.

The music is not nearly as sophisticated as their post-*Rubber Soul* albums. The track called 'One After 909', for instance, is archetypal rock 'n' roll. 'Get Back', already a successful single, is hard-swinging and simple. 'For You Blue', the best and most surprising piece, mixes country-style and a jokey bottleneck guitar very excitingly.

The record droops most depressingly when the freshness disappears, as on 'The Long and Winding Road', which has an excess of strings and brass and choir, presumably the result of the 're-producing' done by Phil Spector, a born believer in the over-spectacular. McCartney's ballads need a lighter touch.

For the rest there are jokes and fragments and other longer songs, of which 'Across the Universe' is beautiful, and if the music isn't enough, there's a fat and impeccably produced picture book to look at – approaching two hundred pages of Beatles photographs and conversations. It pushes the cost of the whole package up to 59s 11d. Memorial tablets never were cheap.

Jesus Christ Superstar: the album

18 OCTOBER 1970

Caught in the crossfire between an older generation, who may regard it as distasteful or even sacrilegious, and a younger who could be deterred or scornful because of its religious associations, life is perhaps going to be hard for *Jesus Christ Superstar*, which is sad.

This is the title of a remarkable 'rock opera' (a misleading label) issued last week as a double album by MCA (£3 19s 10d) and composed by two artists in their twenties, Tim Rice (lyricist) and Andrew Lloyd Webber (composer), who two years ago cut their teeth on this kind of epic by producing *Joseph and the Amazing Technicolor Dreamcoat*, an entertaining but altogether lighter piece which was first performed by a pop group and the choir and orchestra of Colet Court, the St Paul's junior school.

Superstar lasts almost one and a half hours. It is an imaginative re-creation, founded on the Biblical record, of the immediate events leading to the Crucifixion. It uses many rock techniques, as well as those of twentieth-century formal composition, and as an artistic exercise in musical drama is every bit as valid as (and to me, often more moving than) Handel's *Messiah* which, similarly, clothed the Christian story in the language, melodic and verbal, of its day.

Rice has gone further than Handel, though. He has consciously compounded into the powerful narrative some of the *attitudes* of our day. This is most clearly seen in the treatment of Judas.

Without in any way injuring the idea and character of Christ as Son of God which the Bible portrays, Judas is presented far more sympathetically – a realist who had supported Jesus as a liberal reformer, healing and giving to the poor, but who is frightened once his leader begins to act as God, appearing to head up a rebellion against Rome, which Judas believes will cause the occupying power to smash their movement.

Listen Jesus to the warning I give,
Please remember that I want us to live.

Judas protests at the anointing of Jesus by Mary Magdalene – because the expensive ointment could have bought food for the starving poor. His betrayal of Christ is a matter of principle, not of personal gain. At the end, in tortured mental conflict, he is screaming

I don't believe he knows I acted for our good,
I'd save him all this suffering if I could.

Excoriating as is the stark and wonderfully written scene of the Crucifixion, the most anguished section of the whole work is Judas' suicide and the character is given a superb reading by Murray Head (who played in *Hair*). Other names are stellar, including Ian Gillan (of Deep Purple) as Christ, Mike d'Abo as Herod, Barry Dennen (the MC in the London production of *Cabaret*) as Pilate, and a fine new female voice, Yvonne Elliman, as Mary Magdalene. There are also three choirs, more than thirty top jazz and rock musicians (Chris Spedding, Keith Christie, Kenny Wheeler among them), a large string orchestra and a Moog synthesizer.

Despite passages where concepts defeat both words and music, this is a work on a heroic scale, masterfully conceived, honestly done, and overflowing with splendid music and apt language.

George and John minus Paul and Ringo

20 DECEMBER 1970

The Beatles have fooled almost everybody, including their biographers. Paul was intelligently nice, lyrical; John was intelligently sharp, powerful; Ringo was cuddly; George was the grey one, warily keeping his counsel. Now that the magic square is broken, to the detriment of art, George turns out to be, surprisingly, the canniest musician.

None of The Beatles' solo albums has proved especially interesting until now. With the arrival of George Harrison's *All Things Must Pass* (Apple £4 19s 6d), a triple-LP set, aficionados may smile again. John Lennon's coincident first album, *Plastic Ono Band* (Apple 39s 11d) is, by comparison a somewhat miserable offering.

Yet despite the difference in quality, it is the similarities that tantalize. Harrison sits apostle-bearded in gumboots on the cover with four plastic gnomes around him. It is tempting to see this as a view of the dead days of Beatlemania when one examines his lyrics.

> *Wah-Wah – you made me such a big star, being there*
> *at the right time . . . now I don't need no wah-wahs.*
> *And I know how sweet life can be. So I'll keep myself*
> *free of – wah-wah.*

Lennon, too, says it. The things he doesn't believe in now include Jesus, Kennedy, Buddha, Mantra, Bible and, finally: I don't believe in Beatles, I just believe in me, Yoko and me.

Both albums also suffer from over-indulgence and over-production.

Harrison's, for all the beauty of certain songs, could have been cut by half – especially the third LP, an instrumental jam session with Eric Clapton, Billy Preston, Ginger Baker and others. Lennon's is like a wet spoiled cry in the night that goes on too long. Phil Spector, co-producer of both albums, gives them a bang-clanging treatment so histrionic that even the bare instrumentation of John's setting (himself, Yoko, Ringo on drums, Klaus Voorman on bass) seems too heavy, whilst the backing often drowns George's important words.

Harrison, though, is where the sound really is. Without losing simple melodic flair or subtlety, his music is always forward-looking; well-constructed, surprising, cunning in contrasts. His lyrics are full of philosophy, Christian rather than Far-Eastern, and there are some astonishingly gospelly songs, like 'Awaiting On You All' and 'My Sweet Lord', now No. 1 in America. 'Open Up Your Heart,' says Harrison. 'He'll relieve you of all your cares.' And he means Jesus, not the Maharishi. Who would have expected that?

Chapter Two

Some are Special 1971-78

Satchmo: everyman's jazz

11 JULY 1971*

For everyman, Louis Armstrong *was* jazz. The mobile lower jaw, battered lips, streaming sweat, happy teeth, blistering trumpet tone and gravel voice gave three generations around the world their image of the music.

Armstrong's total impact, however, partially obscured the reasons *why* he was, in musical terms, a genius. It is astonishing that a musician as apparently unlike Louis as Miles Davis, archetypal prima donna of modern-style jazz, prickly and acutely socially-conscious, could say: 'You know you can't play anything on the horn that Louis hasn't played – I mean even modern.' Davis is right. Armstrong led the most important musical revolution of our century: yet for years no one realized it was worth reporting.

In the 1920s, when Louis was innovating so immensely, jazz was regarded simply as entertainment music. It was, moreover, black music, not respectable, something nurtured in slums and whore-houses and cheap dance halls. Only a few white critics, writing in minority journals, saw during the 1930s just what Armstrong had done in his famous Hot Five and Hot Seven recordings between 1925 and 1928.

First, he changed completely the nature of jazz and, ultimately, of Western popular music. New Orleans jazz, in the city where Armstrong was born in 1900, was essentially an ensemble art. Cornet, clarinet and trombone played interweaving lines and there were relatively short bursts of improvisation by soloists. After he went to Chicago to join King Oliver's band in 1922, Armstrong increasingly extended the range of the jazz solo so that the music became predominantly, whatever its style, characterized by the extended instrumental solo.

His astonishing technique and imagination raised the sights of every musician who followed him, whether trumpeter or not, and in musical styles other than jazz. He soared to a stratosphere of scale never before imagined for the trumpet, then toppled into long glissandos which revealed infinite series of new pitches. Sometimes he chopped up phrases; sometimes he slurred notes together, varying their shade and weight with immense subtlety. Harmonically and rhythmically too, he broke barriers.

All this he did with a tone simultaneously sweet, full-blooded and glowing. Yet despite these unending variations, he never lost the art of stating a simple melody, seemingly only slightly embellished. Because of this facility he could always communicate directly with diverse audiences. He was, in effect, a wily expositor of the pop song.

* A tribute written following Louis Armstrong's death on 6 July 1971.

Thus Armstrong created a new musical language of rich variety and possibilities which was seized upon by every jazz and popular musician who followed him. Jazz in his wake was no longer a 4/4 music. He changed the ideas of how jazz might be composed, too, and (like Ellington) contributed mightily to the outburst of big swing bands in the 1930s. He also founded a continuing school of popular singing.

To a great extent Armstrong's voice was an extension of his trumpet, and vice versa. When he sang, deep-throated and gravelly, he improvised on melodies, gently re-creating them. Apart from the blues, jazz singing was virtually unknown before he showed how to do it, whilst pop singers fearfully stuck close to the tune (and were usually called 'vocal refrain' on record labels).

From his innovation flowed the musical freedom which enabled Billie Holiday to develop. Gravelly singer-trumpeters – Cootie Williams, Humphrey Lyttelton, Kenny Ball, Jonah Jones – were shown the way. Louis pioneered scat-singing, with consequences for Ella Fitzgerald. The masters of popular song – Sinatra and Crosby, Nat Cole and Billy Eckstine profited from his example of re-creation as, indeed, do even those rock singers today who expand upon simple themes.

'I'm proud to acknowledge my debt to the Rev Satchelmouth,' Crosby once said. 'He is the beginning and end of music in America.'

He never saw any demarcation between jazz and entertainment. So he would mix great music with clowning showbiz routines. To him, it was not at all incongruous to top the charts in the 1960s with 'Hello Dolly' and 'Wonderful World' – which feat, during a rock-dominated era, demonstrated neatly the unchanging universality of his appeal.

His music, of course, did vary in quality through the years. It had to when he was roaring around the world in his fifties and sixties, obsessed about diet and bowels, always fearful that his lips, bruised and battered from a hundred thousand fierce encounters with a trumpet mouthpiece, would be damaged.

But he never lost his ability to surprise and delight with his music. He never griped. 'I must tell you,' he wrote to Max Jones, his biographer, 'that my whole life has been happiness.' A remarkable statement from a man born black in the Deep South as the century began, who, when he headed for Chicago, was told by a white honky-tonk owner: 'Be sure and get yourself a white man that will put his hand on your shoulder and say "This is my nigger".'

But inevitably in recent years there were angry men who accused him of being Uncle Tom, of not acting black enough – conveniently forgetting his angry message to Eisenhower when the Little Rock desegregation issue was hot, and perhaps not understanding that his stage performance was a professional performance, not a statement of political philosophy. Mostly,

Armstrong seemed to have no identity without a trumpet somewhere near.

'You got to live with that horn, haven't you?' he told me once in Amsterdam. 'It's part of you. It makes you unhappy if you can't live with what belongs there.'

Ellington after Russia

24 OCTOBER 1971

Everything about Edward Kennedy Ellington, the Duke, demonstrates monumental cool; everything that is, except his music, which is cool and hot by turns. Towards the end of his second Hammersmith concert last Thursday, during which his orchestra dazzlingly showed just why Duke is the longest-lasting and greatest contributor to modern music, he staged a rampaging piece of soul-rock called 'One More Time', spearheaded by his two singers, which is not at all his usual métier. You could almost hear the purists frowning.

Riding hotelwards later, he recalled that the previous night some of the audience had come on stage, dancing, to join the jubilee. 'If we keep playing that number,' he said, ironically tolerant, 'then the critics can stop wondering what to pan.'

Irony, of a kindly and humane variety, marks the elegant speech of the man and his music (what could be more ironic than the quirky convolutions which Duke plays as commentating counterpoint to his horn soloists?) and it was richly evident in his delightful pronouncements last week, both on-stage and off. Enthusing about his reception in Russia, he remarked that several of his concerts went on for four hours.

'And no one complained – not the audience' (managing to make himself sound surprised) 'not the stage hands, not even the cats in the band. The Russians came to hear our music – no other reason. Some were satisfied, and some were surprised how much they were satisfied.'

The overriding impression of the Hammersmith concert was of the youthful sound of this band of veterans (matched by an increasing youngness in the audience) and the way in which Duke's oldest compositions appear to be modern. His long orchestral work, *Tone Parallel to Harlem*, was the most persuasive instance. Its complicated rhythms, its majesty of orchestral colourings and cunning dissonances, its contrasts of moods and tones were everything that good modern music should be.

The fact that it was played at all was significant. Had Johnny Hodges and Cat Anderson still been with the band, the necessity for lengthy solo spots for them would scarcely have made the performance of a major Ellington orchestral work possible. These ravishing artists were missed most keenly, of course – Cat particularly for his way of giving stratospheric bite to the trumpet section, the only part of the present band which sometimes lacked steam – but Duke faced their absence by simply unlocking other vaults of his treasure-house.

He has found some splendid new musicians, as well as Norris Turney from his last tour. Harold Minerve was a wonderfully positive alto-sax player (more Parker than Hodges) and John Coles a most pretty trumpeter, whilst the old hands – Gonsalves, Cootie Williams, Russell Procope, Harry Carney – played superbly up to standard. Cootie especially, prowling the stage, his trumpet violent and full-blooded, has never been more commanding. He saves himself for solos now and left rather early, presumably taking advantage of the licence permitted to so senior an Ellingtonian.

This was a quite magical concert, Ellington still at the peak of his form, producing newer compositions (his *New Orleans* and *Afro Eurasian Eclipse* suites) whilst never losing touch with the old (like *Black and Tan Fantasy*). He is one genius who needs no razzmatazz for finale. His last stroke was to play a gentle piano solo, 'Lotus Blossom', with only bowed bass for accompaniment, as his tribute to Billy Strayhorn, and with that the music ended – except that at 4 am he was still playing, along with Jacques Loussier, for maybe twenty people in a private suite at the Dorchester. There never, surely, was such a man for music, nor such music from one gigantically talented man.

Riches from heaven

5 DECEMBER 1971

The scalpers are getting $75 a seat for *Jesus Christ Superstar* at the Mark Hellinger Theatre on Broadway; *Godspell* luxuriates in critical balm at the London Round House. Whether this presages a Christian revival, or is merely another bizarre twist in the search of a disordered age for *something* to believe in, poses a question inappropriate for clever snap judgments or puerile lip-curling.

There is, however, undoubted irony in these theatrical phenomena. *Superstar* has made several people, including its young British progenitors, Tim Rice and Andrew Lloyd Webber, rather rich; the *Superstar* album has now sold over 3½ million copies, the fastest seller in history. *Godspell* looks, too, as if it will make money. Whose was the Kingdom of Heaven?

To compare the two shows is, in a sense, unrewarding; like asking whether you prefer beer and cheese after a Lakeland trudge to seeing Brazil v England at Wembley. The experiences are totally dissimilar.

Superstar is an almost frantically ambitious essay of imagination, given on Broadway the kind of spectacularly professional production which Hollywood once used to lavish on Biblical movies. The costumes, staging and technical trickery are overwhelming (as, in parts, is the sheer vulgarity) and such mayhem made the rock opera a predictable butt for the fancier American critics.

Yet it remains a production of immense excitement, brilliant in parts, despite its excesses, with very original lyrics, original insights too into the seven days leading up to the Crucifixion, and music of such splendour. At least three numbers – the title song; 'I Don't Know How To Love Him'; and 'What's The Buzz' – are excellent.

Godspell is a show of negligible musical content ('Day By Day', attractively Bacharachian and the folksy 'By My Side' are nice, but not in *Superstar*'s class) and far fewer pretensions. The spoken words are fine, but since they lean heavily on straight Biblical quotation, how can they fairly be compared with Rice's bravely self-made libretto?

The whole production, indeed, survives on the youthful zest, happiness and humour of the cast, who do a magnificent job of acting, but not especially of singing. There is nothing in the performance to compare with the blues-loaded passion of Ben Vereen as Judas, and the perfection of Yvonne Elliman's Mary Magdalene in *Superstar*.

In a word, *Godspell* is happy but in most musical respects hapless. Where *Godspell* made me laugh (and glad of it) *Superstar*'s musical magnificence really moved me.

Yes and the coming of age

16 JULY 1972

Rick Wakeman, musician with Yes, sits in a studio recording the group's fifth album. Seven keyboard instruments surround him – piano, organ, electric piano, electric harpsichord, two Moog synthesizers and a Mellotron, which can create orchestral sounds of strings, woodwind and brass, in any key, in any combination, from instrumental tapes it contains.

Signs like 'controllers', 'oscillator bank', 'modifiers' litter the electric instruments, which can be combined cunningly by a small digital computer. The music may be fragile and very beautiful; sometimes it suggests several symphony orchestras, an artillery barrage and Dantean screams.

Wakeman began studying piano at five, later studied at the Royal College of Music, is now, early-twentyish, a master musician. The creative flair and technical mastery required of him is staggering; enough, perhaps, to make many symphony orchestra section members quail. Yet the level of musical competence is not untypical of the many-stranded music which, for want of a better word (some would say from excess of both prejudice and ignorance), is still called 'popular', with dozens of sub-divisions – 'rock' and 'pop', 'jazz' and 'bubble-gum' – appended. Such words may, confusingly, hold different meanings for different people. It is easier to call it simply music, the natural music of our century.

Yes began in 1968, modestly. There are five or six of them, depending on whether you call the engineer a musician; and today, isn't he? Now audiences of up to thirty thousand are usual for their concerts in America, where they have toured thrice these past twelve months. Their schedule is harsh, totally dedicated to music.

'We don't mind not seeing the cities we visit,' said Jon Anderson, the lead singer. 'We are involved only in our music, trying to play good sets.'

Anderson composes. His lyrics are often assemblies of images which create mood rather than spell out certainties: 'A dewdrop can exalt us like the music of the sun', or, again from the long title work of the new album *Close To The Edge*:

Crossed a line around the changes of the summer
Reaching out to call the colour of the sky

Anderson is just discovering Ravel. 'I wake up to Chopin and Liszt. I go to sleep to Sibelius. It pacifies the mind.'

He doesn't sound as if he's putting one on. He simply says. 'I played an Elton John album all through today. That's what rock is now. You want to put LPs on at the start, not just pick out tracks.'

It is difficult to describe the new Yes album. It is surprising music of immense sophistication, great talent, mixing conventional and very unconventional modes. It would be as pointless to believe the uninitiated listener could immediately appreciate it as to believe that an Egyptian child would at once enjoy Schoenberg or a sitar player from Dacca would straightaway dig Mahler.

Yet such expectations remain common, perhaps not surprisingly. Radio One leans heavily towards the undistinguished 'bubble-gum' end of the popular music spectrum. And the mass Press too often shows little understanding of the music or its importance. The populars concentrate on the frivols; the qualities, with notable exceptions, report minor 'classical' musicians playing to audiences of a few score friends, whilst major 'popular' concerts, performed before thousands – which may be full of serious artistic content and virtuoso playing – go unnoticed.

Popular music is, of course, still stuffed with nonsense. It has freaks like Alice Cooper, mountains of records by dime-a-dozen tinkle artists, noise for noise's sake and superstars with more charisma than taste, which was true of Elvis Presley in the 1960s – though he woke up with the pointed 'In

The Ghetto' as well as the ability to laugh at himself in his Las Vegas seasons.

But pop's coming-of-age in the last five years hasn't really been noticed by the over-thirty-fives. With conventional conservatoire and symphonic music in an arid state, revealing few new composers (who, even, whistles Britten's operatic arias today as Rossini's once were whistled?), the twentieth-century 'popular' genre is now patently the only music which vividly relates to its age – by which I mean that it reflects it, comments on it, is readily understood by its children. Popular music today, infinitely various, paints the frivolity, disasters, joys, disaffection, protest, yearning for faith, desire to shock, idealism and cynicism of our world.

It is full of poetry, some good, some awful. It bursts with juvenile histrionics, theatricalities (Frank Zappa's shows), love, beauties, cruelty, phonies, honest men, idiot dancing, violence, mass bombardment of the senses and lonely voices preaching strange faiths. It will tear your urban guts out (Tom Paxton's 'About The Children'), tell narrative stories with sparkling panache (Simon and Garfunkel's 'The Boxer'), lay out moving swathes of nostalgia (David Ackles' 'Montana Song').

It has conquered the theatre (*Hair, Catch My Soul, Jesus Christ Superstar, Godspell*) and increasingly seizes the concert hall. It has cantatas (The Who's *Tommy*), symphonies and suites. Both 'jazz' and 'rock' works may be half-hour tone poems or related narrative sequences (Sinatra's *Watertown*) as much as three-minute pops

The case of 'jazz' is interesting. It always was part of the modern popular music stream – an Afro-European-American confluence with many currents. But for years there were jazz versus pop arguments. Now, ageing jazzmen like Buddy Rich and Woody Herman deploy 'rock' traits, and young 'rock' bandsmen (Blood Sweat and Tears *et al*) mix in jazz characteristics. The argument is dead.

Popular music, in a word, is now adult. It is not all serious, far from it, but it has to be taken seriously. If Elvis' gold Cadillac (sprayed with forty coats of paint, including crushed diamonds and tropical fish scales) was once *the* symbol, then Yes are now a symbol equally as important.

McCartney takes Wings

27 MAY 1973

They're closing the Cavern in Liverpool, where The Beatles grew and the condensation ran down the stone walls in rivulets. And I was remembering, oh, round about 1961, when little Paul McCartney was singing and looking as though butter wouldn't melt in his mouth, and the girl beside me gave the Cavern the beady eye and said: 'They tell me this place used to be a fruit warehouse, and no expense has been spared to leave it just like it was.'

Twelve years on, at Hammersmith last Friday, Paul didn't look or sound too much different. His band, Wings, has at last turned into a tight, tidy, very enjoyable rock group. And to observe the erupting audience – stomping, laughing, crushing to get near the action, loving it, wanting more – you'd never have guessed McCartney had been away for almost three years, or that he'd just been torn apart for that pretty limp TV spectacular.

Wings is three guitars, drums, with tambourine, occasional piano, and sharp harmony from Mrs Linda McCartney, who (as I'm not the first to point out) looks strangely like David Bowie. It's fine at hard-rocking numbers, with Paul's belting lead voice abetted by good shouting harmonies. It produces the unexpected: Linda's reggae frolic, 'Seaside Woman', for example. Its message songs are strong, especially the excellent 'Wild Life', toughly ecological. There are still some classy ballads from Paul, like 'Maybe I'm Amazed', his best post-Beatles song. And Denny Laine, once of The Moody Blues, drops in nice reminders of *his* past.

But – and this is the point, isn't it? – enjoyable as the evening was, this is not a supergroup, only a very good band. No one wants the wonderfully-talented Paul to do another Beatles. Yet the audience loved best the simple rock songs, recalling the early 1960s; and the reservation about McCartney remains, that whilst between 1962 and 1968 you could observe an almost miraculous growth in The Beatles' music, how has *his* music developed since 'Yesterday'?

Not, I suggest, significantly. We are enjoying him – good. But I very much want him soon to write three songs as good as 'Maybe I'm Amazed', and one as good as 'Yesterday'. He always was, potentially, the most movingly lyrical of the fabulous four. So, rave on, Paul. But move us when we're silent too.

Cleo Laine: 'Working is living'

OCTOBER 1973

When the English impresario Harold Fielding was planning his revival of Jerome Kern's *Showboat* in London – it's been running over two years now – he wanted Cleo Laine to play the half-caste Julie. She said she wouldn't go into the show just to sing two songs, 'Bill' and 'Can't Help Loving That Man of Mine', which are Julie's ration in the score. So 'Nobody Else But Me' was melded into the show for Cleo. Fielding wanted her that badly.

So, in the last couple of years especially, have a lot of other people. With her composer-husband, John Dankworth, who always leads her accompanying band, she's toured widely in Europe, Australia, the United States, and now Canada during that period. She's had very successful concerts in New York, one at Carnegie Hall, as well as a season at the Rainbow Room. The New York critics raved about her: and the *New York Times* accused Britain of having been hiding one of its national treasures. In her middle forties, she's suddenly an international draw.

Yet despite the evidence of her concerts, she's still pigeonholed by many who know her name simply as a jazz singer. Perhaps that's because she was once a dance band singer; oddly enough she appeared at New York's Birdland way back in 1958, after her husband's jazz orchestra had become the first British outfit to play the Newport Jazz Festival. But now she's so much more.

By sheer application she's become an all-rounder who glides through Schoenberg and *lieder* as readily as Cole Porter or Kern. The two-hour concerts which reveal her comprehensive talents mix an astonishing variety of words and music: James Taylor and Bach, Charles Ives and T. S. Eliot, Brahms and Richard Rodgers, John Donne and the contemporary English wit and ex-Goon, Spike Milligan.

Her handling of this hugely varied material is always highly personal, subtle and, apparently, effortless. 'Where Streisand makes "On a Clear Day" sound like a summons to the local fire brigade,' wrote the British critic, Benny Green, 'Laine *eases* her way into the number, offers a cheerful little improvisation around the theme, and ends up with a soaring extension of the final syllable of "evermore" that would give Yma Sumac a run for her money.'

Yma Sumac is only one of the singers she's been likened to. Her smoky lower tones have been compared with Marilyn Horne's, her ability to scat-sing with Ella Fitzgerald's. The truth is she isn't any other singer; she's just herself. Once a natural contralto, with a one-and-a-half-octave range, she's stretched her voice over the years until she can dart anywhere within a near-four-octave compass. She puts part of the responsibility for that on Dankworth. 'When I was singing with his band in the 1950s, he kept craftily pushing up the arrangements. Later I went to a teacher. She made me understand that it was really mind over matter. If I wanted to do it I could.'

Dankworth's early quiet pressure upon her is only one simple example of the complexity and completeness of their relationship, which has grown into a rare artistic partnership since their first meeting in 1952. She was then in her early twenties and had been a spare-time performer since the age of three. She was born Clementina Dinah Campbell, daughter of a Wiltshire farmer's daughter and a Jamaican immigrant. Their life in Southall, on London's western outskirts, was according to Cleo, 'clean but scruffy'. Her parents encouraged her to sing and by the time she auditioned for Dankworth she'd married, had a son, and been turned down for a job with an all-girl band because she declined to double on bass.

Dankworth, though, wanted her. 'It wasn't exactly a blinding revelation,' he says now, 'but I could tell she had promise.' She got the job, £7 a week, a change of name, the start of years of one-night stands at ballrooms and theatres with Dankworth's bands – and, most importantly, exposure to the ambition which Dankworth had for both their careers. According to Cleo he dominated her at first, bullied her, told her which singers to listen to. In 1958 they married, after a quiet divorce in 1957, and they've been inextricably associated as a musical partnership ever since.

John Dankworth doesn't seem like a bully, not even a musical one. He's a bright, friendly man, born in Ilford, Essex, with Sinatra-ish good looks and easy-going charm, whose career has expanded from jazz to playing Bartok with Yehudi Menuhin and composing concert and movie scores — everything from *The Servant* to *Modesty Blaise*. Yet it's been his drive and his skill at finding and creating a constant flow of unusual new material for Cleo which has been the endless counterpoint to her steady ascent.

It's tempting to cast him as Svengali. He denies it; yet no one seems to believe there would have been a Cleo Laine without John Dankworth. Even Cleo says: 'If I hadn't met him, I would have become someone quite different.'

And that seems true. He's a great doer, always busy. Cleo says: 'My idea of happiness is being completely lazy.' When she first started doing *lieder* she says she hated all the work it involved. Dankworth comments laconically: 'That's probably my greatest service to humanity. Cleo would probably have retired, but I kept bullying her.'

Today, however, Cleo is very level-headed about her success. 'I don't want not to have to work. Nor am I indifferent to whether I make it or not. You see in my terms I *have* made it. I've gradually gathered a public who are very loyal. I'm not a fashionable in-and-out artist. I've paced myself.

And I always wanted John and the kids' – they have a boy and a girl – 'before the jet-setting and the world tours.'

Just about the only 'spurt of real deep ambition' to which Cleo will admit came in 1958. 'I'd had enough of band singing. So I decided to quit and try for the theatre.'

First, she got a part – the lead – in a play directed by Tony Richardson at London's Royal Court Theatre, *Flesh To A Tiger*. But there was no follow-up: 'I was a coloured actress, see. Nobody wanted to know unless my skin fitted the part.' So she began to develop into the kind of entertainment all-rounder she is today. She did the cabaret circuit in England, jazz concerts with her husband, got a pop single record into the Top Ten in 1961 – at the same time as she was singing the Lotti Lenya part in the Weill/Brecht opera, *The Seven Deadly Sins*, at the Edinburgh Festival. She even got a good part in *Valmouth*, a Sandy Wilson musical based on the Ronald Firbank novel.

But it wasn't until the mid-1960s that a wider audience began to understand the phenomenon Cleo was turning into. Two events marked this crucial point in the Dankworths' lives. The first, in 1965, was the release of her *Shakespeare and All That Jazz* record album, an inspired collection of song settings by Dankworth which won her a coveted five-star rating in *Downbeat*, the American jazz magazine. The second, in 1966, was her acting as Andromache in Sartre's translation of Euripides' *The Women of Troy* at Edinburgh. The director was Frank Dunlop – 'the first person to look at me simply as an actress, neither black or white', according to Cleo.

Since then she's balanced her career neatly between acting and singing, but mostly the latter. Her appeal, it seems, is to all those who like good songs of many different styles well (often inspiredly) sung. Her audiences know that her voice is unlikely to be duplicated in their experience. She offers emotional intensity as well as vocal acrobatics. She looks great: her beauty is lush, mature, impishly sultry, matching the low purr of her voice and the low cut of her gowns.

But there's another side to the life of the Dankworths: WAP – the Wavendon Allmusic Plan. It was this brainchild of theirs which led them, four years or so ago, to move into a rambling neo-Gothic rectory at Wavendon, fifty miles north up the M1 from London in Buckinghamshire. The idea was to create a small theatre/concert hall (they converted the stables for that) as well as a musical education centre which would transcend barriers between styles – hence the 'allmusic' of the title.

In the spacious grounds of the house, there are summer camps for kids. Dankworth teaches instrumentalists and Cleo coaches singers. There's a Wavendon Arts Festival every year, jazz weekends, and an average of a concert a week in the old stables.

Without letting WAP devour their lives, the Dankworths still spend a lot of time at Wavendon, and at their villa in Malta. Cleo still likes just lounging around, not doing much. She reads and paints a bit – faces, trees, her husband, their children. She doesn't listen to much music, except by way of work or accident. 'It's around all the time, you see. The kids play cello and clarinet, John's going away at his sax or clarinet or the piano, or he's got Bach or Bartok on the record-player for relaxation. I never need to put a record on myself. Yoga relaxes me more than music. I do exercises every day. It helps me not to get upset by the aggro in showbusiness.'

Indeed, the whole feeling emanating from her is of happiness, relaxation, fulfilment. If pressed she'll admit she wouldn't mind a major movie part or a year acting with a good company, but it doesn't seem all-important to her. In the end, all the questions come back to her relationship with John. Their careers run, sometimes, separately, yet are never far apart.

Dankworth, who trained at the Royal Academy of Music, once said: 'Intellectually, I influenced her I suppose. But critically, she's always influenced me. If you're looking for truth in music, then you just ask her.'

And Cleo seals the compact – yet with devastating honesty. 'John's as important to me today artistically as ever he was. I still have to ask him to explain things to me all the time. I don't read music too well. But, look – you ask me what I'd do if John were to die tomorrow. Maybe you imagine I've never thought about that. But I have. I don't depend on anyone *that* much, not even John – I couldn't curl up and just do nothing. So if John weren't here, I'd go right on working. Working is living.'

Duke's Royal offering

11 JULY 1976

Duke Ellington died just over two years ago. His music, of course, survives through the hundreds upon hundreds of recordings which his orchestra made between the 1920s and 1973. Within that storehouse incredible discoveries are still to be made.

A minor masterpiece, for such it is, has been given to the world, very appropriately this month. Bicentennially speaking, with the Queen's visit to the United States so fresh in mind, it is marvellous that *The Queen's Suite* should now be available for the world to hear. It has been at last released, together with *The Goutelas Suite* and *Uwis Suite*, on Norman Granz's glittering Pablo label (2335 743, £3.25); and thereby the story begins.

In October, 1958, Ellington met the Queen for the first time at an arts festival in Leeds which the Earl of Harewood, her cousin, had organized. It was a happy occasion. The band played nobly and Duke himself – riding on the crest of his revival after the 1956 Newport Festival – was benignly content. Asked by the Queen when he had last played in England, he replied with characteristic finesse: '1933, Your Majesty, years before you were born.'

In the months after his return he wrote a six-part suite as a memento, recorded it at his own expense, and sent the solitary pressing to the Queen at Buckingham Palace as a unique gift. Despite endless entreaties he would not allow the record of *The Queen's Suite* to be issued whilst he lived; only rarely, and then usually on private occasions, did he play the piano solo from the *Suite*, 'Single Petal of a Rose'.

The series of pieces now revealed is among the greatest of Ellington's works. The superb reed section of the 1960s – Hodges, Procope, Hamilton, Gonsalves, Carney – play some of his most mystic, ethereal ensembles, with Hamilton's clarinet and Hodges' alto sax in especially mellow form. The trumpets (including Clark Terry) and trombones sound continually majestic, and the scores vary from lyrical to idiosyncratically exotic, notably 'Apes and Peacocks', an inspiration from the gifts the Queen of Sheba brought to King Solomon in The Bible, which Duke read so avidly, over and over again.

Above all, there is 'Single Petal of a Rose', which guests at a London party in 1958 heard Duke in the process of composing. A most beautiful piano impression, fit to be ranked with the best of Debussy or Chopin, it has long been my favourite Ellington solo.

Mostly, Ellington did not find the immediate inspiration for the pieces in England. Displays of beauty in America while he was travelling – a mocking bird in Florida, evening insects in Ohio – and the majesty of the Northern Lights seen in Canada were the springboard for his ravishing music. *The Goutelas Suite* is a bonus on the album. Not as impressive as *The Queen's Suite*, it remains delightful. This work, remembering Ellington's inauguration of a restored French chateau in 1966, when crowds of children greeted him in the snow with flaming torches, contains one of the few fanfares Duke ever wrote as well as other felicities. A record in a thousand, if not a million.

Evita as masterpiece

14 NOVEMBER 1976

Jesus Christ Superstar, the most important opera of recent times – although Covent Garden hasn't heard it – is still filling the Palace Theatre after five years. With *Evita*, their new opera, Tim Rice (lyrics) and Andrew Lloyd Webber (music) have surpassed *Superstar*. It is quite simply a masterpiece.

It's not yet on stage, although it was brilliantly exposed in an audio-visual presentation to launch the double-album of *Evita* (MCA, MCX 503, £5.99) last week. *Evita* is a record, as *Superstar* was, and when it moves to stage or screen, as it must, it may not even run like *Superstar*. Musically, however, it is an immense advance.

The reason for hesitancy on predicting *Evita*'s future is almost entirely its subject. This is the life story of Eva Peron. 'A cross between a fantasy of the bedroom and a saint,' as Juan Peron sings in the opera, sounds a recipe for instant commercial success. Yet somehow Argentina could prove too remote, Eva too suspect a heroine, for certainty.

The composers treat her ambivalently. At times you are captivated by the back-street actress who made it; but relentlessly the counterpoint of opposition, of the realities of the totalitarianism her popular appeal disguised, is thrust into action. Since, however, she has the best tunes, and most moving words, the creators of *Evita* seem *emotionally* under her spell.

Those best tunes are tremendous. Lloyd Webber's score is, in beauty and dramatic impact, overwhelming. One recurring theme alone – 'Don't Cry For Me Argentina' – has the romantic sweep of Tchaikovsky and, given the elegiac twist of Rice's ultimate lyric ('Eva's Final Broadcast'), wrings the heart as few tragic operatic arias do.

The score is, in all ways, a triumphant synthesis of modes: churchy choral singing; upbeat rock; Latin-American rhythms; flowing romantic melodies; punchy, witty lyrics. Sometimes I was reminded of *Carmen* (especially *Carmen Jones*), sometimes of the best Broadway musicals, always of the team whose *Joseph* and *Superstar* have established a brilliantly personal style.

Superb performances come from the interpreting artists, particularly Julie Covington as Eva. C. T. Wilkinson (Ché), Paul Jones (Peron), and Barbara Dickson are nobly in support. The rock musicians include Ray Russell and Hank Marvin; the London Philharmonic Orchestra is conducted by Anthony Bowles.

'They said of *Superstar* that everybody knew the story, so it would fail,' Tim Rice observed last week. 'Of *Evita*, they say, nobody knows the story, so it will fail.' If taste or justice survive, the doubters will again prove horribly wrong.

Yes at the summit

30 OCTOBER 1977

Rarely is it that twice in a few days the immense range of popular music, the peaks and horizons of possibility, are so wondrously landscaped by artists of differing traditions. That benison was the work last week of Yes and Stan Getz.

For Yes, younger electronic masters, Wembley Pool – their haven for six nights and sixty thousand listeners – was on opening night like a cathedral. An audience intent on the music, except when the acolytes were invited to participate, the choral harmonies keening, Rick Wakeman's powerful organ pealing, Jon Anderson's modern counter-tenor spinning words like psalmists' verses and finally, a forest of arms raised in worshipful salute.

The return to live concerts of this magnificent British band was a triumph not often equalled even in the world of rock hyperbole. And they, unlike most other present demi-gods, merit the applause. They couple the driving excitement of rock with all those reflective, lyrical, imaginative and virtuosic blessings which come from other kinds and qualities of music. Virtually unmatched they stand.

Oddly, despite their continuing hold on the popular imagination, a minor critical backlash assails them currently. This, perhaps, is an inevitable part of pop culture (as well as of the musical politics of envy) but the horizons which Yes have shown – the larger-scale uses of rock, sophisticated technique, symphonic sweep, without ever losing their vital rhythmic roots – are now, mercifully, part of our expectation. Popular music was never only about sweat, stomping, sneers and sex.

The return to Yes of Rick Wakeman, bearded like the pard, is good for the band and for him. He's not straining so much with his battery of keyboards, content to cement the whole sound together without excessive pyrotechnics. Steve Howe's varied guitar effects, especially his chiming Spanishry, hot and languid in turn, remain superb, whilst Jon Anderson's tone and words give Yes a unique dimension.

Certainly his lyrics – oblique, unusual images – invite charges of pretentiousness. But that is to ignore their metre, muscularity and, at their best, concentrated provocativeness. 'In charge of who is there in charge of me' is still one of the memorable lines of modern pop poetry; like Yes generally, Anderson raises the sights.

The band gave Wembley fullish measure, though why waste time with Donovan at the start? There were ecstatic laser tricks and waterfalls of smoke accompanying their venerable symphonies, 'Close To The Edge' with 'And You And I'; a happy mixture from their new album, including the driving 'Going For The One' and the long, most beautiful 'Awaken'.

For maybe twenty minutes they played through a joyous jam session, each musician igniting the others, fierily improvising with the audience urging. Few rock bands could have done it with such panache, few jazzmen either. Cleo Laine, who with John Dankworth was in the throng, said cheerfully that it would be interesting to sing with Jon Anderson. So barriers melt.

Stan Getz is melting misconceptions too during his season at Ronnie Scott's Club. He has moved into a more heavily rhythmic environment. There's that mellow-toned exile, Rick Laird, on bass, a percussionist as well as the admirable Billy Hart on drums, whilst his new keyboards man, Andy Leverne, uses electronic together with acoustic instruments. He's also a composer, and Getz plays a lot of his work during the first set.

Not everything is perfect, but it's fascinating to find Getz exploring, and to be reminded so dramatically that he's not only the world's most exquisite balladist on tenor saxophone (and still a bossa nova lover) but also a happy, inventive swinger. Getz is fearsomely good at fast tempos, and he plays these days as if he's continually smiling at the world, sax locked into flying fingers like another limb.

Ballads, though – yes, it is unchangeably the ballad which distils the imperishable art of Getz. For purity of tone, sweet and smoky, for elegant and moving interpretation which makes words seem redundant, for the gift of freezing an episode of reflective emotion unforgettably in time, Getz is unrivalled.

Cleo: a touch of class

6 NOVEMBER 1977

Something enormously important was proved at the Palladium last week: that music, jazz-influenced music, spiced with classical tones, can be glorious box-office entertainment provided you keep the faith and *present* it right – with wit, discipline, contrasts, love, conviction and class.

Such a lesson oughtn't to be surprising. In the 1930s' heyday of bands and singers in theatre, they knew you had to make a show, do a presentation, not just blow and hope. Many rock bands know it today too.

Class is the key, of course. Cleo Laine, at fifty still the best singer in the world, and John Dankworth provided it in a three-hour marathon which was totally spellbinding and, at last, drew from a British audience the kind of sumptuous standing ovation with which Carnegie Hall and overseas arenas regularly regale them.

It's been long enough coming. I remembered twenty-five years ago (New Brighton Tower Ballroom) hearing Cleo sing with Dankworth's Palais swingers. Green party frock, like band singers used to wear, plugging through ballads, rough diamond. Now the diamond is polished perfection.

Wisely, Cleo came on first at the Palladium to set the evening's tone. The picture montage preceding her had been sickly showbiz; but that voice dispelled fears. She bounded (vocally) for ten minutes, left on a high note (her four octaves at work) and then gave it over to Dankworth.

His opening half with an excellent orchestra was so good it threatened to upstage her. He recalled the Palais and bebop days: reminded us of Miller, Goodman and Kenton; brought on John Williams whose guitar chimed through Albeniz, Bach and beautiful Rodrigo; and wound up with a joyous quintet jam on Goodman's 'Slipped Disc'. There hasn't been a band show like it in years.

Cleo, in dazzling black, began her thirty-song essay with variations on 'Blues In The Night' – a wonderful grass roots touch – and thereafter rarely put a note wrong. She sang her strings of beautiful ballads (outstandingly, Ralph McTell's tragic 'Streets of London'), duetted with Williams, jazzed exquisitely on 'Riding High' and 'It Don't Mean A Thing', did her joke songs – and continually surprised us.

Her encore of Sondheim songs, especially 'Broadway Baby', showed what a dazzling lead musical actress she would make. Her art, certainly, has always been dramatic, whether in theatre or on concert stage.

Does her voice remain as good? Probably. It's smokier now, carries some scars from years of hard road work. Maybe she attempts fewer high-note exercises. But for conquering tone, total command of interpretation, she is untouchable empress.

Joan Armatrading, a different singer, but equally dramatic, is still on the way up, so rich in promise both as composer and performer. Unlike Cleo Laine, however, she's as yet predominantly an album artist. Her stage command droops as the music stops, and her colleagues never seem to get the sound right.

They were filming for BBC's *Sight and Sound* at her Hammersmith concert on Thursday, but I hope you at home heard it better than did the theatre audience. The sound oozing into the hall was like blancmange with sharp rocks in it – muzzy words, overamplified drums, poor balance, spiky keyboards.

In Joan's deliciously sharp bank-raid saga, 'Opportunity', you couldn't hear the supporting singers' dialogue; the song was ruined. Meantime, the lights blazed on (and off) the audience's heads; not the best way to win friends for TV live shows. The singer looked a touch bedazzled too.

Still, the quality of her quirky, astonishing songs survived – from 'Down to Zero', through the poignant 'Willow', to 'Tall in The Saddle'. Her blues ancestry shone through, and her solo spot, with churning guitar-playing, stunned the hall.

If Cleo is preciously rare, with no one quite like her, then Joan too – given, as her remarkable song has it, love and affection – might one day merit similar adjectives.

When Eva came on stage

25 JUNE 1978

No man's art is an island: and so there are many things which almost anyone who looks, listens or reads must already know about the magnificent, original, compelling *Evita* of Andrew Lloyd Webber and Tim Rice.

Here, therefore, I declare a moratorium on particular superlatives, yet begin with others.

Evita, tracing the career of the charismatic but awful Eva Peron, is quintessentially about words and music. These, created and coalesced with genius by Rice, librettist, and Lloyd Webber, composer, are its heart and ensure that the work, staged or unstaged, is a masterpiece, as readers may recall has been my view since November, 1976, when the record was unveiled.

It is, thus, with sounds – only minimally changed from the record – that my story begins, an order of priority intended in no sense to detract from the miraculous wand which has been waved over *Evita* by bluff Hal, the undisputed American Prince of musical directors, whose glittering lineage stretches back to *West Side Story*.

Evita is a quite marvellous modern opera, exceeding in stature even *Jesus Christ Superstar*. Lloyd Webber's score, so full of glorious melodies apart from the well-known 'Don't Cry For Me Argentina', is an unparalleled fusion of twentieth-century musical experience. Echoes of the past, Tchaikovsky, Puccini, and church choral music – shimmer hauntingly through. But it is the interweaving of pop, rock, jazz, Broadway, Latin and other elements which makes the brew so astonishingly potent.

As you listen, these ingredients become strikingly apparent. Is not the show's most perfectly constructed song, 'Waltz for Eva and Ché', in the Broadway tradition? Does not 'Buenos Aires' remind one of the Latinate explosions in *West Side Story*? And whence springs 'Another Suitcase In Another Hall' except from the torchy rejection ballads of classic popular modern composers like our Cole Porters and Kerns?

Lloyd Webber is perhaps the most remarkable musical child of his generation. He has heard much, sensitively absorbed it, and produced his own completely original and personal synthesis.

In Tim Rice, he has a partner of perfection. Rice writes trenchant, witty, modern lyrics superbly married to Lloyd Webber's ambitious score – a score so skilfully orchestrated that I am amazed to have read elsewhere no comments yet upon this aspect, nor tributes to those invisible musicians who play it so well under Anthony Bowles' direction. Criticism of musicals should begin with the music.

This, however, is not Wagner but *modern* opera in the tradition primarily of twentieth-century popular music. So one's enjoyment of the libretto is natural and easy. Practically every word of Rice's can be instantly savoured by the audience. *Evita*'s excellent cast, their fine diction enhanced by microphones, can achieve meaning, nuances and subtlety which make it an opera for our time, satisfying our hunger for understanding.

Everything, too, is *sung* in *Evita*. No lumbering 'book' links it, but elegant and powerful recitative which continually points up character and sums up inevitably in brusque form Eva Peron's progression from bed to bed, ambition to megalomania.

That recitative also reminds one continually of the evils of the Peron dictatorship, its greed, the brutalities wreaked upon thousands of Argentinians. The words printed with the original *Evita* record demonstrate this unmistakably, and the austere, sombre stage version makes the message still clearer.

Which brings me to the sorcery of Harold Prince and the interaction of his supremely relevant stagecraft with the music – or, rather, should have brought me to it – as well as to the wondrously revealed talents of Elaine Paige (Evita), and all the other facets of the artistic diamond which is *Evita*. To these things, I will return.

Encore *Evita*

2 JULY 1978

The breathtaking opening of *Evita*'s second act (to resume last week's story) distils both the work's meaning and Harold Prince's achievement in interpreting the opera of Tim Rice and Andrew Lloyd Webber.

Set arrogantly high on a balcony above the people are Peron and his crew. Eva Peron, glittering in bejewelled white, cruises on and begins to sing softly, with calculated alertness. 'All you will see is a girl you once knew, although she's dressed up to the nines.'

The song becomes 'Don't Cry For Me Argentina' and then, suddenly, she is ranting – 'Peron . . . his noble crusade . . . fire those cannons' – like any crude rabble-rouser. The transformation is remarkable.

Elaine Paige, playing Evita, is here revealed as an artist with range, no mere Merman-like belter, despite her explosive dynamism, but a subtle dealer in contrasts, interpreting for us Evita's technique. She wooed the masses, flattered them, gave them handouts, belittled herself – all as a prelude to the fiery oratory which enslaved them.

This balcony spectacular, stamped with Prince's hallmark, is immensely more effective because it contrasts with what surrounds it. Prince believes in economy. He doesn't maul fine words and music by reckless staging.

Prince's sparingly-used *coups* also include superb formal blocks of moving bodies representing army and aristocracy, and a marvellous revolving door through which Eva kicks out her lovers. For the rest, sounds speak virtually for themselves, framed by austere settings, harshly lit, cold with menace.

This adumbration of the evil Peron régime offsets any musical tendency to romanticism as surely as does the characterization. Joss Ackland's Peron is a squat toad. Evita glitters, but only as does the cobra's head before the strike. The drily cynical tone of David Essex's Ché, a waspish chorus, is neatly apt.

'Political' reaction to the opera in some quarters (depicting evil on stage, etc) have amazed me, and wouldn't have done much for Will Shakespeare either. The devil has always had *some* of the good tunes, but of glorification of the Perons or sentimentality about their dire régime *Evita* has very little.

A horrific drop-curtain (Peron atop dead, tortured bodies) greets the audience. The text bombards us with acid comment. Evita cheats, plots, lies, steals. Police thugs haunt scene after scene.

The miracle is that from such bleak material has emerged so impressive a work of art. Its secret – musically and theatrically – lies in one word. Style.

Style is David Bowie's prerogative, too. After his endless image shifts, he has now so abandoned flamboyance that its absence becomes, paradoxically, a new style.

Why did he remind one sometimes of *Evita* at Earls Court last week? Perhaps it was the harsh white lights; perhaps his opening, as downbeat as *Evita*'s with sounds of dirge and doom in *Warszawa*. This time, Bowie gave us a retrospective with huge revivals from *Ziggy Stardust*. Not his finest concert, but tremendous artistic value, with the hammer-blow repetitions of 'it's too late' in the magnificent 'Station to Station' ringing like civilization's knell.

Chapter Three

Rock and Pop 1964-72

The Stones, Supremes and Bill Haley. Cream, The Who and Pink Floyd. Simon and Garfunkel, Ike and Tina Turner, Tom Paxton . . . These are some of the artists included in this chapter, and their names indicate the strain which is at once placed upon terminology – hence the almost defeatist choice of a title. The umbrella phrase 'rock and pop' can only partially suggest the music and the events of the period, as the words deal only with a tiny fraction of the people who were performing at the time. (Yes, I'm acutely aware of those musicians – or unmusical charlatans – who *aren't* covered.)

These were years when the musical revolution spawned by rock 'n' roll changed the face of the entertainment world. Instead of 'concerts', appearances of rock musicians became imperial (or quasi-religious) occasions in monstrous arenas. In Britain, pirate radio boomed and Radio One was born. The best-seller charts were transformed. With every year, rock 'n' roll became more sophisticated, more political, more poetical, more pretentious, more mystical, and ever more fragmented into sub-divisions. The Rolling Stones, all sex and raw power, made do with voice, guitars, drums and over-kill amplification in the early years. Bob Dylan was more or less a voice and a guitar to begin with. But the swift development of synthesizers and other electronic instruments provided new dimensions for rock. The Beatles' *Sergeant Pepper* album in 1967 was only one symbol of how popular music could become orchestral. (It was also a symbol of much more – a kind of unified youth culture, 'seriousness' mixed with entertainment, tangential lyrics which suggested social criticism, drugs, mystical experience, etc.) The phrase 'rock opera' was first coined. The media devoted ever-increasing time and space to popular music. As the 1960s died and a new decade began, the future seemed to lie with bands like Pink Floyd, who created works of symphonic length and used every trick of electronic sound and dramatic lighting to overwhelm their audience. Yet in 1972, The Stones were still around – and rock had more tricks to play in the years which followed.

Stones start rolling

24 MAY 1964

They are the ones who look, to disbelieving bourgeois eyes, like primitive hoodlums: long unkempt hair, ashen cheeks, disorganized clothes, and a surly look. The ones who get turned away from restaurants because they don't always wear ties; the ones whom parents of all shades of respectability, having settled for cosy co-existence with The Beatles, are reputed not to want their daughters to marry – or their sons to ape.

Even in the hysterical world of pop music statistics the swift killing made by The Rolling Stones is surprising. Their first LP record deposed The Beatles from the top of the charts immediately it was issued late last month and is still there; in four weeks it has grossed over £200,000. The Stones get from £400 to more than £1,000 an appearance. And although their music has scarcely scratched the transatlantic record market, they leave tomorrow on a North American tour, ambitiously far-flung by British pop group standards.

Last week, their itinerary read: East Ham, Birmingham, Cannock, Stockport, Sheffield, Slough. In the next three weeks they will holler through New York, Toronto, Philadelphia, Los Angeles and San Antonio (Texas). They are doing more than anyone to restore the equilibrium of Decca Record Company executives who saw The Beatles (and the Epstein stable) slip through their fingers into EMI's welcoming bosom.

There are several pat explanations why these Stones, though far from Beatle-sized, have become the new love affair of the young. The most convincing is that the hard-core teenage idolators felt deprived of their in-thing once The Beatles made their jolly, brash noise acceptable to parents, became embryonic All Round Entertainers and started being seen around Oxford senior common rooms and talking to the Duke of Edinburgh.

The young are possessive about their idols: and it has become axiomatic that those idols flourish on parental disapproval. When The Beatles became famous, The Stones were lying around to be thrown at the adult world. Their music, generically called rhythm and blues, is harsher, wilder, more negroid and less 'commercial' than that of The Beatles and is sometimes, of its kind, very good. Their appearance and behaviour are guaranteed to evoke the birching-and-conscription syndrome among the elderly of twenty-five and over from Birchington to Bath.

The Stones, five Southerners aged from nineteen to twenty-two, called Mick Jagger, Brian Jones, Keith Richard, Charlie Watts and Bill Wyman (he is married with a child), neither contradict nor confirm this reading.

But, after the fashion set by The Beatles, they are articulate about it. They talk straightforwardly and sharply, sometimes pleasantly, sometimes crudely, with a mocking conscious intention to shock. All went to grammar or art schools; Jagger studied at the London School of Economics for two years; two have parents with 'professional' backgrounds.

Jones says it has been their image rather than their music which has established them since they turned professional a year ago. Not until they were *seen* widely in Britain did they catch on; they believe they must now be seen in America to cause similar mayhem. The image and the music are now inseparable.

Though there are lurking suspicions that they set out deliberately to out-Beatle The Beatles, they claim their clothes and long hair were not contrived. They just happened to be like that. But they are very conscious of the burning commercial need to keep their hair long now. 'We don't think we're ugly,' said Jagger. 'It's you who's ugly, because you've got a straight nose and ordinary eyes,' said Richard.

Jagger says he grew his hair long because he was once *told* to get it cut; and their answer to a question about the hysteria which greets them on and off stage was another stereotype of teenage-revolt vocabulary. 'It's very basic,' said Jones. 'It strips everyone of their inhibitions. It's honest.'

Outside their Birmingham hotel the sad, patient girls waited hour after hour. 'We're always trapped in hotels,' said Jagger. 'When I've no one to talk to, I make plenty of phone calls. I've nothing important to say, but I phone.'

When they went down for lunch, Watts and Richard had no ties. The restaurant manager said they must wear them. After protracted negotiations ('Did you put on clean underwear today?' Watts asked the manager) they went to get ties. 'We're not going to do ourselves out of anything for the sake of being nonconformists,' said Jones.

They thought this sort of reaction to them was becoming less common. Jagger and Richard said they were invited by Caroline Maudling – 'socially you know' – to a cocktail party at 11 Downing Street on Budget Day. 'I met her at a party,' said Jagger, 'but I don't really know her. She probably thinks it's hep, or I'm invited as a curiosity piece, or she might fancy me, you never know.'

He even claims parents don't hate them as much as journalists think. 'We get lots of letters from parents who say we're nice.'

For the other parents – those wanting to draw the sting of these young men who seem to them disturbing, quaint or even menacing, Beatle history suggests the answer: accept them, buy them – and smother them.

Supremes and the sound of Detroit

21 MARCH 1965

Detroit is not, historically, a fashionable city for art forms of any kind, even pop music forms – unless you count the external bizarreries of the automobile and their effect on Pop Art. No more was Liverpool till the early sixties. Both cities tend to be self-sustaining and inward-turning. Merseyside, despite its escape route to the sea, is Britain's Middle West.

What happened to refurbish Liverpool's image – the arrival and deification of The Beatles – has also, indirectly, created a new one for Detroit in this country. Once The Beatles confessed that Detroit groups were their early idols and part of their inspiration, Europe cautiously began to get interested in the noise that city was making, which came chiefly from a whole school of very similar artists who record for the Tamla Motown label. It's ironical that there was no mass market in Britain for a wild American group sound, with heavy overtones of blues and gospel singing, before our local imitators stimulated the appetite for the original.

Last year, though, the Detroit sound began to make up for being a little before its time. And the group which set the pace was The Supremes. This week-end most of the Motown top people, led by The Supremes, begin their first concert tour here.

'We are,' says Berry Gordy, head of Tamla Motown, 'very honoured the Beatles should have said what they did. They're creating the same type of music as Tamla Motown – and we're part of the same stream.

'But like other British singers they're from another country as far as we're concerned, and so they don't sound the same as Americans. If they'd imitated American groups perfectly they wouldn't have gone over so well here. The Beatles or Dusty or Georgie Fame, they're all different enough to have created a new sound, a fresh sound. The instrumentation's different, so is the tone of voice.'

There is, conversely, not much danger that The Supremes would be mistaken for other than Americans. There is too much of the tradition of American Negro music, especially that half-jazz, half-pop style called 'race music', in their sound. Though 'rhythm and blues' (the current euphemism for 'race music') and its derivatives have been mashed around in Britain for some time, the American style of it, commercial or otherwise, is usually quite easily recognizable.

That style was also popular enough to make The Supremes the only Americans apart from a bespectacled Tennessean called Roy Orbison to oust British artists from the top of our pop charts last year. They did it in

November with a song called 'Baby Love'; earlier a simple, chanty thing called 'Where Did Our Love Go?' had reached No. 2.

The most typical beat of The Supremes is heavy and rocking. Above this one of the girls (almost invariably Diana Ross) sings a simple, jingly lyric line, arranged in short punchy phrases, while the other two (Mary Wilson and Florence Ballard) chant responses to it, or simply echo it.

Diana Ross has a sweet, rich voice, one which is genuinely jazz-inflected in its ability to slur and syncopate; the chanters have a sharper, tinklier tone, but the edge is somewhat taken off it by diminished volume, which makes them sound as if they are singing in the next room. The similarities between this call-and-response sound and American Negro gospel music are obvious.

'Certainly the basis is gospel-flavoured,' says Berry Gordy, 'but it's not a conscious thing. This is just something we *feel*, and therefore produce. We've never stopped to think about it.'

The Supremes, in other words, are doing what comes naturally, what springs easily from their musical background as American city Negroes. Toned down, of course, for the mass market. So are the other Motown groups. The Supremes may be the smoothest-sounding – the others are wilder and harsher, though with the same very close, inside-tight harmony – but there is a generic feel to all of them, even in their names. The Miracles, The Marvelettes, The Temptations, The Contours, Martha and The Vandellas are the other leading groups, most of them included in the 'package' now in Britain. Mary Wells, Marvin Gaye and Stevie Wonder, a blind boy prodigy who plays wild harmonica, fair piano and drums, and sings shrill and electric, are some of the solo artists Tamla Motown has produced.

Practically all were raised around Detroit and it is extremely difficult to tell the groups apart, even though some are men, some women, and some mixed. The men are invariably counter-tenors, or something like, and chant just as high and wild as the women. It is much more revealing to talk of the 'Detroit Sound' as a generic than it was to talk of the 'Liverpool Sound' when that phrase was OK.

'Looking back now,' said Mary Wilson when The Supremes broke through last year, 'it seems like we spent seven years sort of half working at our singing before things began to happen.' They might, like most other Motown artists, have stayed far longer on the church social and talent contest circuit but for the business flair of Berry Gordy, who is in his early thirties. It was he who discovered The Supremes, who had been friends since childhood, and the growth of his empire reflects the increasing power and confidence of the Negro in America.

Six years ago he was simply a songwriter, and he still writes masses of the material used by The Supremes and others of the school. The Beatles, too, have used his *Money* and other Motown songs. In 1959 he founded his own record company, calling it first Tammie (after the movie, which he liked), then Tamla (someone else, he discovered, had a record company called Tammie) and finally Tamla Motown, for obvious reasons with a firm based on Detroit.

Within three years, using only artists he had discovered himself around Detroit, he had pushed the gross sales of his company's records to over $4 million annually. Tamla Motown was, and still is, virtually a hundred per cent Negro operation, both in its artists and its executives. By last year the American public, black and white, had made the firm (studio address: Hitsville, USA) the most successful of all the independent American record manufacturers – those outside the handful of giants who own the many major labels.

In May, 1964, Tamla Motown artists occupied ten per cent of the places in the American Top 100 record charts, which was a fair achievement at a time when British artists had taken over more than a quarter of the placings. This weekend the EMI company has launched the Tamla Motown label in Britain, by arrangement with Gordy.

He told me last month that the company is still expanding and, for the first time, signing artists he had not discovered himself. Recently he added Billy Eckstine to his contract list.

Though this was probably inevitable – and though The Supremes are still fun whoever they record for – it will seem odd if Tamla Motown becomes just another large record company. In a world of giants it has had a powerful and readily recognizable identity. Without it there might never have been a beat boom. Certainly the beat, and The Beatles, would never have been quite the same.

Bill Haley's distant comets

5 MAY 1968

Beside the rich varieties of today's pop, rock-and-roll in the Bill Haley style of the middle fifties seems as relevant as a penny-farthing to an Aston: a part of evolution, now sadly anachronistic.

Not that you would have known it at the crowded Albert Hall last Wednesday when the rockers of yesteryear, drape suits and brass-bound leather jackets dusted off, held their revival meeting and greeted Haley's Comets like rediscovered messiahs.

Sociologists would have made a feast of it. The audience was mainly twenties to thirties, and virtually exclusively twenty to fifty; not a teeny-bopper in sight. While Haley played, that sixth of the audience nearest the stage stood solidly and swayed in rows or clapped or sang. There were sporadic solo dancers around the hall and a line of rockers, nearly all male, demonstrating at the fringe of the stage. The rest of the audience, the majority, sat fairly passively. They had come, presumably, hoping for blood.

They didn't quite get it, though there was a whiff of violence about, with studded belts removed and whirled like standards in battle. Music suffered, of course. The best group of the evening, The Quotations, who tried to dramatize the monotonous rock beat, were booed, pelted and, in the case of their drummer, injured for their non-conformism. The announcer was also struck down when a crowd invaded the stage as Haley fled from it.

Musically, this was back to the dark ages of pop, relieved only minimally by the skills of Duane Eddy, the guitarist. Hard rock, stripped naked this night, was one good riff and a handful of phrases boringly repeated until they disappeared from sight. Haley's Comets are unchanging and in their plump middle age rather sad. 'Shake, Rattle and Roll' and the rest are churned out; the bass player still climbs his instrument; the ugly saxophone squeals of Rudy Pompilli ride above the noise. A depressing business.

The Cream is off

1 DECEMBER 1968

The British trio called Cream played before ten thousand people at two full-house farewell concerts in the Albert Hall last week. They have broken Beatles' attendance records in America. Yet few people in this country who judge pop by the average TV programme devoted to the music will even have heard of them.

This is indicative not only of that dreaded cliché, the generation gap, but also of the gap of taste *within* generations. Now the group is no more, freely disbanded because its members want to pursue individual musical paths.

It contained some highly skilled, if perverse, talent – especially the guitarist, Eric Clapton. But its Albert Hall show was misconceived, an attempt at a gigantic *tour de force*, with the accent on force. I have never heard louder music. It destroyed itself in sheer decibels. The juggernaut of sound assaulted the stomach as well as being a danger to the ear-drums. It was mind-fragmenting music, involving one in what the pop avant-garde fashionably calls total experience.

I don't want total experience in a concert hall, whose amenities are frankly not suited to it. I want *musical* experience – and music is contrasts of volume, subtleties of colour, sudden silences, as well as harmonic cleverness and din. The promising Yes (a group, naturally) showed such qualities earlier in the evening. Their 'Something's Coming' was marvellous. But the audience, devoted and hypnotized, appeared to want only Cream, or the nasty Taste, destroyers of blues and Gershwin alike.

Parentage of pop

11 MAY 1969

Progressive pop, as they call that music which sells albums and fills concert halls whilst rarely making those ridiculous charts, progressed backwards at the Albert Hall last Thursday. Or perhaps it was sideways. It surely came out from underground and owned up to its lineage (jazz and earlier popular music), a confession which should assist a cartload of contemporary pundits to sort out their historical hang-ups.

First there were Clouds performing *Big Noise from Winnetka*, which Ray Bauduc and Bob Haggart used to do with Bob Crosby back in the 1930s, right down to the drumsticks playing on the string bass – only this time bass guitar, which is noisier.

There was Ian Anderson, leader of Jethro Tull, playing flute Roland Kirk-style – pastoral or yelping, with voice-over and pizzicato finger-hole stopping. You could mistake his chat for a seaside comic's and his demented pixie leg movements for a vaudeville stooge's.

There were drum solos from Jethro Tull and Ten Years After, just as long, dreary and applause-pulling as any in the last thirty years of the jazz-pop mainstream. This kind of pop concert is, endearingly, even creating its clichés in the way the big jazz events did in the 1940s and 1950s when they, too, conquered the philharmonic halls.

These repetitions include the ever-popular lead-guitar speciality number, all ear-crushing volume and electronic squealing with one soloist sounding much like another, as did the honking tenors in Jazz at the Philharmonic jam sessions; the obligatory standing ovation; the inevitable attack on the Top Twenty by the compère (applause) which compares with the audience laughter which would greet a reference to Guy Lombardo twenty years ago.

Do not mistake the message. This was a fair concert. Jethro Tull were the stars. They have good flute-playing to set against the necessary but inevitably samish guitar sounds; they have good musical ideas and know the value of contrasts in moods and harmonies and volume. Ten Years After were exciting, but disappointing after the subtleties of their *Stonehenge* LP, smashing their effectiveness in unrelieved volume. But who can be deluded that what is happening here is so very new? This is a twentieth-century heritage, not master Presley's.

If pop wants to be regarded as an art form (and who but most disc jockeys and over-sixties in spirit could possibly treat it as if it were not a contender?) then it must be judged by exacting standards. Such standards imply that *Tommy*, the provocative double album by The Who (Track Records), cannot be discussed in one paragraph.

It is a pop 'opera'. From it comes that mysteriously oblique single 'Pinball Wizard', now (unexpectedly) No. 4 in the charts and musically the most surpriseful record in them. The opera is about the 'dead, dumb and blind kid' of the single's lyric and the album, another watershed in pop, requires the lengthier judgment of next week's episode to explain its value and its failure to achieve a very ambitious goal.

Build-up to *Tommy*

18 MAY 1969

Take this proposition: that jazz and pop are more interesting to write about than other music, simply because the discussion not only centres on musical values but goes to the heart of much of our century's social history.

Anyone who has heard a few of the thousands of Negro blues will see the historical point. An arguable case is easily built up, even from random pieces of evidence. Lorenz Hart's brittle lyrics put an era in aspic, as Cole Porter's 'Love For Sale' embalmed a case-history. A mass of musical sentiment engulfed the last war, from 'Lilli Marlene' to 'We'll Meet Again'. Where were the symphony writers when popular music made 'Buddy Can You Spare a Dime?' for the Depression? Cultivating their gardens?

Post-1960 pop has gone the whole social hog, displaying every symptom from alienation to generation gap, idealism to puppy whines. Now The Who's new double album, *Tommy* (Track Records), arrives to represent rock's first major narrative, ninety minutes of 'opera'.

It is dynamically of its age, from the harsh-and-soft of its sounds to the histrionics of its plot. Tommy becomes deaf, dumb and blind from the shock of seeing his father murder his mother's lover. He is bullied by his cousin, assaulted by his uncle, learns to live in his inner world, becomes a pinball wizard solely by touch. Miraculously cured, he is at first a kind of messiah, but finally, advising his followers also to exist within themselves, he is rejected.

Make what message, allegory or myth you like of that – but the bones of the story are one reason for the failure of *Tommy*. It sets out too calculatedly to shock, like a movie begging for an X certificate, or a paperback jockeying for prime space on the counter. Pete Townshend, the composer, is the Harold Robbins of rock.

There are other reasons. For all the cunning of the playing and recording, three guitars and drums simply can't sustain the ninety-minute test. There is not enough surprise or contrast, insufficient quality in the lyrics, inadequate range in the voices. But many passages have a seizing power and artistry. Failure here is to be measured against very high standards of musical ambition.

Crosby, Stills and Co.

11 JANUARY 1970

In a multitude of ways Crosby, Stills, Nash and Young represent the summit at which the best rock music has arrived. Rock rubbish is still with us, but there is also the music which they and many groups like them play; fresh, literate, brilliantly performed, and a blend of highly diverse influences – rock through folk to Bach.

Thus 'pop', a ridiculously inadequate word, has reached an adulthood which the CSN and Y concert at the Albert Hall last week exemplified. For one and a quarter hours they played what Dave Crosby called 'wooden acoustic music' – compositions exquisite in their easy bluesy rhythms, redolent of folk music's nostalgia, but intricately melodic and subtly constructed. Each player is a master of the acoustic guitar, and the group's light-toned close-harmony singing is beautiful to hear. It has all the control and skills of traditional close-harmony groups from way back, while sounding totally modern.

Later in the evening, CSN and Y changed to electric guitars, switching style from what it's convenient to call country rock to the tough acid rock whose blow-torch power is the conventional idea of late-sixties pop. In this last hour, with the aid of a drummer (Dallas Taylor) and bass guitarist (Greg Reeves), they sacrificed the blessed individuality which their other style bestows. They played, though, with marvellous skill and an infectious enjoyment which seemed to hint at a send-up.

This group (two Americans, one English, one Canadian) are totally absorbed with music. Decibels for decibels' sake, pelvis-pushing, simulated sex and the rest of the rock ragbag have nothing to do with their music or their easy informality on stage. Together, or as soloists, their art demands attention as close as would be given to a classical string quartet – and gets it from ever-growing audiences. Craftsmanship and care are their watchwords, as the Crosby, Stills and Nash album issued last year on Atlantic, before Neil Young joined, continues to proclaim. It could come to be known as the watershed LP marking musical sixties from seventies.

Simon, Garfunkel, Paxton

3 MAY 1970

The Albert Hall looked almost austere. For once – more accurately, for twice – the stage did not groan under massed banks of sci-fi speakers, their glowing red eyes presaging total pop blitzkrieg. This was the week when the words came back, not destroyed by millions of decibels, but sung with crystal clarity at two concerts of memorable excellence.

First, Simon and Garfunkel last week-end, then Tom Paxton on Thursday. In their not so different ways they showed the quality which is at the heart of today's popular music. It was a necessary demonstration, for the huckstering, hysterical world of pop is made for fakery, and inevitably those who shout loudest set its tone.

Neither Paxton nor Simon and Garfunkel shout. They perform on stage without frills, using only acoustic guitars and the naked frame of the melodies and words they string together, though oddly their albums deploy extra musicians. Both Paul Simon, who writes most of the songs for himself and his partner, and Paxton offer material which gets to the guts of our society without being pretentiously boring or pseudo-revolutionary.

There's a sentence of Paxton's which his hand-outs make much of: 'I got off the soapbox a long time ago, but I didn't quit caring.' Listening to his work it seems completely fair, despite the persuaders. And it fits Paul Simon, too. These singers, with the gift of reaching out to a mass audience, are chroniclers of the age. They comment, but always with subtlety and wit.

Paxton, untrendily balding, is a very attractive personality. His roots are deep in folk music and his repertoire includes a number of pretty songs with titles like 'Wish I Had a Troubador', which he delivers in a light, wispy voice that disguises the toughness of what he is often saying.

He has, however, much stronger songs which deal with Forest Lawn and Joyce's Molly Bloom, with corruption and contentment, with rumbustious city Saturday nights and sad urban love affairs. He is a craftsman with words and rhymes, but Paul Simon is perhaps the more poetic lyricist, grasping the free flow of modern idiom brilliantly:

So long, Frank Lloyd Wright. I can't believe your song
is gone so soon. I barely learned the tune

He and Garfunkel, bland as choirboys, sing the most beautiful harmonies, and that is as deceptive as Paxton's sound. You don't have to hammer your chest to show you're tough.

Ike and Tina: raw and sexy

7 FEBRUARY 1971

Their records, which are scarcely inconsiderable feats, can project Ike and Tina Turner only in part. To *see* their revue, a rare happening in Britain, is to understand all. The experience catches facets of the raw uncomplicated urban soul and blues music of black America in all its directness and vitality, reveals what Detroit and Chicago were about before Tamla Motown polished and marketed the city sounds.

Which is to imply nothing against the Motown assembly line, a producer of great entertainers, but simply to say that the Turners, as well as the singing Ikettes and their Blood Sweat and Tears-like backing band, are something quite else. If the Supremes are delicious seducers of male equanimity, then Tina and the Ikettes in action are (metaphorically, of course) rapists, who could confound many an unwary boy.

Liberty Records, who sell their albums, are sending them around a European trail (which reaches Hammersmith next Saturday) with the apparent intention of projecting them as the sexiest act in popular music. The company don't have to work very hard at it; they probably *are*.

The Olympia Music Hall in Paris, one a.m., was perhaps an especially friendly venue for the Turner ritual. Charles Aznavour had brilliantly preceded them. The place was squirmingly over-full, people fringing the stage, snap-happy photographers blazing away and plainest-clothed *flics* stomping around. It could have been a tight situation.

Surprisingly, the Turners roused stormy enthusiasm yet, simultaneously, held the audience, controlled them, sent them happy away. Perhaps it was that there was so much going on, it took all one's hearing and seeing to cope. The band swung joyously. The Ikettes, all harsh tight harmony and eternally swaying, dancing limbs, combined sacred and profane vocal traditions in that unique black, American way. Tina Turner – Ike plays swift guitar and holds the music together – was purely another magazine of explosive added to the alchemy.

She is a frenetic sex symbol with a voice like honeyed sandpaper – able to make 'Son of a Preachet Man' really sound like the wicked song it is, and an inspirer of dementia when, finally, she dances under strobe lights behind clouds of billowing smoke. For aficionados, the only answer is first to witness, then to recollect emotion in non-tranquillity, perhaps with their new album, *Workin' Together* (Liberty, 39s 11d/£1.99½).

James Taylor seeming set

11 JULY 1971

'I seem to be set for life,' James Taylor told the people in the programme for his Festival Hall concert on Friday. Right. You sense he's got it made for ever.

String-bean shaped, lank-haired, he crouches over his guitar singing alone in a whiny but very musical voice that is out of folk and Dylan and Western sage-brush. His playing is out of both jazz and Bach. He picks the guitar so that it comes out sounding like harpsichord, and he has superb strength of line, holding back or pushing forward the inter-weaving bass string notes fractionally to create jazz-like tensions.

The words of his songs make nice stories and images, and the melodies are often memorable. 'Something In The Way She Moves' (not the George Harrison number, but the one whose chorus begins: 'I feel fine any time she's around me now') is marvellous, and other songs like 'Going to Carolina in My Mind' and 'Fire And Rain' indicate why he seems booked to be the Jim Webb or Dylan of the seventies. He's cool, too, very laconic and funny, playing the audience like a trout-tickler, and the humour bursts into his songs. 'Chilli Dog' is splendid, in the tradition of funny pop songs celebrating food.

It was a very regal concert. Carole King, who has the No. 1 single and album in America right now, was also on the sellout bill. *Time* magazine has called her the new Queen of Rock. Not so, despite her ten years of song writing. 'Up On The Roof' and 'Natural Woman' are fine songs, but strung together her work tends to sound all the same, her thumping chattering piano seems histrionic, and her voice is all shout, no softness.

Pink Floyd: looking like hell

20 FEBRUARY 1972

It looks like hell. The set is dominated by three silver towers of lights that hiccough eerie shades of red, green and blue across the stage. Smoke haze from blinding flares that have erupted and died drifts everywhere. A harsh white light bleaches the faces of two of the four musicians to bone as they crouch among the cauldron drums and snaking circuitry of the sound equipment.

Pink Floyd in performance at the Rainbow Theatre (Finsbury Park) is an experience for the strong. The sound, too, is sometimes vertiginous. Much of the music created by their two guitars, drums and assorted electronic keyboards is calculated and controlled. But it is overlaid with a maze of extra tapes which titillate the ears from all sides with extra-terrestrial electronic sounds, whispers, cries, snatches of prayers, chugs, glugs and the susurrant keening of wind and rain, all operated from a massive console in the stalls, like a mini-Houston space control room.

If all this sounds like *The Inferno* reworked, you would be only partly right. The ambition of Floyd's artistic intention is now vast. Yet at the heart of all the multi-media intensity, they have structure to their music, beauty of form (the passage beginning 'Us and them' in their new hour-long work *The Dark Side of the Moon*, for instance) and an uncanny feeling for the melancholy of our times.

'And then one day you find ten years have got behind you, No one told you when to run, you missed the starting gun, And you run and run to catch up with the sun, but it's sinking . . . Hanging on in quiet desperation in the English way The Time is gone the song is over.'

Substantial words, substantial performance. In their own terms, Floyd strikingly succeed. They are dramatists supreme. Themselves almost self-effacing, tip-toeing around the gloomy stage, they let their voices and instruments, echoing and exaggerated, do it all. I wish for more contrast of volume and of mood, as also for less preoccupation with melodramatic mania in their music, but can scarcely argue if their particular vision is not my own. The sell-out Rainbow audience on Thursday (sustained by the theatre's own diesel-driven generator) gave them temple-like devotion. Twelve thousand people in four nights is some congregation!

If you believe there's no laughter in cork, however, listen to Cheech and Chong's album *Hard Rock Comedy* (A and M, £1.50). It's like a cross between Tom Lehrer, Bob Newhart and Lenny Bruce. It swipes with cheerful, often vulgar, and sometimes profane shafts in many directions – at religion, law, the drug culture, rock music itself. It is, like it or not, a humour of our times.

Exiled Stones, living Dead

28 MAY 1972

The Rolling Stones are remarkable. They've lasted ten years, outlived their peers, survived mutations of taste. Perhaps they won't last much longer, but a decade in pop is like a lifetime. This week they start a thirty-city American tour and offer a new double-album (*Exile On Main Street*, Rolling Stones Records, £3.69).

And although they've mellowed a little, they're not too different now from the band of the early sixties who projected the harshest, nastiest, sweaty-sexiest and most pointedly offensive musical image yet to frighten all law-abiding Britons with daughters under twenty-one out of their minds.

Their last album, *Sticky Fingers*, was excellent. It had variety. They'd absorbed some of the exciting and electric post-1967 developments in rock. They revealed new moods and new musicality. *Exile On Main Street* sadly forgets much of all that.

The album will be (already has been) over-praised. It contains some good songs, 'Hip Shake', 'Casino Boogie', 'Let It Loose', for instance. It has interesting, if strictly limited, use of horns and backing singers, as had *Sticky Fingers*. Keith Richard's rhythm guitar drives the engine with hot-rod persistence. But it also has some of the worst rock singing around (blurred phrasing, unpunchy, balance-killed), several extremely boring tracks, and a dreary sameness of feeling.

It's said this is the essence of Stones style, produced out of themselves alone in the relaxed aura of Richard's home in southern France. If that's so, then themselves aren't enough. Too often the album wafts the mustiness of a quaint historical monument. The aged deserve respect, but music today is so much more than this.

Hear the Grateful Dead for music that's liberated, rich, inventive and ever-surprising. Since they burst six years ago from San Francisco, they've given us virtuoso sounds, which mingle R and B, boogie, country, jazz and chamber influences in dazzling sequences. If their present tour has eluded you, then take sustenance through any of their six albums – from *Anthem of the Sun* (1968, £2.09) to the latest double-LP, *Grateful Dead* (1971, £3.69) – which have been re-released by Warner Brothers. That really *is* a monument, artistically superb, to the living.

Chapter Four

Rock and Pop 1973-6

It was still the time for supergroups: Genesis or Emerson Lake and Palmer. But the times they were a-changing. Bob Dylan and The Stones reminded us that rock could produce its own kind of nostalgia. David Bowie looked both forwards and backwards. Reggae had arrived and punk rock was on the brink of arriving. There was even a moment, as 1974 dawned, when it seemed that popular music might perish altogether, rock-stock-and-barrel, in the face of more important world events connected with oil and raw material crises. It didn't, of course, and some tentative predictions I made went down the drain. As a record company president observed at the time: 'When the Romans had riots on their hands and the place was falling apart, it was sand for their circuses they imported first, wasn't it?'

A gig with the Guru

22 JULY 1973

Christians have – to name but a few – Wesley, Hymns A and M, the Glasgow Orpheus singing the 'Hallelujah Chorus' and, in latter days, *Godspell* and *Superstar*.

Balyogeshwar Parum Hans Satgurudev Shri Sant J. Maharaj, otherwise Guru Maharaj Ji or Perfect Master or Lord of Creation, has got a fifty-piece pop band called Blue Aquarius and a bag of rousing Fun Thirty songs.

At the feet of the Master
We can really let it grow,
Really let it flow,
Because we're all love, love, love
Love, love, love (repeated)
By His grace

That's the climax of one stormer in which the singer's also 'listening to catch His orders in the very midst of the fight'. Remarkable it is – the fastest harnessing of contemporary musical idiom to a religious cause since the Salvation Army brought in brass, tambourines and martial and musical hall sounds last century to give a sharp kick in the pants to Handel, Psalms and Gregorian chants.

Fast, oh yes. Three years ago there were only a handful of Western devotees for the Divine Light Mission, which is Guru Maharaj Ji's movement, started by his father in 1949. Now the boy of fifteen who compares himself with Christ, Mohammed, Krishna and Buddha has many thousands of followers in Britain alone and Blue Aquarius is a slick, block-busting aggregation of full-time musicians who tour the world spreading the gospel of the Guru's zippy, inexplicable faith.

Inexplicable, oh yes. To get in harmony with God, man must have knowledge of God. To get that knowledge, turn only to Guru Maharaj Ji. The knowledge is, literally, unspeakable. It cannot be explained; so there's no reason to explain it . . . This is a shorthand, and quite possibly unfair, summary of G. M. Ji's story. But the music will tell us far more.

Is it not nicely ironic, after we've grown accustomed to Western pop stars plugging gurus and adding sitars and tablas to their groups, that a faith coming out of the East should ride into battle to the sounds of Afro-America? Last Tuesday, among a deliriously cheerful and devoted audience at the Hammersmith Odeon, I heard song after song which was zestful twentieth-century pop fodder.

Blue Aquarius are good: big band brass and reeds, plus string section, guitars, percussion, organ, Moog, piano. All pros. All followers. Britons, Europeans, Americans. Some of them come from name groups: ex-Dando Shaft, an ex-Bee Gee, I've heard. There's a big vocal group, girls and boys, looking as pristinely innocent as did the old Seekers.

They zap into an instrumental, like a TV-movie thriller theme, the sort Quincy Jones writes. On bounds the leader, fat and check-suited, looking back-view like young Cab Calloway. That's the Guru's brother, nineteen, Shri Bhole Ji, part of the family business, Lord of Music. He doesn't seem to do much for the band, but they do it all for him.

There's excellent pastiche of every Afro-American pop style – gospel, soul, blues, rock 'n' roll, jazz, Detroit-sound to follow. You can hear James Brown, Ray Charles, Elvis, Isaac Hayes, the Platters, Satchmo, Pink Floyd and the Eurovision song contest right in there. Polished solos stream fluently forth, as do lines like 'to lose my crazy mind and fall in love with you' (ooh-wah, ooh-way) – only it's not girls they're singing about, but G. M. Ji. They do the 'Saints Come Marchin' In' too, and 'Amazing Grace', and an immortal couplet, 'Oh, sad Guru, there's nothing left for you'.

It was really just fine. The audience was enraptured. They seemed very happy: bowing with hands together, chanting, sporting flowers and badges, imbibing incense, but not smoking. The ushers were fierce about smoking. Followers give up smoking, drugs and drinking, they explained. Smoke repels them.

I've read elsewhere that the Divine Light Mission is capturing the Lower Middle Class Young in Britain. That may be right, although I'm not much good at spotting old-fashioned class by clothing any more. It's supposed to be the LMC that was captured by revivalist sects like Methodism too. But I was only there for the music.

And the music was *so* American. Like everything else. Divine Light's language is old-fangled NYC hip. 'The Lord of the Universe has come to us this day and he will turn you on.' G. M. Ji speaks with an American accent. And the movement's verbalizing mixes sundry mystic titbits with American analogies rooted in consumerism, motor cars and go-go objects. There's a weekly paper, *Divine Times*. There's Divine Sales, which is moving from selling jumble into Just Revelations, a strong line in soaps, bath oils, shampoo.

Many people think it's a load of old codswallop. Others say, well, if it makes people happy . . . or, well, they laughed at Jesus too . . . Well, I say I was only there for the music. And if you take G. M. Ji's thing at its own estimate, who can say that the Devil today has all the good tunes?

Moody Blues, happy families

30 SEPTEMBER 1973

The boardroom, smooth and pleasantly wooded, looks out on Cobham High Street, deep in executive Surrey heartland. The bass guitarist savours what, in part, belongs to him.

'This electrician I met told me about a man in the local who was telling his mates: "A lot of people would like that house, but one of them bloody Rolling Stones has got it." I've lived in that house five years. That's how much impact we've made on Cobham.'

The guitarist isn't a Stone, but one of The Moody Blues: John Lodge. He's right about the Moodies' image. They've made it almost by stealth. 'We've never been the in-band. Just a well-kept secret,' says Lodge.

Yet the Moodies, playing in London this week during a world tour whose extent is impressive even by mad pop standards, are among the biggest half dozen or so groups in the world. Between now and early 1974 they'll play solo concerts to about a million people in Britain, Europe, the USA and the Far East; they've reached four hundred thousand people at one mass rally in France.

It's not, however, their drawing-power or their ability to sell records – seven gold (or million-selling) albums in the last six years – which makes them remarkable. It's more their longevity, their life-style and their musical qualities. In a pop world scarred with collapses, hassles, break-ups, hypes and disasters, they have achieved the near-impossible by staying together.

Among pop bands of high world reputation, probably only The Beach Boys and The Rolling Stones date back as far as The Moody Blues, who were a Birmingham rhythm-and-blues band in the year of the Mersey sound, 1963. They even had a No. 1 in the singles charts, 'Go Now', in 1964, and then spent two debilitating years trying to repeat the trick, flogging around the club and ballroom circuit.

Lodge joined the band in this period and it's been unchanged since. It was failure as much as anything – they'd slipped from £250 to £40 a gig – which gave them the impetus to come back. They tore up their old material, started writing their own songs, and bought a second-hand Mellotron for £300.

With this instrument, which by programmed tapes produces orchestral backgrounds of strings, brass and woodwind, they began a trend which has widely influenced popular music. They *thought* orchestrally, almost symphonically, and their first album, *Days of Future Passed*, was made with a symphony orchestra. It was in effect a suite, each song a movement: a 'concept' album as it's known in the trade. Where that has led, with bands like Yes and Jethro Tull's *Passion Play*, we now know.

Their best-known song, 'Nights in White Satin', was on that first album, but they didn't break through at once. The British pop public was puzzled. Many people thought their music pretentious, a danger of which they're well aware. Not least, they've had to prove that they can produce on stage the rich variety of their studio sound.

Their next album, *In Search of the Lost Chord*, established their hard-core following, but it was ultimately success in America – again, the experience for many British groups since – which ensured their future. They went there in 1968, among the first British bands to hit California when flower-power and the 'West Coast sound' were relatively new.

The tour was troublesome. Sound systems were often inadequate and the travelling schedule was harsh. Once the band found themselves running a mile in a blizzard along a freeway after their van broke down, clutching guitars and suitcases, to catch the last plane that would get out of snow-bound Detroit for days.

Yet it was here that they found a new and crucial audience. 'America saved us,' says Lodge. Their steady progress thereafter was like that of an author whose back-list finally becomes as potentially best-selling as his new novel. Last year, when the Moodies' latest album, *Seventh Sojourn*, came out, their *Days of Future Past* had a new vogue, rising to No. 1 in the American charts for a period whilst *Sojourn* was still at No. 3.

They came back from America, too, with firm resolutions about future life-style.

The Moodies, after unhappy early experiences, have no manager. They manage themselves, promote their own concerts. Two of the five, John Lodge and Graeme Edge, handle contracts and accounts, although the whole band will then have to agree to any arrangements.

This co-operative mode of living is made easier by geography as well as temperament. Once the five Moodies lived in one room. From 1969 onwards they all came to settle around Cobham, all married, all had children. They used to travel up to London but, as Justin Hayward, their lead guitarist, explains, 'We found we'd got locked into the commuter system we'd tried to avoid.' So they moved their headquarters to Cobham itself, founded their own record label, Threshold.

'It's easy for us to be friction-free, because we're a band without leaders,' says Hayward. 'Each man contributes a song or two to our albums, so we find personal artistic freedom within the band. I guess our contrasting personalities help, too. Once we were five. Now, with wives and kids and the people close to us, we're a community of around thirty-five. We won't work if any of us has a good reason not to. You've got to have time to bring up families, to live a life outside the band.'

Lodge expands on this. 'We've been very lucky because we've had time to adjust. Nothing has ever happened overnight. It's been a slow hard grind and we've been very strict with ourselves. It's only eighteen months ago that we stopped being on a wage.'

For The Moody Blues, who can get a six-figure sum for a mass-venue concert in America and won't take less than a million dollars gross out of a tour there, money has bought enviable independence. They have splendid houses, the Rollses and all the other accoutrements of pop success, of course, yet their lives still seem centred on music and on families.

They have other interests, certainly. Ray Thomas, their reeds player, lives on an estate with a lake where he fishes endlessly; Hayward and Mike Pinder, who plays Mellotron, spend a lot of time developing electronic equipment. But most days, when they're not touring or being part-time businessmen or family men, they spend playing acoustic guitars on their own, stringing new words and music together. Each has a recording machine at home, where, by over-dubbing, they can lay down symphonies with themselves.

They've had the time, too, to become reasonably proficient on a vast range of instruments – say, around a score or more, including pianos, organs, guitars, Mellotrons, cellos, ukeleles, sitars, flutes, oboes and harmonicas.

They think their music has progressed, not in style, but – to use Lodge's words – 'The band's tighter, more fluid, more reflective of what we are as we've grown older.'

'Earlier this year we got a lot of calls from America complaining that a song of mine, "Dawning is the Day", was being used as backing to an Air Force recruiting commercial on TV,' says Hayward. 'We hadn't given permission, of course, and we soon stopped it. But the nice thing was it was the fans who told us.'

The future, though, is still missing. As Hayward says: 'We're now getting our first generation fans bringing their kids to the concerts. Maybe we are all over thirty now, but we can't conceive we won't be playing to a large audience in ten years' time, or in twenty for that matter.'

Happy days are here again?

6 JANUARY 1974

The pre-Christmas exhortation outside a Californian supermarket read: THESE ARE TOMORROW'S GOOD OLD DAYS. For popular music, prophetic. Our various crises – with less of everything that makes records, noise, light, mobility and showbiz confidence possible – are already undermining the pop bonanza along with everything else.

Small rock bands complain they can't get to take their vans around to one-nighters. Even big rock artists moan that the shortage of paper and vinyl is delaying album releases. I've heard laments about the impossibility of playing guitars with frozen fingers in unheated halls, of Moog synthesizers going out of tune with voltage reductions, of new bands shunned by record companies, now alleged to be interested only in sales-proven artists. The pop industry has come to depend too heavily for its own good on electricity, plastics, petrol and excess.

So allow me – as you would expect – to discover sparks of cheer amid the dark.

The decibel level in some pop has now reached overkill and will benefit from restraint.

There are too many records released. Fewer will probably mean less adventure, but perhaps also more discrimination and higher quality.

Live performances will become more special, not merely repetitions of artists' latest albums. Audiences will demand better value. The ludicrous fees some rock acts charge may be forced down.

Perhaps, even, some of the simpler, older traits of the modern popular music tradition will be re-emphasized: the lone guitarist-singer, the solo pianist, the less amplified band, the long residency at a single club, café or hall rather than the frenetic business of one-night stands.

The paradox is that in America traditions like these have never died. Visits on East and West coasts before Christmas showed me, yet again, how distorted a view we here get of popular music in the United States, which remains the country that mostly created the pop styles of every generation this century.

It's natural, I suppose, that the communications channels, generally seeking the 'good story', should so often present popular music in terms of its extremes. So you are far likelier to be told about the latest freaky antics of an Alice Cooper or Tiny Tim than to learn that thousands of singer-pianists still perform the works of Rodgers and Hart, Lennon and McCartney or Bob Dylan in bars around most American cities.

Now you may think me deranged to be talking about simpler pop delights just when Bob Dylan has begun his first American concert tour for eight years. In the unlikely event you haven't heard, six million people or more wanted tickets for his forty concerts, which must surprise even the tour promoter, Bill Graham, who ran the legendary Fillmore rock halls.

Yet consider Dylan. It's over-simplifying, certainly, but the one-time rebel messiah of pop – creator of 'Blowin' In The Wind' and 'Times They Are A-Changin' – has increasingly appeared to disappoint the generation he once seized, spokesmanlike.

Of his later albums, *John Wesley Harding* was in the simple folk tradition; *Nashville Skyline* was pure country-style ('redneck' America in excelsis); and *Self Portrait* was almost middlebrow pop. His new album, *Dylan*, on CBS, is embarrassingly second-rate, and whether Dylan chose the tapes or not (he's switched labels recently) they show what he's been up to in recent years.

And yet all those people want to see this retired revolutionary, this rule-breaking idol. Nostalgia it is, partly. Curiosity and charisma too. But maybe also they understand, with Dylan, that the wide sweep of popular music encompasses more than the latest rock fads of brutalism, high camp, and yobbery. They could be more catholic in their appreciation of pop styles than rock agitprop would sometimes suggest the popular audience is, and even charitable enough to forgive Dylan his lapse in taste.

And so . . . certainly I heard masses of rock in America, some nauseating and some, like The Beach Boys and Grateful Dead in California, very beautiful. But there were also piano bars everywhere, Harry James playing for dancing, and Cy Coleman singing his own show songs – 'Hey, Look Me Over', 'If They Could See Me Now' and suchlike razzmatazz – in cabaret.

He rhymes, does Mr Coleman, Romans with omens, amazes with dazes, eight a.m. with mayhem. The Cole Porterish crackle of rhymes is still the thing in many American popular songs.

In Las Vegas, Anthony Newley was working to a dining room containing five thousand people. He's wry, Newley. 'Will I have to learn to eat organic food, listen to Ravi Shankar in the nude?' he sang in a new song with the refrain 'Here comes the middle-aged silent majority Geritol rock 'n' roll star.'

Middle-aged, too, are Morgana King, a superb singer still relatively unknown here, and Mose Allison, like a latterday Hoagy Carmichael, but both were pulling in youngish audiences at West Coast clubs. I remember likewise a sax-led quartet in San Luis Obispo playing strict tempo as if Select Flannel Dances at drill halls had never gone out of fashion, and a coffee shop on Big Sur sporting this announcement: 'Come On, Come On, Come

One, Come All, To Sunday Services in God's hall. If life seems troublesome and often hard, Join us Wednesday at eight in the maintenance yard.'

So, more old traditions, musical and otherwise, survive in America than we sometimes realize. Bill Graham in San Francisco, counting the Dylan cheques, still talks about being 'hooked on the sweet smell of success' and has a sign on his door too: 'Yea, though I walk through the valley of the shadow of death, I shall fear no evil, for I am the meanest sonofabitch in the valley.'

I asked a record company president about his expectations for pop in a harsher, less secure world. He grinned. 'When the Romans had riots on their hands and the place was falling apart, it was sand for their circuses they imported first, wasn't it? I guess we'll survive.'

Genesis: rocking the boat

20 JANUARY 1974

After two hours of music and mime, costume drama and light-show, comes the ultimate *coup de théâtre* from Genesis.

As menacing music crawls through the speakers, actor-singer Peter Gabriel stands black-cloaked like a wicked mad monk in an ancient creepy movie. Then POUF! (if that's the word) an explosion blinds us. Through smoke he moves heavenwards, on wires, still singing, making cycling motions. He is lowered, lifts a violet-lit tube before him, eye make-up glowing. Final chords crump, smoke belches, curtain falls.

The thunderous standing ovation to that closed curtain lasted for fifteen minutes last Tuesday at Genesis' historic opening night in the Theatre Royal, Drury Lane. They're an in-group and no argument, as the rock papers keep telling us.

Genesis have added theatre vengefully to rock music, and with madly variable success. The musicians playing with Gabriel are excitingly accomplished, using their guitars, Mellotron and sundry electronic aids to create impressively symphonic sounds – by turn gently pastoral, hard-rocking and colourfully chordal, all in territory similar to that commanded by Yes and Pink Floyd.

Gabriel, though the dominating figure, is less convincing. He's a fairish actor. His costume changes are striking, but lean heavily on stock horror movie and grand guignol touches. His introductions to Genesis' strange songs are largely pretentious verbiage masquerading as surrealism.

I don't doubt it's rock heresy to say that. But the novelty of the Genesis mixture, and the quality of some of their music, can't disguise the artistic poverty of parts of the recipe. Fantasy, which is the band's hallmark, is dangerous ground; the gap between the intriguing and the boring is narrow. When shocks are the keynote, they have to be really imaginative to seize the mind through two hours.

Aren't many of Genesis' tricks really rather cornily old – flying bats and masks back-projected for example? Are easy laughs raised around words like 'brassière' really mind-stretching (a current vogue phrase used to describe Genesis' performance)? And, much more important, is human-kind so totally ugly that not one noble gesture, verbal or visual, can be found in Gabriel's vocabulary to delineate it?

So – Genesis are interesting, ambitious, often moving, often funny. But they're *limited* still and, at times, chillingly reminiscent of what I've read about Berlin cabaret in the 1930s.

Dylan: not remaking the world

3 FEBRUARY 1974

Long, long, ago, sometime in the 1960s, Bob Dylan was saying, 'I accept chaos; I am not sure that chaos accepts me.'

Today, in a song on his eagerly anticipated new album, *Planet Waves* (Island £2.30), he is telling us, 'It's never been my duty to re-make the world at large, nor is it my intention to sound the battle-charge.'

So many of the changes which have marked Dylan's progress are summed up in *Planet Waves*. Once he appeared to be the spokesman for a restless and politically-discontented generation, who picked up his songs as their battle hymns. Now he is a private person singing about private affairs, pausing every so often to clobber those who intrude.

He's thirty-three now, and it's a long time since he was a frizzy, thin-faced boy from Minnesota, weaned on the pure folk tradition of Woody Guthrie. It's some years, too, since he began remorslessly demolishing the image of prophet-leader with which 'Times They Are A-Changin', and 'Blowin' In The Wind' invested him. His music is the evidence.

Recall the shock when he sang with a loud electric rock band on his 1966 tour and the folk-faithful spurned him. That was the prelude to two years of silent withdrawal following a serious motor-cycle accident.

Then the albums, if not the tours, began to happen again. And such albums! *John Wesley Harding* in 1968 was a musical return to folk-like simplicity, a stark contrast to the then pop environment of flower-power excesses and shattering electronic sounds. Later, his *Nashville Skyline* celebrated the poor-white American country style. And *Self Portrait*, in

1970, was even more baffling. Sentimental it was, with 'Blue Moon' and strings and girl choirs, and a very revealing song ('Copper Kettle') where old men sat around a fire, cut off, talking about revolution, but *doing nothing*. Faithful Dylanites howled in anguish.

It was also in that year, 1970, that Princeton University gave him an honorary doctorate and Dylan shuffled nervously whilst his praises were spoken, then ducked out without saying a word. That was in character. Outside of his songs, he's never said much.

From 1970 to 1973 he was, again, largely silent – until the announcement last autumn of the major American tour he began last month, his first in eight years. The unprecedented demand for tickets has shown how his messianic appeal is undimmed.

Planet Waves, recorded last November, goes a long way to explaining why. It is a fine and fascinating album. Musically, it sums up what Dylan has given to popular music. He taught his contemporaries (Beatles, Stones, all of them) that rock and folk and country styles could be fused into a muscular, stripped-down sound which was infinitely flexible in its musical uses – and that's the sound of *Planet Waves*, beautifully played by The Band, his five-piece backing group.

This unpretentious flowing style strikes like a cold shower at a time when pop music is dominated by yobbery, bizarreness, theatrical posturings and sheer 'wallpaper' tedium. There's vitality, shot through with tenderness, irony and some anger in the album. And can Dylan still *phrase* a lyric! That harsh, dry voice inhabits the memory.

The Album was originally called *Love Songs*. Many of them are, indeed, love songs of a sort – straightforward and personal. But others are edged with menace: and Dylan speaks often in enigmatic, powerful images. He's a songwriter, not a poet, but many of his phrases shine with the concentrated surprise of good poetry; he changed his name from Bob Zimmerman out of admiration for Dylan Thomas.

Of the ten songs on the album, four are especially effective. The doom-tinged 'Going Going Gone', where he spits out 'I've just got to cut loose before it gets too late', is one. The three others are the fast and happy 'On A Night Like This'; his 'Wedding Song', where the bride is cast as a refuge for Dylan from a world over-anxious to possess him; and, finally, 'Dirge', bitterly powerful and mysterious.

It's tempting, again, to say that in 'Dirge' he's castigating the fans who tried to make him conform to their image of him. And the message is clear enough. He wants to be alone. He wants to be alone and himself; he's 'searching for a gem'; and 'I've paid the price of solitude, but at least I'm out of debt.'

Dylan's standing today is paradoxical. He rejects, yet is accepted by millions. And isn't he, despite his evolution, still a man of his age? There is an inward-turning mood today, affecting young and old, characterized by non-involvement, a search for privacy and a tendency to look backwards. *Planet Waves* mirrors it in a definitive, disturbing and haunting collection of songs.

ELP's never-ending show

21 APRIL 1974

Welcome friends, shouted the banners, to the show that never ends: Emerson, Lake and Palmer. So it seemed. For two uninterrupted hours last Friday, this immensely spectacular three-man band pounded the fifteen-thousand-capacity Wembley Pool into adoring submission, no mean feat even in our age of electronic overkill.

ELP, as they say, are too much. Undoubtedly. For musicians of such awesome virtuosity they play too much of nothing special. They could do with more pools of quiet, fewer repetitions, more contrasts in mood and volume. Then they might unreservedly be kings, for they have rare gifts of invention and surprise.

Their sound, and the encyclopaedia of influences within it – Bach, jazz, Moussorgsky, rock, Aaron Copland, ragtime, Art Tatum, classical organ, The Beatles among them – is light-years ahead of most people's musical experience. But that's a place some travellers may not wish to be.

ELP are now four years old and trail profitable clouds of glory (and three juggernauts for their equipment) wherever they go. Their visual impact is tremendous. A triumphal arch rising to the roof; fireworks and a marvellous side-show; batteries of lights pulsing sympathetically with the music; and Keith Emerson leaping into the audience to play the long magician's wand which feeds back to his electronic synthesizer.

Emerson (ex-Nice) remains the dominant musician. From his varied keyboards he creates maniac symphonies and devouring tones. Electronic storms race around the vast arena through encircling loudspeakers. He makes the grand piano, playing its keys or sweeping its strings, even grander.

Greg Lake (ex-King Crimson) is the foil, with voice and guitar. His voice has passion. He sang two fine songs alone; not nearly enough. Carl Palmer (ex-Atomic Rooster) is both brilliant and the drummer most likely to wind up suffocated beneath his fifty-seven varieties of equipment. His solos are unique. He bangs gargantuan gongs and a dozen drums whilst tolling a large bell with his teeth – and stays in time. Formidable.

The show was, effectively, an ELP retrospective. They began with

Copland, the Parry-Blake 'Jerusalem', and Ginastera's First Piano Concerto, the last two from their latest album, *Brain Salad Surgery*. They revisited all five of their albums, notably *Tarkus*. The audience adored it; and as music of total immersion, it was sensational. But that, sadly, is not enough.

Ken Russell's *Tommy*

30 MARCH 1975

Of course you should see Ken Russell's *Tommy* – and Grand Canyon, the Amazon rain forests, and even Niagara Falls. You know what you're likely to see, but you want to see them for real, and they *are* something, aren't they . . .

Tommy is something; a *tour de force* (such force), in so many ways absolutely stunning. Russell never lets up. With anticipated cannonades, he bombards the senses. Few spectaculars are in the same league.

Mounds of writhing bodies, maimed characters, ghastly machines, among which the Acid Queen's shiny iron maiden, studded with hypodermics, full of skeleton and writhing snakes, is memorable. Memorability indeed is always there. The Marilyn Monroe church; Elton John as the defeated Pinball King in monstrous boots; Ann Margret – like Roger Daltry's, a brilliant performance – as Tommy's mother drowning amid an emetic flood of foam and beans in her luxurious white pad; these images live on and on.

But the questions remain. Does the visual explosion add much to the oratorio which The magnificent Who originally created six years ago?

By rewriting and establishing a more orderly plot line, the movie regularizes the somewhat elusive parable which The Who first recorded. That to me is a loss, not least because the music becomes massively less important and is often maltreated.

Certainly the sounds match the film; both are over-stated. But there is scarcely one track on the *Tommy* movie double-album (Polydor 2657 014 £4.42) which improves on the original. Elton John's 'Pinball Wizard', for example, is fine when it's sound *plus* sight; but in sound only it's banal compared with the biting originality of The Who's effort.

Inside the cinema, even, the unrelenting blast of the music in Quintophonic sound is ridiculously too much. It was the starkness, the subtlety, which so often uplifted passages of the first *Tommy*.

So, the music has been sadly aggrandized to mirror Russell's bloated vision. It has its moments, of course. The 'See Me, Feel Me' theme is magically used, especially as a counterpoint to the ghastly Christmas party. 'I'm Free' is magnificent.

But then, 'See Me' was similarly used originally, so what's gained? Yes, *Tommy* is some movie; I prefer the old album, some silences, and imagination left to roam.

Springsteen off the streets

23 NOVEMBER 1975

For Bruce Springsteen you will surely have heard the publicity mills grinding already. Latest runner in the rock messiah stakes, this remarkable twenty-six-year-old street minstrel from New Jersey hit London last week.

At last, the hoardings at Hammersmith proclaimed, Britain's ready for Bruce Springsteen. He wasn't quite ready for Britain, though. He opened forty-five minutes late. No one even slow-handclapped. It's old-fashioned, they tell me, to mention such things.

Is it worth waiting for? Well, yes. And that says a deal for Springsteen, because he's been blown up like a balloon. Compared to Chaplin, God save the mark, when his jerky gestures and shapeless cap and stumbling about the stage are a dead ringer rather for rock's Norman Wisdom.

Springsteen is also compared to Bob Dylan, Mick Jagger and a largish cast. 'He's a rock 'n' roll punk, a Latin Street poet, a ballet dancer, an actor, a poet joker, hot rhythm guitar player, extraordinary singer and a truly great rock 'n' roll composer.' Thus Jon Landau of *Rolling Stone*. Rock's hyperboles make one fall about.

Yes, his voice has the acid scrape of Dylan's. He also plays harmonica. But he leaps around like Dylan doesn't. He can whisper and command silences more effectively too. He doesn't moralize much. He simply *describes* – scenes of rough tough urban New Jersey life, the bleak sidewalks and the scruffy beaches and the hellholes of chemical living and the hot-rod no-hopers in language so evocative it sets him *apart* from the street, no longer its child.

His melodies are competent, but his lyrics are the thing: the surprising, extravagant language is as poetically remarkable in its context as was Dylan Thomas' for his particular world. So, powerful as Springsteen's stage show is, his three albums remain his glory. You could scarcely hear a word at Hammersmith. How ridiculous.

His group (the E Street Band) is an all-purpose driving outfit, but nothing special. The two keyboard players are best; the saxist blows as ugly a sandpaper sound as has afflicted my ears in years.

His best three songs are 'Meeting Across the River' (which can't be properly done on stage since its magnificence grows from a gorgeous trumpet counterpoint by Randy Brecker on record), 'She's The One' and '4th of July, Asbury Park'.

Simon in the mainstream

14 DECEMBER 1975

Many musical extravaganzas will mark the bicentennial of the United States next year; but none will more strikingly or gloriously show what American music has meant to the world than the magical two hours which Paul Simon offered at the Palladium last week, so aptly on the brink of 1976.

Sheer perfection it surely was. His clear simple voice is a marvellous instrument for his own telling songs of wistful social observation, of unmalicious but biting comment. 'The Sound of Silence', 'American Tune', 'Fifty Ways To Leave Your Lover', 'My Little Town', 'Bridge Over Troubled Water', 'The Boxer' – the titles suggest, sometimes proclaim, the world this diffident genius in jeans inhabits.

His melodies are strong and pure, too. The best are memorable; even the more intricate are haunting. No wonder the audience stood and stood, cried and cried to win encores. Absolute unmatchable triumph.

Yet it was not only Simon they applauded, but the exquisite texture of the whole. He surrounded himself with superb musicians – Toots Thielemans, guitarist/whistler/harmonica player supreme; Hugh McCracker (guitar); David Sanborn (sax); and more, including a string quartet.

He used them in the best American manner – as Billie Holiday, Ella, Sinatra have: to sustain, to solo, to produce dazzling counterpoint and obbligato. Yes, there was jazz and blues in there. There was gospel music too, from the explosive Jesse Dixon Singers whose voices rang like trumpets, who make handclapping an art, who uplifted Simon to unexpected emotional peaks.

Thus were the styles of the American mainstream brought together in an incredible shrinking act, for these artists made the theatre as intimate as a club. Simon belongs to his age, but also to those which preceded him. Like all singers whose songs will last, he is a descendant, not a trader in instant sensation.

Unforgettable was his beautiful 'American Tune', sung solo towards the end – hymn-like in feeling, which is yet another strand of modern American music. A concert, then, in a class of its own, during which he played much from his outstanding new album, *Still Crazy After All These Years* (CBS £2.99).

Bowie and Bassey

9 MAY 1976

Shirley Bassey and David Bowie on successive nights. So contrasting, yet so similar. She a peach in maturity; he fragile as a stick-insect, and just as elusive to discern, define, deny. Similar? Certainly. Both are children of our time, climbing out of Tiger Bay and Brixton, and so, enabling audiences to identify with them, are archetypal popular music idols.

She feeds middle-aged fantasy, epitomized in beautiful songs like 'Yesterday When We Were Young'. He encourages a younger army, bored with their external characters, to seek within themselves alternative egos; as artist-hero, he kills off his past roles – Ziggy Stardust, spaceman, bi-sexualist, rebel – like clockwork, with only the orange coxcomb of his hair for continuity. His disciples dutifully ape him.

Both, too, are beyond normal criticism, defying purely musical assessment. Bassey over-sings (but thrillingly) and cannot perform except with total commitment. Bowie over-plays (but rivetingly) and demands attention by his extravagant idiosyncrasy, which is as professionally adamantine as hers. She devours the audience; he incites it. Each earthquakingly demonstrates the power of personality.

Shirley Bassey sang, in all, to twenty-five thousand at the Albert Hall last week. Tuesday, second house, was an outstanding triumph. Standing ovation after standing ovation, the emotion aroused by her beauty and her passionate singing flooding the arena.

She is at her peak. She still goes over the top sometimes, which is Bassey magically being herself, but she knows more about light and shade than ever. She whispers the final note of 'The Way We Were'; within 'Something', the orchestration leaves momentary sounds of silence. Her world conquests are richly earned.

David Bowie entertained fifty thousand at Wembley. On Monday, after a boring surrealistic movie, greeted with cynical derision, his casual entry was spellbinding. He has murdered Ziggy, appearing glitterless in plain black trousers, waistcoat and white shirt, looking like a refugee from Isherwood's Berlin cabarets.

The lighting, with Bowie trapped in harsh white cross-beams, was rock's most brilliantly theatrical effect. He sang fourteen songs, and when the hundreds of mini-Bowies leapt on seats, miming every gesture, he played with them, smiling.

He's rejected soft orchestrations (as on *Space Oddity*) for a thunderous rhythm-and-blues backing, which is tiresomely flairless. It ruined 'Stay', the best of his *Station to Station* album. But Bowie's personal performance was monstrously successful, more of a charged-up crooner than an Alice Cooper rival.

Is he sinister? There are, undeniably, visual Nuremberg overtones. Bowie-obsessiveness is sterile. But mostly, I suspect, he's the prisoner of his own publicity, his need to keep changing his image. Musically, he's limited as yet. It's where he ends up that matters. Meantime his own lyric, 'Fame, bully for you, chilly for me, gotta take a raincheck on pain,' may yet be his epitaph.

Stones in aspic

23 MAY 1976

Today's gigantic pop occasions are often more religious gatherings, symbols of togetherness, than places to hear music. How can it be otherwise when ice hockey arenas and football grounds accommodate the worshipping multitudes? Amplification in such spaces inevitably crucifies the sound. It becomes crude noise.

So it was with The Rolling Stones on Friday when, to frightening homage, they opened their six days at Earls Court. If you want to hear their music, buy their albums. Earls Court (and The Stones) is about experience, worship and recognition of the ties which unite the generation that grew up in the changing world The Stones have always thumbed their noses at.

Thumbed their noses at, yes – and gestures more obscene. But The Stones are clever. They've emphasized sexuality, outrage, aggressive self-confidence, teenage solidarity; but they are not really street-fighters. They may have terrified parents in the 1960s. Now they're armchair rebels, leaping up occasionally from their tax haven to record or tour, cannily maintaining contact with their audience as it ages, as do they.

The Stones are virtually nostalgia now, bad boys in aspic, more a circus than shock-troops, toning down the outrage of their records. The miracle is that they are still at it; still, for so many millions, the emperors of ecstatic independence.

Friday's fans looked, on average, around twenty-five. Outside the arena, Saturday's queues were already bedding down. The Hari-Krishna disciples were handing out joss-sticks. Camels could have gone through the needle's eye about as easily as the eighteen thousand customers finally squeezed through the few turnstiles. Many were still outside when the show started thirty minutes late.

They missed little. The warm-up act, The Meters, are an ordinary band shrivelled in the barn of Earls Court. In the interval, clowns and men on stilts clumped sadly around with a steel band before The Stones gave the audience its chance to perform.

The Stones are really about beginnings and endings. The middles tend to be less exciting. What an opening it was though. Aaron Copland's *Fanfare to the Common Man* played, searchlights criss-crossed and The Stones appeared inside a gigantic 'crown', whose spikes lowered to provide the stage on which they cavorted.

The audience were aflame for 'Honky Tonk Woman' and a spurt of newer compositions. Then they settled down to comparative quiet, including the melancholic 'Fool To Cry'. Keith Richard and Ronnie Woods ripped out flamboyant solos before the guest pianist, Billy Preston, danced madly and Jagger joined in. The climatic build-up began.

The music grew cruder, the pranks more outrageous, and the downstairs audience climbed on their seats, arms uplifted in worship. Jagger, Tarzan in breeches, swung over their heads on a rope, sprayed them with confetti, threw water over them, and finally, over himself.

The music was 'Jumpin' Jack Flash' and other hysterical old battle anthems. Jagger leapt, flapped, twitched, flailed – the eternal rag doll. The Stones gave value, as always, if that's what you wish to buy; but the scene of the real action has moved elsewhere.

Marley on the march

30 MAY 1976

Popular music has been 'political' for centuries. Even in the fashionably despised Tin Pan Alley days there were epics like 'Strange Fruit', about Southern lynchings; the Depression anthem, 'Buddy Can You Spare A Dime'; the Duke Ellington revue, *Jump for Joy*. Bob Dylan was more of a traditionalist than was apparent.

Yet in a world where rebellion has soured on the tongue of so many rock stars – sourer still when those stars effect classically playboy life-styles – there's one kind of political pop which has raged through its homeland and, like no other, bitterly reflects the volatile condition of that place. Reggae is the music, Jamaica the source.

In Britain, reggae is often heavily diluted – light, bubbly and, with its metronomic beat and limited melodic content, increasingly banal if listened to at length. Reggae played by Bob Marley and The Wailers, who have thrust themselves into the popular mainstream with exceedingly successful visits here during the past two years, is quite different. Their new album, *Rastaman Vibration* (Island £3.25) is searingly strong, nakedly political.

Michael Manley rode to the Jamaican premiership with a reggae campaign song, 'Better Must Come'. In an island with dire ghettos and a thirty per cent unemployment rate, Bob Marley's bland voice and sweet backing sounds sit oddly with the violent advocacy of his words. He speaks for the Rastafarians, a revolutionary religious movement which mixes calls for a return to Africa, or 'black African' culture, with pot, worship of Haile Selassie, and Old Testament thundering against 'Babylon', which means any enemy of their particular brand of black power.

There's no doubt that, whatever one's view of this music, it's among the world's most genuine popular styles; it's of the people, addressed directly to them with its references to racial grievances and social tension. One song on the new album, 'War', takes for its lyric a Haile Selassie speech calling for insurrection in Africa. It can't, in any serious assessment of our world, be ignored.

Footnote on Punk

28 NOVEMBER 1976

Maybe you've heard of 'punk rock'. Perhaps you don't wish to hear about it. But listen, briefly.

Punk rock is the generic term for the latest musical garbage bred by our troubled culture, British and American. It features screaming, venomous, threatening rock sounds. It's not totally illiterate musically; the punks have been practising. But musically, it isn't much.

It isn't new. The pendulum principle works in pop as in life. Early rock 'n' roll was a scream against Tin Pan Alley's bland commercialism. And when yesterday's rebels flaunt their fortunes, flee to tax havens, there's bound to be a reaction from under-nineteens bred in social deprivation.

So punk-rockers hate Mick Jagger (also, Led Zeppelin, Yes and Genesis) as much as they hate critics. They hate love, over-nineteens, 'dishonesty', escapism, long hair, dogs; suburbia, newspapers, teachers, drugs, etc. They love hate, aggression, apathy, lust, alcohol, anarchy. They wear hand-me-down clothes and safety pins all over, including in their ears.

Johnny Rotten and The Sex Pistols are punks. They sing 'Anarchy in the

UK', which ends with a scream: 'Destroy'. Clash and Damned are other bands. 'Love: something you feel for a dog or a pussy cat', says Rotten, according to a writer called Caroline Coon who has been plugging the music in *Melody Maker*. Rooted in 'urban reality', she says it is.

She's recounted various jolly Rotten anecdotes about spitting at people, throwing bricks at passing cars, drawing the dole; also about the cigarette burns and knife scars on his limbs. A BBC TV interview with Rotten was re-done several times because the obscenity level was so high. Punks like spoiling things – say, pouring beer on carpets, or polluting the atmosphere personally.

Popular music has many faces. It has always had a punk face. It has also, this century, evolved faces which, musically, have dignity and joy. Punk will fade. Its apologists are ludicrous. There are ways to protest about the putrid faces of both pop and society without relapsing into barbarism. Punk is anti-life, anti-humanity.

You will probably hear much more about it, although not from me, for it will be exploited by writers desperate not to be thought 'old' and record companies without shame. When it dies, it will not be mourned.

Chapter Five

Rock and Pop 1976-8

Towards the end of the 1970s, upheavals and confusion. There was New Wave, inevitably, but not only that. Mike Oldfield could still round off a remarkable feat in the charts. Acts as diverse as Bette Midler, Abba and Pink Floyd had (to understate it) their moments. There were words, too, from an American writer, Greil Marcus, which summed up the problem of predicting where popular music, and especially rock, might go in the next decade: 'Rock 'n' roll is a combination of good ideas dried up by fads, terrible junk, hideous failings in taste and judgment, gullibility and manipulation, moments of unbelievable clarity and invention, pleasure, fun, vulgarity, excess, novelty and utter enervation.'

Mike Oldfield: on the tubular route

5 DECEMBER 1976

'When I was ten I found my guitar was a better way of communicating than words,' said Mike Oldfield. 'I still feel that way.' Today, he communicates through many other musical instruments, but 'only fools around with them'. Guitars, and his remarkable musical imagination, which pours out romantically haunting melodies with the abandon of a young Debussy, have been the foundation of the artistic phenomenon now marching again with his new box of records.

It contains fresh versions of Oldfield's three major compositions – *Tubular Bells* (1973), *Hergest Ridge* (1974), *Ommadawn* (1975) – together with less substantial exercises like *In Dulci Jubilo*. It has quickly entered the sales charts.

This is surprising, for the original records have already sold thirteen million copies around the world, and *Tubular Bells* (eight million sales) has proved a rare block-buster. Only last month did it disappear from the top thirty album charts in Britain, having remained there for three-and-a-half years, a feat approached solely by Simon and Garfunkel and The Beatles in latter-day history; it was unchallenged at No. 1 for fifteen months until *Hergest Ridge* displaced it, so that Oldfield had numbers 1 and 2 in the charts. For a forty-minute symphonic composition to enjoy such manic commercial success on record is unparalleled.

Oldfield is twenty-three. He began work on *Tubular Bells* when he was seventeen. He created the record essentially alone, playing everything on it, as is increasingly the modern virtuoso style. He's had more help since then, but he controls recordings of his work as no great composer of the past could.

It is with some of them, certainly, that he should be compared, for although he moves in a 'pop' environment, his records part of the commercial music machine, he is scarcely like a rock star. He hates glamour and he hates London – 'a side effect of mental illness,' he says – preferring to live in rural isolation, presently in Gloucestershire. He is shy, introverted, gentle, with a face which might naturally reside in a stained-glass window. He has made a lot of money, inevitably, but he cannot be aligned with the business men of classical music, those who churned out their music for princely or religious patrons. Oldfield reminds one more of the wild, sometimes tragic romantics: Keats, Shelley, Tchaikovsky.

Because he loves the countryside, however, do not type-cast him as a nostalgic or an anti-technologist. 'I wouldn't be where I am but for technology,' he explains. Thus *Tubular Bells* exists only partly as a score. Its substantial life is in a set of tapes and instrumental parts created by Oldfield himself. The new version (as with his other works) results from the re-mixing of those tapes, with additions and subtractions of tone colours, even melodies.

Whether the world will prefer version B to version A is not the point. Oldfield, a perfectionist, still isn't satisfied. He defends a joke ending to *Tubular Bells* – a jolly 'Sailor's Hornpipe' recorded at three in the morning, with a surrealistic alcoholic BBC-type commentary by Vivian Stanshall – as 'an acoustical experiment in youthful outrageousness – but funny'. He thinks he can still do better. The symphonies of the past are frozen in their magnificence; today's symphonies can be in a state of eternal change.

Oddly the inspiration for *Tubular Bells* was Sibelius, his Fifth Symphony. Oldfield heard it in a 'horrible flat in Victoria' when he was eighteen and at a spiritual nadir. 'I'd had a very painful growing up – though I think it will be worth it – and I had so much energy, not knowing how to use it. I saw much unbelievable beauty in Sibelius, not tranquil but a huge and powerful beauty. It seemed to me what life ought to be like and wasn't.'

Naive, that statement? Perhaps. But there was nothing naive about the years which had preceded his eighteenth birthday. His father was a GP in Reading, who moved to Hornchurch in Essex when Oldfield was thirteen and still practises there. His mother, who died two years ago, suffered from mental illness for years.

'How could I not love my parents?' says Oldfield. 'But my childhood was domestically turbulent. I needed domestic security, and it wasn't there. I've had similar problems to my mother's, but I'm a generation on and I can cope with it all and turn it to creative use. I'm devastated, because now I might have been able to help her. Earlier I couldn't. So it was pills, tranquillizers, electric shock treatment. I felt so helpless.

'That was why I became so immersed in the guitar. By the greatest stroke of good fortune, my father bought me one and taught me a few chords when I was seven. Every day I'd come home from school and lock myself in my room and play.'

At eleven, he was already halfway to a virtuoso. He played at folk clubs, writing his own songs, listening to established artists like Bert Jansch and John Renbourn, ignoring electric rock.

A year later, he was dabbling in electric rock, running a band ('a mixture of The Shadows and early rock 'n' roll') but he was happier playing a residency at a Reading folk club. The family's move to Essex put him into a grammar school which he describes as 'abysmal'. He left at fifteen after an argument with the headmaster over his hair-style and, more importantly for him, after visiting a studio to see Mick Jagger recording.

His sister, Sally, six years older, was responsible for that introduction; she'd known Marianne Faithfull at school. And with Sally, he plunged. 'We did a recording, "Children of the Sun", and got a contract with Transatlantic. It was a short-dress, bare-feet act and they wanted to turn us into a happy flower-power duo. I couldn't stand it. So I had a lean year living off my father, trying to run an electric band, and at sixteen I auditioned for Kevin Ayers.'

His two years with the Ayers Whole World band were crucial, even though he grew increasingly unhappy with the music. He met David Bedford, whose brilliant compositions, ranging from avant-garde conservatoire exercises, through suites and oratorios, to rock orchestrations, have recently done so much to bridge the world of different musical styles. Bedford played for a time in Whole World, and later often collaborated with Oldfield; in turn, Oldfield has played guitar in works like Bedford's *Star's End* and *The Odyssey*.

Whole World also taught Oldfield the hard lessons of professionalism. 'We were trailing everywhere to gigs, but technically and creatively the music became abysmal. People would get drunk, we'd struggle to find the right notes, so we'd turn up the amplifier and the feedback and do somersaults.

'I got mixed up in drugs, too, because it was fashionable and everyone was so bored. Pot, LSD, all of it. I've realized since how absolutely lethal it can be, and I've dropped all that long ago. But so many of the people I knew haven't, and artistically they're stuck precisely where they were, or worse.

'Towards the end I had a total panic attack. I couldn't carry on. I was rarely meeting any honest sincere person, only people who were on drugs or without hope. The music business seemed like a wilderness. I knew I'd got to change. Kevin rented a house in Tottenham, and we all lived there. He lent me a tape recorder and I started work on *Tubular Bells*.

'I took my demos to various companies. Richard Branson of Virgin Records was prepared to take a chance. I moved into The Manor (a recording studio in Oxfordshire) for a year and kept working. I mixed it three times to get it better, and then we held up the release to coincide with a concert at the Queen Elizabeth Hall.

'The concert didn't please me. I was so disappointed – but then everyone stood up and applauded and applauded, and that was the start of it.'

Tubular Bells, originally released on May 25, 1973, was Oldfield's springboard. Not only of itself. It became the theme music for the sensational movie, *The Exorcist*, and there followed a saga of an unauthorized release of a section of it in America, and a symphonic version by the Royal Philharmonic. Oldfield, however, went to live with a girl-friend in a house on a Welsh border hillside facing Hergest Ridge and began composing again.

'Hergest Ridge is wild, hilly, a fantastic place. And that's what I wrote next, but it wasn't what they expected. Not Tubular Bells Part Two. It's involved and complex because I'd been accumulating so much more inside me. Influences like Ravel and Stravinsky, Led Zeppelin and heavy rock.

'There was a backlash. People didn't like *Hergest Ridge*. I was upset, because parts of it were fine, but the criticism was very good for me. I've had too much praise, and I hate it when people say I'm fantastic.

'So I said to myself, right, I'll show you. And I went on to do *Ommadawn*.'

I said to Oldfield I thought it was his best work. He agreed. 'But just wait. I've spent a year building a studio at this beautiful farmhouse, fourteenth century, I've moved into in the Cotswolds. The studio's like a chapel. High-ceilinged. I think I can *really* make something there. David Bedford gave me a wonderful record of medieval music last Christmas. So you can guess my next influence.'

Will success spoil Michael Oldfield? He dresses simply. He drinks mostly beer. He rolls his own, strictly with Old Holborn tobacco. He practises judo (learned it at evening classes), rides a horse, spends hours on the trampoline ('a great sport'), and, like Duke Ellington before him, is obsessed by creating music.

He looks at the very long nails on his right hand – 'you need them for picking the guitar, but they make a terrible clatter on the piano' – and talks about one of the problems of success.

'Hangers-on. I'm trying to get rid of them. I'm successful, they say, and in a position to help people. There are people who have some talent, and once you've helped them they start thinking because I'm nice and quiet and polite they can be just as successful.

'Honestly, I'm not prepared to do it, and I can't see how people with any self-respect can behave like that. It's not the money they're after, even though they ask for it all the time. It's the glory. So I suppose I'm adjusting to the world, growing up. In the last year I've had a hell of a battle and I've lost several friends. That I'll have to learn to live with.'

From Pink to black despair

20 MARCH 1977

Around ten thousand souls in the Empire Pool, Wembley, as there were for each of five nights last week: Pink Floyd's sound – dense, heavy webs of chords and yearning runs played on guitars and electronic keyboards – floods the arena. But it's the moving images on a giant screen which engage eye and mind equally.

The song unfolding is 'Welcome to the Machine', superficially a piece about disillusion after early dreams of pop-star glory. The messages to the eyes, however, are much more overwhelming. First, a menacingly obscene metal monster confronts us. Then, revolving images of faceless tower blocks. Suddenly, blood cascades around them.

The eye is dragged across this bloody ocean. Its dancing waves dissolve into a myriad human hands, stretching imploringly. A tower appears again; the bloody hands still reach out towards it. Meantime, the music spins on . . .

All this was part of the second half of the Floyd concert, when the five-strong band played their penultimate album, *Wish You Were Here*, as they had devoted the first half completely to their new album, *Animals*. Those who have never experienced a Floyd concert can scarcely conceive how different it is from the usual daily experience of three-minute pop bursts on radio.

This is all-engaging (or all-deterring) musical and visual experience. Entertainment? Scarcely. Arguably, it's closer to sombre modern conservatoire music. Equally arguably, it's a variation of theatrical catharsis in parts, as Floyd intensify the dark side of their various moods.

Rarely, if ever, can so-called popular music have dealt so relentlessly in images of bleakest pessimism. Words emerge, not always clearly, in blackly broken skeins: 'sometimes it seems to me I'm just being used,' or '. . . running over the same old ground . . . the same old fears'.

What you see underlines what you hear. The incarnadine ocean is just one example. During *Animals*, huge inflated figures of grotesque human beings float over the audience, collapsing into ignominious deflation; so does a pig.

A send-up? Sick jokes? What Floyd believe of humankind now? Who knows? Floyd retain their vast following. Their music has moved closer to a central point between hard rock and intellectual 1970s 'wallpaper'. Their presentation is the ultimate in brilliantly staged theatre of despair – except for the final mirror-plated revolving wheel, whose silvery beams immaculately wash the audience. It would be comforting, but probably misleading, to interpret this as a late symbol of hope.

Another, more cheerful face of popular music in our time was beaming last weekend at the Festival Hall: Oscar Peterson. He entranced two capacity houses, as his richly virtuosic piano style – full of contrasts, dynamics and virtually an encyclopaedia of jazz piano history – was bound to.

The melodies he chooses, too, are so aptly good: a rich sketch-book of mid-century song, from 'Skylark' to 'Misty'. Peterson, a piano genius, is even better in an intimate club setting, but no concert hall could quell his joyful sound.

The crowds came for Peterson, of course, since his TV shows have widened his fame. But they may have departed marvelling equally at the orchestrally dazzling guitar set played by the lesser-known Joe Pass. His shining art can be seen more intimately at Ronnie Scott's Club for the next two weeks.

Harry Chapin: an eye for losers

10 APRIL 1977

It is scarcely possible to rank Harry Chapin among contemporary singer-songwriters, for he stands virtually alone. It is also hard to believe it has taken so long for so sparklingly original a talent to play a solo concert in London.

He managed it triumphantly after thirty-four years and six superb albums at the New Victoria last Thursday. The hall was not quite full, which will not happen again. No one who was there can fail to persuade six other people along next time.

Chapin's gifts are liberally in evidence on his albums, of which the last three (all Elektra) reveal the most: *Verities and Balderdash*, *Portrait Gallery* and *On The Road To Kingdom Come*. They show how his inspiration springs from the daily encounters of American living, yet also how the situations he depicts are often allegories for the universal modern condition.

'Cat's In The Cradle', about a father-son relationship, is typical Chapin. The son worships the father, wants to grow up like him. The father is too engrossed in business. 'There were planes to catch and bills to pay, he learned to walk while I was away.' Suddenly the boy is grown, married; the father is alone. Now the son is too busy to visit. 'He'd grown up just like me,' as the painful punchline observes.

As dramatic narrative alone, that song is compelling. Similarly, Chapin observes a meeting between an old man and a waitress in a café; a chance encounter of old flames in a taxi; a crucifixion by metropolitan critics of a singer from the sticks who never opens his mouth in public again. 'Music was his life,' sings Chapin. 'It was not his livelihood.'

Chapin has an unerring and pitying eye for life's losers; not heavily tragic losers, but those for whom the pieces never quite fall together. Simultaneously, he celebrates the strength of the human spirit which survives loneliness, discovers the comic moments of episodes with which his listeners can continually identify. In that coincidence lies the secret of the best popular songs.

Chapin sings in a clear, pleasant voice, using unfussy melodies and arrangements played by a small backing group within which a cello provides haunting counterpoints. His stage personality is captivating. He did as he wished with Thursday's audience. As he hunched dumpily in his chair, tousling his hair, talking wittily and relevantly about the circumstances of his songs, himself, and his musicians, not a soul stirred, except to laugh or applaud. The final standing ovation was spring-heeled and genuine. London will see no more absorbing concert this year.

Earlier last week, at the Albert Hall, Glen Campbell and Jimmy Webb had a larger audience, without stirring them so deeply. Campbell is excellent at what he does, in intonation and style as true to his Western roots (born in Delight, Arkansas, once a cotton-picker) as Chapin is to his Greenwich Village background. Yet where Chapin gets inside every song he sings, Campbell seems too often a spectator, smoothing out tunes and meanings alike. Few shocks, few insights – just a pleasant flowing country-ish sound.

He can, it seems, do anyone's music. Still slim and lithe, he was once a Beach Boy (1965), and revived their hits fluently. He imitated Elvis. He rocketed through the *William Tell Overture* on guitar with the finesse of a computer print-out.

He has the great good fortune often to sing Webb's fine songs – 'Wichita Lineman', 'Galveston', 'Macarthur Park' – and here performed several. Webb himself sang 'Didn't We' which, like the others, is already a modern classic. But the gloss of Campbell's breezy performance will not endure like the grittier 150 minutes of Harry Chapin's.

Magical Mystery Train

24 APRIL 1977

'Rock 'n' roll is a combination of good ideas dried up by fads, terrible junk, hideous failings in taste and judgment, gullibility and manipulation, moments of unbelievable clarity and invention, pleasure, fun, vulgarity, excess, novelty and utter enervation, all summed up nowhere so well as on Top 40 radio, that ultimate rock 'n' roll version of America.'

Popular music has already, in this age of theatrical rock, become a phenomenon involving careful looking as well as listening. If the words are as provocatively interesting as those above, then it should soon be a subject where reading is also mandatory.

So let me welcome their source – a book called *Mystery Train* by a youngish American critic, Greil Marcus. Having made its reputation in America, it is, at last, available in Britain in softcover (Omnibus Press, £1.95). It should be eagerly sought out, for there has never been a more well-written, imaginative, scholarly, infuriating, crackling, gladdening book about rock music.

'Images of America in Rock 'n' Roll Music' says the sub-title and that's really the point. For Greil Marcus uses a handful of modern popular artists – a brace of bluesmen, together with The Band, Sly Stone, Randy Newman and Elvis Presley – to illuminate and interpret two centuries of the American Dream. What he terms 'the stakes of life in America' are given dimension by these artists, whilst American social and historical ideas add stimulating overtones to the music.

This, of course, is how the best (and occasionally the worst) popular music should be viewed. It can often be a fascinating social document, fit to be treated seriously – which doesn't mean dully. Greil Marcus is serious, and he'll smoothly rope in de Tocqueville, Raymond Chandler, Walt Whitman or Lyndon B. Johnson to make a point.

With Whitman he is especially in love. Whitman, we're reminded, once wrote that he didn't want an art that could decide presidential elections: he wanted an art to make them irrelevant. Greil Marcus sees original popular music artists in roughly this way. They interpret the feel of American experience, provide guidance and understanding for those who seek it – a philosophy which works with hand-picked artists, but in a business as commercial as popular music needs considerable qualification.

The serious and stimulating purpose of much of this book shouldn't, however, overshadow its many less exacting pleasures. Greil Marcus has a remarkable knowledge of pop trivia and a flow which makes most other music writers seem ponderous.

'When Elvis was drafted I felt a great relief, because he made demands on me. It was close to what I felt when the politics of the sixties faded – an ambivalent feeling of cowardice and safety.'

Of Randy Newman: 'His best songs implicate the listener. He goes far enough to wonder if everything might not be worth doing, which means he is far enough gone to wonder if anything *is* worth doing – such as pursuing an audience.'

Of some modern singer-songwriters: 'Truth telling is beginning to settle into a slough where it is nothing more than pedestrian autobiography set to placid music framed by a sad smile on the album cover.'

Such quotations only partly demonstrate the qualities of Greil Marcus, for it is from counterpointing arguments, rather than through aphorisms, that he gains his effects. Dealing with a music of hyperbole, he can fall victim to it himself – over-inflating Randy Newman's talent, for example. Living in a society of paradoxes, he allows them to pockmark his writing. That, however, is virtually all I can say in modest qualification of *Mystery Train*'s many kinds of excellence.

Punk on film

4 SEPTEMBER 1977

The language of popular music is a quicksand. No sooner had 'punk rock' recognizably reared its scabrous baby head last year than justifications for it had to be invented by those who must live with it to survive – from particular record companies to writers desperate not to be thought out of tune.

Terminology came first. Instead of punk, the phrase was 'new wave'. Today the phrases are sometimes used interchangeably; or 'new wave' may indicate bands with more skills and pretensions, 'punk' the cruder outfits. There are endless variations on the themes.

Further explanations and justifications range from the socio-political (worth listening to, since punk has sprung out of contemporary moods and conditions) to the musical. Isn't it great, runs the latter argument, that excitement is back in rock, that bands can just get up and play again without dragging round seventy tons of special equipment like all those dreary supergroups and tax exiles?

The theoretical attractions of that argument are obvious. But it ignores the nihilism of much punk, the elements in good popular music of all styles other than 'excitement', and isn't even historically accurate. Bands didn't cease to emerge in the early 1970s; there were hundreds of non-punk newcomers.

Punk/new wave is, then, still very much here. On the swing-of-the-taste pendulum basis, that's unsurprising – after a period of over-sophistication in rock, back to basics. It has an audience; it has hype; it has made inroads in the pop charts; it is within most record companies' catalogues. But it is changing and will change further.

Musically, some bands have become more skilled. Many are, virtually, old wave 'heavy metal' outfits – strident, but with considerable technique; they would probably be around if punk had never been invented. Lyrics have been made less obviously outrageous to escape radio bans. The final irony will be when the first punk supergroups emerge to gladden showbiz accountants' hearts.

Movies, too, will come – but none will have the brutal honesty of the remarkable documentary currently showing at the ICA Seminar Room. Called *The Original Punk Rock Movie*, it is a jerky forty-five-minute selection (not one hour as announcements misleadingly claim) drawn from 8mm film shot by a black disc jockey, Don Letts, at the seminal punk club, the Roxy.

Many of the bruited bands are shown performing and acting up in a way which no film will ever capture again. The obvious elements are there – from the relentless emptiness of the music to the obligatory flashes of tattoos, swastikas, pins in lips, sniffing and suchlike exhibitionism, including a barbaric cut-by-cut display of self-mutilation.

Popular music has produced nothing uglier or more joyless than these documentary fragments. New wave may, ultimately, have some musical (or other) bonuses. But those tightrope walkers who plug punk so indiscriminately could find living with their adjectives less easy after viewing this sad panorama.

Abba: money, money, money

5 FEBRUARY 1978

No recent popular music phenomenon has matched Abba, the Scandinavians who made it by winning the 1974 Eurovision Song Contest with the catchy 'Waterloo'.

One statistic – fifty million records sold, outstripping The Beatles in their heyday – indicates the commercial success. Artistically, the reckoning is less certain. Not that their music is inconsiderable; it is jolly, accessible, safely sexy, brilliantly constructed for the middle-road market. It's just that its dollar harvest seems wildly disproportionate to its musical merit.

Musical values, however, take little account of Abba themselves, a situation partially rectified by a magnetic documentary about the foursome, *Abba*, which in ninety-five minutes, under Lasse Hallstrom's deft direction, exotically covers their 1977 Australian tour – concerts, backstage flashes and some fantasy inserts connected with a wearisome sub-plot about a radio reporter pursuing them.

This movie will stun you and, if you enjoy their always competent music, delight you. Over a score of hits there are beautifully photographed concerts, and a visual concentration on the principals of unyielding rigour.

Super-super superstars indeed. At one rainstormed show, their reception is fantastic: not even The Beatles at Shea Stadium exceeded this. In Adelaide, Perth, Melbourne, sixty-year-olds endlessly join the teenies in romps at their concerts.

Why? 'They are,' says one grandmother, 'so nice and clean and tidy.' Just so. Safe as cornflakes, family sunshine, one of the few groups to pull in *all* ages except, I suspect, the no-fooling 16–21s who consume Yes (or Rotten, according to taste).

The movie's clever, loud. Even warts are cosmetically painted on. A cop has cottonwooled ears at a concert; a child believes they show off too much; a cab driver says he hates them. There's even a kerbside philosopher, quoting St Mark, to remind us that Abba means Father.

Abba themselves – by heaven, such impact! Were ever a group more wholesomely handsome? The men, very hairy and Vikingesque, master musicians; the girls, beautiful and talented, and with endowments so additional as to mock any principles of fair play for us mere mortals.

Anni-Frid Lyngstad, the redhead, radiates energy, grace and punchy humour. The blonde, Agnetha Faltskog, has – well, almost everything, but outstandingly, a rear view so divinely proportioned and so relentlessly presented (above long Scandinavian limbs) during the movie as to drive all males between sixteen and six hundred crazy. Someone, some day, somewhere will sell (maybe already has sold) postcards of it as others sell views of the Taj Mahal. Certainly everything else about Abba has, as the film demonstrates, been sold: buttons, cushions, balloons, shirts, fanzines, dolls, all that pop-machine *garbaggio*.

What the film doesn't do is to tell you what Abba *think*. They are so tremendously outgoing, giving so much of themselves, how long can they survive? But who are the people behind the mask? What goes on in the mind two feet above the bottom? Is 'Money, Money, Money' the name of the game? End of story. But see it this month, and marvel.

The forty-year Transfer

19 MARCH 1978

It's much too glib to pigeonhole Manhattan Transfer, who enthralled Palladium audiences last week, as high priests of nostalgia. Their music certainly conjures shimmering memories of days past – but their spell is far more potent, their magical brew more subtle.

What they have done is to distil the essence of the best popular sounds of the past forty years, to dress them with classiest harmonies and arrangements, add beauty, style, humour and remarkably fine singing voices. The result is a musical entertainment to overwhelm eyes and ears, smash barriers, enchant equally the generations which swayed to Glenn Miller or knelt to The Beatles.

If ever there was proof that the best elements of each pop vogue survive, this brilliant American quartet – two women, two men – provide it. Ellington, Woody Herman, gospel, Tin Pan Alley, Elvis, high school rock, blues, Motown, Piaf – everything revives with their touch. Rarely was technique more magisterially deployed than in their breakneck vocal parallel of Herman's 1947 anthem, 'Four Brothers'.

That's an obvious *tour de force*: the loving treatment of tunes as varied as 'Cherokee', 'Java Jive', 'Where Did Our Love Go' and 'In the Dark' is just as impressive – but they explode, too, with the dynamic Alan Paul haring through the audience in black leather, evoking the cruder, more rumbustious myths of rock 'n' roll.

It has taken ManTran around five years to move from being fun take-off players in coffee houses to their present position as major musical and theatrical artists. They make sense of recent musical history, delightfully expand its glories and its foibles, make it sound of today as well as yesterday.

Hard work, natural endowments and musical intelligence are at the heart of the transformation. All four have excellent voices, an infectious sense of humour, radiant handsomeness and sex appeal.

The tall redhead, Laurel Masse, undulates torchily and as hypnotically as Abba's Agnetha Faltskog; but in her case you remember the voice as well as the voluptuous rear view. ManTran might even be called the thinking (and listening) man's Abba.

Part of their charm may be gauged from their new album, *Pastiche* (Atlantic K50444, £3.95); but the dazzling delights of their stage marathon – over thirty songs in 2½ hours – inevitably is missing. They are giants.

Bring on the heavy horses

14 MAY 1978

There is no denying the power, wit and freshness of Jethro Tull. Among British bands, they are almost unique; magnetic and magnificent after a decade of music making.

They are, however, almost too independently original for their own good. There is, through their many albums, a discernibly logical line in leader Ian Anderson's development as a composer. But the superficial twists in the band's career have sometimes left those who ride the bandwagons of pop taste – desperate to be thought in vogue – bewildered and insecure.

Hence the spiteful attacks which greeted Anderson's *Passion Play* in 1973; hence, also, the critical reserve in some quarters for his last album, *Songs From The Wood*, and his new one, *Heavy Horses*.

The infectious splendour of Tull's recent British concerts, the clamour of the audiences – how, at the Hammersmith Odeon, they rose to *Heavy Horses*! – and the riches revealed as the band play retrospectively, amply answer the grouches. Anderson, so much his own man, has leapt the generation chasm, still winning young followers while retaining the old with his substantial repertoire of excellent contemporary music.

He is, he's said, trying to fashion an English sound while still remaining a rock band. That, I think, does only scant justice to the magical mix of blues, folk, rock and jazz (listen, please, to his flute improvisations) which Tull pours forth. Yet the Englishness is unmistakeable.

It emerges in his pastoral songs and acoustic gentleness. It's seen also brilliantly encapsulated in *Heavy Horses*. Anderson lives in the country, loves horses, would never be without them. 'Think what it's like to be cut off without petrol.' The song grew from that feeling, and from reading an article about Clydesdales while touring in America.

The feeling is there, his emotions and his way of life outside entertainment reflected. Isn't that what good popular music is about – honest feeling springing from experience? 'Heavy Horses' is a fine song glowing with evocative images. Yet Anderson's realist enough (his honesty is too fierce for some) to confess that Clydesdales can't cope with the agricultural development he's undertaken on his Skye farm; he has to use tractors.

So, this is the enduring, enquiring, idiosyncratic, fascinating nature of Tull. Their concert performance reflects it. Bare stage, except for staccato lights mirroring the moods, as Anderson and his five splendid companions produce flute, guitar, percussion and keyboard solos and walls of sound fit to conquer.

They do it all with a humorous, ripe theatricality which, in its self-micking zaniness, is totally winning. David Palmer's mortician's stance at pipe-organ, John Evan's impish obeisance to Harpo Marx, and the careful support of the other musicians to Anderson's gymnastic exuberance produce one of the world's peerless performances.

Despite their longevity, Anderson and Tull have, I suspect, only just begun to surprise us.

Bette Midler: excess story

24 SEPTEMBER 1978

Bette Midler is the only artist I have ever seen who could simultaneously, and fairly musically, send up Dorothy Lamour, Mary Martin, Carmen Miranda and assorted Hollywood clichés whilst singing 'The Moon of Manakoura' and ricocheting around the stage wearing a mermaid's tail in a crazy electric bath-chair.

She lives by excess, revels in going over the top, pulling into the magnetic field of her unquenchably iconclastic spirit every mockable facet of the work she inhabits. She is unique, America's most original entertainer, a comedienne and actress who can sing when she gives herself a chance between falling on the floor, swearing, bumping and grinding, and being outrageous about everything sacred from Joan of Arc to royalty. The singing, in a sense, is the point, for she's made the popular music of our age the framework around which she drapes her multitudinous talents. As her records have promised, and last week's triumphant Palladium shows confirmed, she is a witty musical parodist, from The Andrews Sisters and 'In The Mood', through bounding rock 'n' roll to tortured Streisandish ballads. She could have made her name for that affectionate, bitchy gift alone.

But her records and her powerful musical persona could scarcely have prepared anyone for the full impact of her Palladium first half. For seventy-five minutes, between songs, she told bawdy tales, scored off politicians and peasants, royals and renegades, all at a blistering pace which would have destroyed other artists.

The pace is part of the Midler illusion. She can be highly offensive and crude – over the top as usual – but she moves so fast that no barb or vulgarity festers. She has, too, a glittering vocabulary, like a Broadway moll who has swallowed *Roget's Thesaurus*, which is superbly deployed with every suggestion of total spontaneity.

That, however, was only the first half. The second began with high camp music from the 1940s and more lewd tales. Then, suddenly, she was sitting on a bench, miming and singing a string of desperately sad-funny songs, throwing in poetry and character sketches in a *tour de force* which suggested a cross between tragic Judy Garland and Charlie Chaplin's universal pathos.

The audience was stilled, enraptured. They recognized the vulnerability beneath the crust of flashy sophistication. And that remarkable surprise was her final stroke. She received the kind of tumultuously genuine reception which only a star who is many stars in one can evoke.

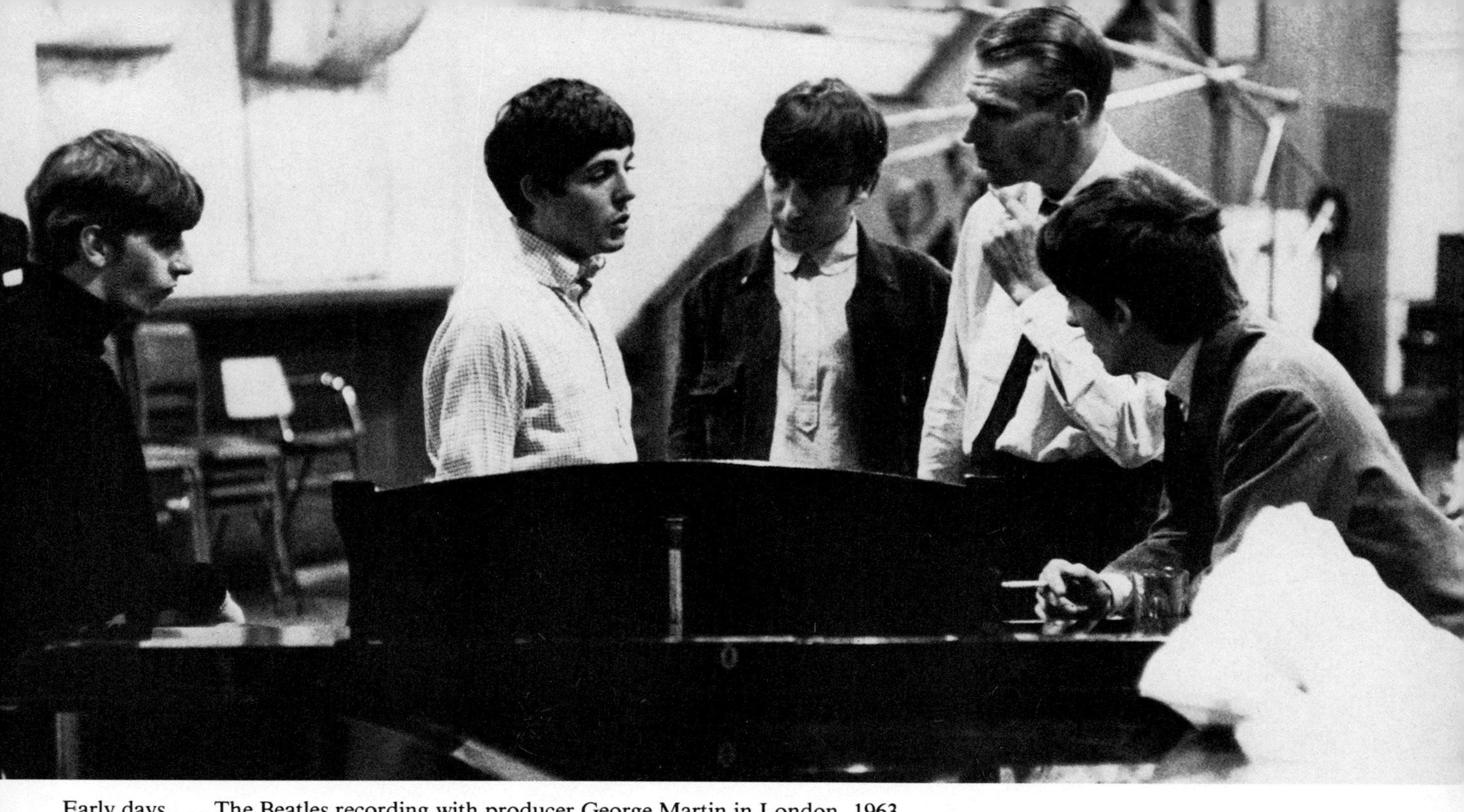

Early days . . . The Beatles recording with producer George Martin in London, 1963.
Photograph Derek Jewell

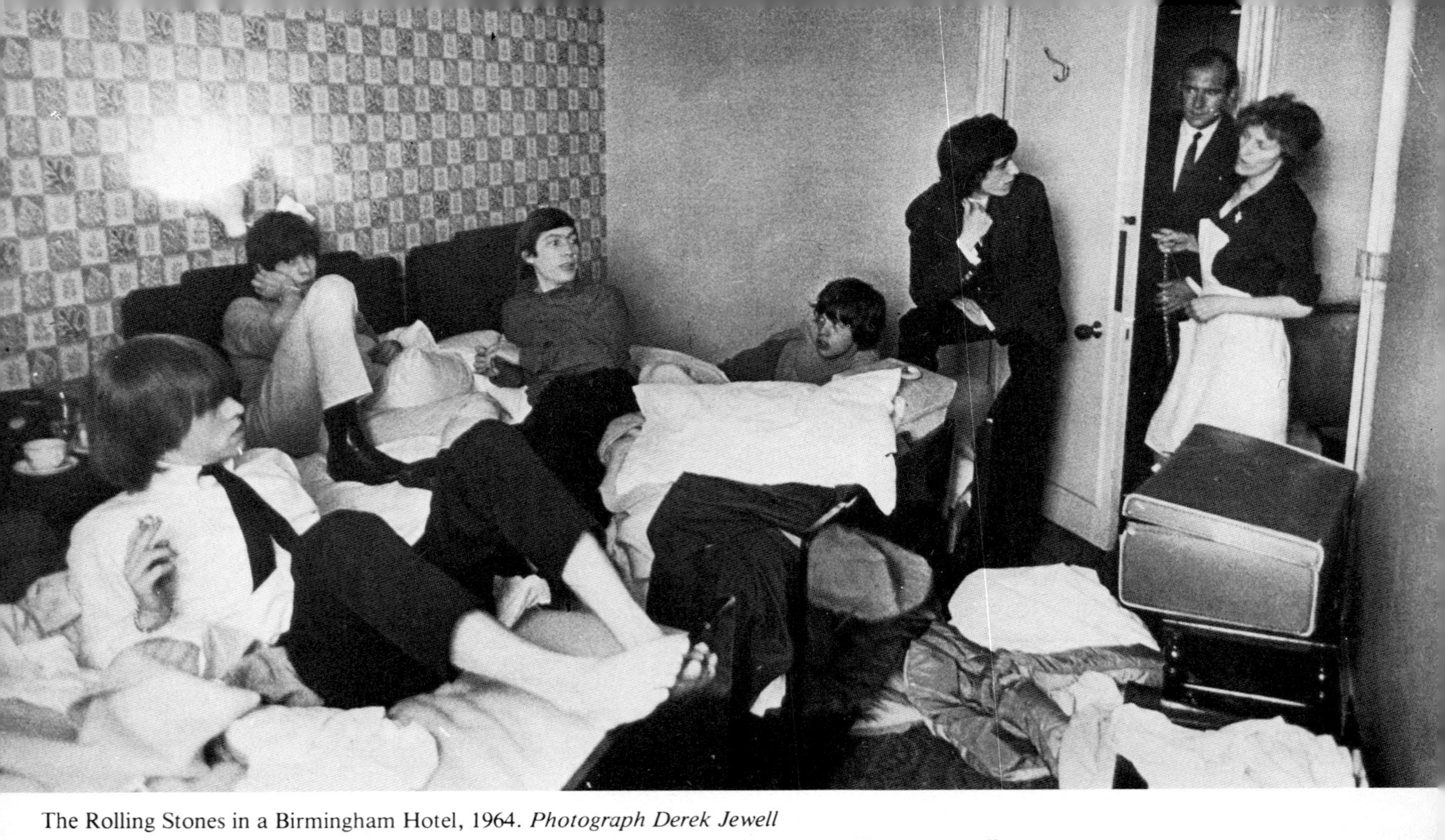

The Rolling Stones in a Birmingham Hotel, 1964. *Photograph Derek Jewell*

Duke Ellington (with the author) at the Dorchester, London, 1964: 'You know me, I'm a great talker. I'm always duly flattered by being asked.'

Above: A great idiosyncratic: Roland Kirk.
Photograph David Redfern Photography

Frank Sinatra: opening the cave of nostalgia.
Photograph David Redfern Photography

Liza Minnelli: from the beginning,
definitely diamond.
Photograph London Features International

Abba: safe as cornflakes,
family sunshine.
Photograph London Features International

Tina Turner: a voice like honeyed sandpaper.
Photograph London Features International

Chapter Six

Jazz: four portraits

It's often accidental that one writes about an artist at length: a magazine wants a piece at a particular time (which happened with Ornette Coleman, originally commissioned by *Encounter*) or one's enthusiasm for a musician is given the kind of free rein which extended programme notes for a tour allow (as with Benny Goodman). So these four portraits are not necessarily of the people I most admire in jazz. They do, however, reflect so many of the qualities which have drawn me admiringly to jazz during the years I have been writing on popular music. Among these, the sense of history and perspective engendered by jazz provides a touchstone in what sometimes has seemed a disordered and totally transient musical world. Since early in the century, jazz and its great practitioners have given blood and muscle and brain to the body musical. Jazzmen's skills have set standards to be emulated: their ideas and innovations have fuelled changes in more 'commercial' areas of music; and in recording studios around the world, their ability has on thousands of occasions created a glittering setting for the voices of (frequently less talented) popular artists. Jazz itself – mostly a minority art form in the 1960s and 1970s, but showing amazing qualities of survival – has undergone all kinds of change. The old labels of traditional, mainstream, bop and so forth seem very inadequate today when 'free' jazz, jazz-rock, 'crossover' music and the rest have become the vogue. Some part of the ferment is captured, I hope, in the portraits of this chapter and in the brief sketches of the next. Benny Goodman is history, an unchanging giant in a time of uncertainty. Sonny Rollins represents the idiosyncrasy of jazz, as does Ornette Coleman, who suggested new ways (like them or not) in which the music might move. The Modern Jazz Quartet were as individualistic as any group in history; having evolved their special brand of 'chamber jazz', they ignored criticism and in doing so won for themselves (and perhaps for jazz) a large, faithful audience. They were also, I suggest, pioneers in showing how popular and classical styles of music could interact on each other. Those new horizons of 'fusion' were to have a major effect on popular musicians of every kind in the 1960s and 1970s. The MJQ did finally break up in 1974; their twenty-two years as a unit was one of the most remarkable of all exercises in survival.

Ornette Coleman: punch a button and blow wind

NOVEMBER 1965

For the first time his voice had risen assertively above the grubble and whine of the traffic outside. He was on his feet, swinging the saxophone harness he had only meditatively picked at before.

'Do you know the most stupid statement I've ever heard? Around the time Louis' (the sound is hard, chopped up – 'Lew-iss') 'Armstrong had made "Hello Dolly" – you know that thing? And there's this agent saying "Louis, you can get to be the greatest man in the world. I can make you so rich, you'll never have to play another note" . . .'

His arms were now stretched out, the sax cord wound tight around a finger.

'Do you dig what I'm saying? This man who plays the most beautiful trumpet, and here's someone trying to fix it so he never plays another note. Cutting him off from what he can do best. And you ask me why I don't dig agents?'

The blast was over as suddenly as it had blown up. Like a climax in his music, which springs from no set pattern of harmonic progression or length of phrase or metric repetition, the eruption had been unpredictable. It was also untypical, of this conversation at least. Mostly, Ornette Coleman sat relaxed and spoke quietly, choosing his words with no apparent care, yet with the didactic hammering you might have expected from the man who six years ago set the jazz world by its ears with his playing and his principles, and who has since seemed almost trapped in his own mystique.

It was a quite unexpected meeting. No PR releases said he was coming on his first visit to Europe – primarily to appear in a film whose score he had written and to play seven concerts on the Continent. He simply arrived in London, and the grapevine only worked after he was encamped in a Queensway flat. Indeed, though he had been the first musician to do anything radically new with jazz since the bop revolution of the 1940s, he might as well (to British searchers) have been dead for the last few years before a concert hastily arranged near London showed how very much alive he is. Nothing recorded by him since 1962 has been issued and the names of men who have been encouraged by his example to attempt something similar–Archie Shepp, Albert Ayler, John Tchicai – have become nearly as familiar as that of the leader of the revolution himself.

It was very different when he first arrived in New York in late 1959, after years of obscurity playing with rhythm and blues bands, and a period in Los Angeles as a lift operator studying harmony and theory textbooks in his spare time. He carried a white alto saxophone made of plastic then – bought originally because it was cheaper, but soon to become almost a textural trademark – and the sounds he produced on it seemed for a time to divide the whole jazz world into camps for or against him.

What he seemed to be trying to do to jazz was, in effect, what 'serious' composers had done to concert-hall music fifty years earlier: to throw over accepted canons of structure and harmony and tonality. That someone had to come along to do this was probably inevitable. Charlie Parker had shaken up jazz once (and had, incidentally, been reviled as much then as Coleman was being reviled in 1960), but the vast school of imitators he had spawned were in a rut. A pleasant, even rather creative rut; but still a rut.

There had been, and still are, minor currents deviating from the main flow of 'modern' jazz, of course: a growing aggressiveness in the music of many younger Negro players, for instance, with heavy use of 'soul' elements, based on blues and gospel music forms. That movement (like the writings of James Baldwin, and perhaps like the brusque stage antics of Miles Davis) reflected the increasing passion of the civil rights struggle in America, and its racial overtones have since become as repetitiously boring as the more customary reverse pattern is both boring and vicious. There had also been diversions, like 'Third Stream' – an attempt to blend jazz and classical techniques; and there were to be fads, like bossa nova. But no one was trying to do to the guts of jazz what Coleman then proceeded to do.

His jazz was quite divorced from the traditional concept of improvisation based on chord patterns, which Parker had not departed from but had simply idiosyncratically enlarged by stressing the harmonic as well as melodic possibilities. Coleman's music seemed virtually atonal. He played notes which were unfamiliar, and because of this caused some critics to say he couldn't play in tune, when in fact he was simply extending the number of notes jazzmen have always played which do not coincide with the tempered pitches of classical Western music. What was often missing in his music compared with theirs was the ultimate return to a familiar tonal base – the 'resolution' which usually gives 'out of tune' jazz notes a point of reference and creates their particular piquancy.

In the familiar jazz pattern of tension (caused by stretched or smeared notes) and release (the relief created by a return to conventional tonality), Coleman did not always bother with release. He turned his phrases to suit himself and not to drop into eight-bar shapes, which his jazz contemporaries tended to do.

It was all a bit much for some ears – and Coleman laid himself still more open to attack by insisting in print on his right to do it.

Before I met him, I looked again at the sleeve notes to the first Coleman

LP issued here. 'There is no single *right* way to play jazz,' he was saying, insisting that 'modern' jazz had in fact become a rather settled and conventional thing, full of predetermined effects. His music had even grown a name – 'free group improvisation' – which in print sounded rather like what they'd been up to in New Orleans forty years earlier, except that Coleman really meant *free*. 'We do not have any idea what the end result will be,' he said, and it often sounded that way. Some of his tunes gave me no pleasure at all, though it is a wonderful thing how aural tolerance matures with the years; in others there was, even at first hearing, a beauty, and a daring, which could leave you breathless. Not everyone, naturally, would agree with me.

For a time he seemed to be producing, and recording, madly – not least, one suspects, because some members of the jazz establishment (like John Lewis and Nat Hentoff) championed him. Then, after a concert at New York Town Hall in December 1962, the well – certainly as far as Europe was concerned – suddenly seemed to dry up. Coleman retired into himself. Only early this year did one really appreciate he was stirring again: a performance at an American university, a date at the Village Vanguard in New York, compositions – for the film and for a Pirandello play at Princeton – and stories of a new-found proficiency on violin and trumpet as well as saxophone.

Now here he was: a taut, friendly man in a bare room, without mystique, not shy about talk, letting his coffee grow cold.

Early conversation was a desultory scuffling round the facts of recent months. 'I'd just finished conducting this film score with a chamber orchestra – more or less classical instrumentation. That drained me, so I thought I'd better take off. See the world . . .' And so on. Then: 'You're talking about me. Let's talk about music.' The difference didn't seem apparent, but one had to try. Had he changed at all in his music, in what he was trying to do.?

'There are imperfections I've tried to avoid. I've come to know more about the forms of expression which suit my instruments. My work is more free, but it has more order. I mean like this. I'm still trying to play something you haven't heard before. But the tools I'm using are maybe more perfected. So there's more order.

'Eighteen months I've been studying violin and trumpet. And orchestral composition. By myself. I've been playing so long that the very best way is the way in which you yourself like to study anything. I had notation lessons with Gunther Schuller till I found I knew more about it than he did.

'That part of my music which is written down – well, there are some things I wouldn't write down because I know I couldn't get them played right. But beyond that I'm seeking honest spontaneity. I really believe you can play music without having any preconceived notion of thought about what you want to express. Why not? You just punch a button and blow wind. A person doesn't always have to relate to the past to play something in the present. Basically, when you write down notes it's like a computer. It can be repeated. And isn't that a limit to a form of expression? I don't know exactly what is the depth of emotion that music will allow a performer or an audience to experience. But I do know there are more experiences to be had in music than in anything else. And I don't want them to be limited in any way . . .

'People are always asking the wrong questions in music. What have questions like "Who are you?" or "What gives you the right?" or "Was that the way it was done before?" to do with making music *today*? Aren't they very insecure questions? You don't have to get permission to die, why do people seem to want it in order to live? I'm against that way of thinking: the attitude that says "I knew Spike Jones, I knew Louis Armstrong, I knew Stan Kenton, I knew Ornette Coleman. Now, please, can I play?" I'm more interested in the present, not in history. Isn't it a very painful thing to always be wondering if you're doing the right thing so much you end up doing nothing at all. You know what I mean? . . .'

The thing with Coleman is that you think you *do* know what he means: the general drift of it, anyway. And it does not always seem particularly remarkable. His talk can even grow soporific. But as he spurts these great loose-hung banks of words he knifes you sometimes: with near-private language which makes you grapple, with a phrase, with spice of gossip.

'I'm not talking to you. Just thinking aloud. And I'm not supposed to be thinking like this, do you know that? If a Negro hears me, he says I'm trying to be a white man. If a white hears me, he says "My, that's a clever nigger". So I'm losing both ends. I'm always talking instead of doing.'

He does seem genuinely to believe he has travelled some way towards acceptance. Particularly he likes playing at universities, where he feels the interest in what he is doing is most free of prejudice. But the reservations are always explicit, and the irony implicit.

'Now that other groups have started trying to do what I was trying to do, the whole thing's less insecure. My music is *passé*, I hear, so when that happens acceptance of it must have increased, mustn't it? I'm thirty-five now and I've composed, I suppose, over a thousand tunes, and sixty or seventy of them have been recorded. And is that valuable? I'll tell you I don't know what *value* is. I've sold lots of records, yet I haven't been treated fairly. I've played honestly, yet I've been misunderstood. So what is value?

'The truth is, I've been exploited. As a gimmick. I feel I've never been paid in any manner of money because of what I'm *really* trying to do, but for quite different reasons. Those who control bookings have a tendency to play you against people and people against you. It's all class categories or racial categories, and I'd rather be a human being than live with any of these things. It's very painful' (the word keeps recurring in his conversation) 'to find out there's nothing you can do without someone else asking how well it was once done. Why place the future in subjection because of the past?

'I've found that in music today it is possible for an individual to play without relating to the musical past. You *can* eliminate any kind of stereotyped attitude now, and there are growing to be as many different types of music as you want. People come up and thank me because I'm trying – and it's not a race-conscious thing, or class, or origin, or anything like that. You don't have to get a degree in humanship to do this kind of music.

'The newer musicians in New York – those you've asked me about, that you call the "avant-garde", and that's OK if you want to say that – well, I've heard them all and I've played with them all. They're like me in some ways – they all seem to be playing from the same key. Cecil Taylor, he has the most consistency in what's good. But I haven't heard from them a true conviction of human ability – *their* ability. I know that they feel they've got to be accepted before they can create. So I don't worry about them because I don't worry about that . . .'

Coleman was less tolerant of some long-established jazz musicians. And you may draw your own conclusions about his views.

'Duke Ellington is one of the few Negroes allowed to exist at the level of a pop creator. And he's written beautiful music. But I've never seen him take a stand for jazz.

'You know, so many writers have told me what Duke Ellington is. But does he know what he is himself? There have been many Duke Ellingtons. He is a character created by a certain group of people and put in the system to balance it. There were ten or fifteen other Negro bands that were a bitch, just like his. But they weren't allowed to go on existing. Uncle Tom isn't a word I use. But I suppose that is what he is. A glorified Uncle Tom.

'Miles Davis, he treated me so bad. He asked me to write something for him, and I did, and later I went round to see him. And someone comes to the door. You'll have to make an appointment, he's too busy, all that stuff. And I'm saying I'm not a bill collector, I'm not trying to assassinate him. But it's still that same old soft-shoe dance. People have made him so big now, they protect him from what he can do best. And there's this attitude of not caring anything about people. Shutting yourself off. Yet people dig that, do you know? They really dig it.'

Ornette Coleman sounded puzzled by all this. Baffled rather than bitter. 'All these people telling you what you are. Can I talk to you or do I have to go through ninety thousand people to talk to you?' A little later he made a specific denial – 'No, not bitter. Just depressed at having to accept a lower standard as a human being' – and if bitterness was there, he certainly disguised it well. He also sometimes sounded as baffled by what was inside him as he was by the behaviour of others. 'I really believe in music, but I don't claim to *need* it.'

Throughout the conversation he hadn't used the word 'cat' once; nor the word 'man' as a finishing jab to a sentence. For an interview with a jazz musician it made a change.

Surprising Sonny Rollins

5 DECEMBER 1965

The candle dripping grease in the corner was baffling. London's newest hotel, and this was the only light in the room. Outside the leaves were raving about in a very black autumn night.

'I always have my candle,' said Sonny Rollins. 'It was taught me by a guy I used to practise with. When I'm playing saxophone I light the candle and blow real close to it. If it flickers it shows there's air escaping around the reed. And that means my embouchure isn't firm enough. I left it burning because it's restful. Can you see to write, though?' In his fashion, Rollins pays a lot of attention to detail. He was sitting there, explaining how much he had enjoyed a visit to Japan, when a maid knocked, came in, deposited a sheet and left. Her eyes looked suspiciously through me, Rollins and the candle. Understandably. There was a shuffle of embarrassment from Rollins. He had, he explained, no small change to tip her for providing him with clean sheets every day. But, I said, don't American hotels change the sheets? 'They weren't for my *bed*. See, I do my exercises every morning on the floor. Yoga. She's been giving me the sheets for that. It's nicer than sitting on carpets.'

Rollins is his own man. Going his own way. What might seem affectation in others flows quietly, with complete naturalness and dignity, from him. He is a big man who walks and talks softly. There may well be an element of the joker in him, but he disguises it well. Not a flicker of conning. His personality hangs together. He is consistent and very determined.

There is the matter of his sabbatical, which in the jazz world is now quite celebrated. In 1959, when he was twenty-nine, Rollins was very successful indeed. He had been said by Miles Davis, among others, to be the greatest tenor saxophone player in history. He was certainly at that time the most influential since Coleman Hawkins and Lester Young, and has continued to be so; his hard-edged, large-toned sound and the daring methods of improvisation have coloured the style of all the modern jazzmen, from John Coltrane to Roland Kirk. Rollins, though, felt that playing for hours in public night after night was draining him, making him go stale. 'I was,' he later explained, 'filled with question marks.'

There are those who cry all the way to the bank over the effect of public taste on their art. There is also, occasionally, a Sonny Rollins. His reaction was simply to stop playing in public. For two years.

'It wasn't easy. I had royalties and things, but my wife had to go out to work. I didn't want that, but it had to be done. And we have no children. I studied and studied and practised and practised. I really explored my whole way of playing. Changed it.'

Much of the time Rollins played indoors, but he was worried about the neighbours. So he took to going out and sitting on the Williamsburg Bridge, near his New York flat, and playing there. 'I think the people liked it. Nobody interfered. They used to stop and listen for a time, morning and evening. I could play as loud as I wanted, and with the skyline and the water, well, you get feelings you don't get inside a building. That's only natural, isn't it?'

When Rollins did return to public performance in 1961 he was not so much a changed man as simply more himself. He was a better jazz musician, though even now he is often attempting so much in his playing that it is not always easy to follow or enjoy. He had become, unarguably, so much an individualist that there was no longer any point in young players trying to copy him.

'Sonny Rollins,' as Barney Wilen, a French disciple, put it, 'fears nothing.' Steve Lacy, an American musician, said of him: 'I've never seen anyone in love with the tenor saxophone the way Sonny is. He really loves that horn and understands it.' And Jim Hall, one of the really great guitarists, described working with Rollins as 'like watching Picasso paint or Thomas Wolfe write.' The best capsule description of jazz I know is Whitney Balliett's: 'The sound of surprise.' No one fits it like Rollins. Every time he plays it is as though he were testing himself – pushing his instrument to its limits, exploring it, revealing textures which no one suspected were there before. He is, it would seem, not the first man you would imagine a British director inviting to write film music for a major commercial production. But it has happened. A few weeks ago he became the first musician to create ('compose' is not quite the word) an uncompromisingly jazz background, using a small group, for a British feature film. The film, *Alfie*, is based on the Bill Naughton play which starred John Neville in the West End. It has Michael Caine in the title role of a Cockney philanderer whose *affaires* (if you read the play one way) begin to change the man; especially one in which a girl has an abortion. How did an American jazzman, I wondered, feel about making music for a film showing Londoners in London? 'Well, I didn't do research into Cockney music, if that's what you mean. I haven't tried to write folk melodies jazzed up.'

What he did, in fact, was to begin with a number of themes. He and the six British musicians he asked for ('Some of the best musicians around. Not around London. Around. Period.') would watch a section of the film. Then Rollins would play a little, explain what he wanted. The musicians would try out the idea, then try it again, perhaps building on it. 'They were able to pick up the inflections in my playing.'

The British tenor player picking up his inflections on the soundtrack is one of the uncles of local jazz, Ronnie Scott, and Rollins says that the pianist, Stan Tracey – who had played with him earlier this year – helped a lot with the music. 'We had these themes,' says Tracey, 'and we just twisted them about according to what was required. Like once Sonny just said: "Play Alfie's theme, but distort it so it's still recognizable, with undertones of gloom".'

All this sounds like a group effort at improvised composition, with Rollins as master-mind. And it took a week's playing before they were satisfied with the final twenty minutes of sound which the film will use. It is an unusual, and exciting, way to create music for films and the result is something very special, both in jazz and in the cinema. I have heard the music, and it is very, very beautiful; not at all 'difficult', but straightforwardly lyrical, with a cheerful main theme you whistle after hearing once. 'His music never tries to outplay the film,' says John Gilbert, the associate producer of *Alfie*.

'It reflects Alfie's character, yes,' said Rollins. 'Whatever that may be.' He might have been joking, but his powerful face did not crease. 'Along the way I found everybody had different ideas about him. In the end I listened only to myself and the musicians. The music starts kind of jaunty. Then we show what happens to him. It gets sadder, plaintive, lonely. Look, I can't quote myself as saying it's good, but is *is* good. I know it. It's strong.'

Tracey says laconically: 'Out of chaos comes sense, and nobody knows why.' Rollins came to get involved with *Alfie* because on his first visit to London last January, the director and producer of the film, Lewis Gilbert, and John Gilbert, his son, (as well as Harold Pinter), went to Ronnie Scott's Club to hear him play. John Gilbert had been trying for years to persuade his father to use jazz in a film, and his fervent advocacy of Rollins, together with the music they heard at Scott's, decided Lewis Gilbert that here indeed was their man. They can have been in no doubt after hearing Rollins that he was, in Tracey's words, 'one of the different ones'. His performances were rather strange.

When announced on the opening night he did not spring to the bandstand, but stayed at the bar, sounding off exploratory flurries of notes. On the stand Tracey and the other accompanying musicians looked silently perplexed. Rollins then slowly walked, still playing, to the stand, mounted it, and blew an unbroken sheet of sound for twenty-five minutes. This was his opening number. He made what the Victorians might have called a brave sight – tall, broad shouldered, with shaven head, goatee, and a full nose that gives his long face a wickedly solemn appearance. He rarely stood still, prowling the stand and pointing his saxophone all ways – this, he says, because it sounds different as he bounces the sound off various parts of any room. His playing was dazzling: a kind of musical explosion churning up wit, sarcasm, virtuosity, beauty and zest. After about an hour he left the stand, still playing, and blew his way to the band room/office at the back of the club.

'We stopped being surprised after that first night,' recalls Tracey, 'but we never had any idea what would happen. We'd rehearsed three numbers with him earlier that day, and that was the last time we ever played them during the month he was here.'

Every night became a guessing game. Rollins once walked on to the stand, started playing 'Night and Day', and kept it going for the whole set – forty-five minutes. Next set he returned and did 'Night and Day' again – for forty-five minutes. Another night he finished his show, said goodbye to the audience and, apparently without premeditation, started on 'Goodnight Sweetheart'. He then ran through every 'Goodnight' tune known to Archer Street. Time: forty minutes. It reminded his listeners of the occasion in an American night club when he finished his act out in the street, playing under a lamp-post – 'just to see how it would sound' – with the audience watching him from the club entrance.

Between shows, Rollins never left the club. He would be in Scott's tiny office 'playing his saxophone or looking in the mirror doing his exercises', according to Tracey. 'Isometric exercises,' explains Scott. 'Twitching his face muscles. He said he was trying to straighten his nose. But I think that was a put-on.'

'I first came to London,' Rollins said when he was here for *Alfie*, 'against the advice of my agent. He was worried I couldn't bring my own group. But I'm glad I did. I get feelings here like in no American city.' 'He may be a New Yorker,' says John Gilbert, 'but *Alfie* is a film about the big city which lends itself to jazz. It doesn't really matter *which* city. To me the saxophone is a lonely instrument. This is a film about a lonely person.'

After a score of years in jazz – he was virtually a pro before leaving high school in New York, and had played with most of America's top modern musicians – Rollins remains optimistic about the state of jazz. He has had a very full musical life, including spells with Miles Davis, Art Blakey and Bud Powell, as well as leading his own groups, and his thinking reflects this.

'Jazz is just beginning really. It's making inroads into hitherto unwelcoming areas of musical performance. Well, isn't it just the greatest music there is? Active, vital, the Bach of today. It has invention, as all the greats had in their time. It's the music of today, tomorrow, the world. Do you know the person who writes a jazz score now is almost recognized as a human being?

'People are stopping generalizing about what jazz is and isn't. In the world today only a fool can live by generalities. You can't be that lazy. So jazz is being used in films, even in TV Westerns. I just don't know where jazz *can't* be used.

'I'm a band leader. I've had a lot of experience, worked with great men, and they've taught me and carried me along. This background has enabled me to make a good living. Very comfortable. There's nothing my wife and I need we don't get. I feel fortunate and I'm thankful. People are always saying this club's closed and that thing's happened. But jazz goes good all over the world. I don't see why anyone can't make a living if he advances and wants to play more and more and contribute something.'

Ronnie Scott recalled the other day that when he went to visit Rollins at the same hotel, the American had two saxophones propped up on the bed on pillows; as if they needed to be nursed, taken care of. 'I think,' said Scott, 'that was a bit calculated.'

Perhaps it was. But you get the feeling that if Rollins is joking for some of the time – and he betrays no overt sign of it – he's laughing at himself as much as at the world. And that makes a change.

Still King Goodman

30 SEPTEMBER 1971

The age of Swing may be long past, but the man who was called its King is wonderfully alive, proving still, as he has been doing at regular intervals since he gave up the grind of leading a band for fifty weeks a year, that today's musical climate allows all kinds of exotic flowers, ancient and modern, to flourish.

Benjamin David Goodman was sitting in a London hotel room savouring the prospect of his European tour. He looked pretty perky for rising sixty-two, a bit plumper than in his prime, a touch greyer, with heavy hornrims where once there used to be rimless or thinly gold-framed spectacles. It was probably the habit of snatched meals from the hard years of one-night stands and dance halls and theatres that made him eat a club sandwich for lunch. He was in braces (or, as they'd say in New York, suspenders) and the mayonnaise kept squirming from between the bread and meat and lettuce on to his face. Because he was talking about music, he never seemed to bother much about wiping it away.

'Sure, I like doing what I'm doing today,' he said. 'The musical scene's changed, of course, but it has its advantages. By the time I stopped leading my regular band in the forties, I needed a rest. Can you imagine playing maybe five or six shows a day for seventeen weeks at a theatre? Now it's concerts, working four or five months a year, and that's fine. Sometimes it's swing, sometimes I'm playing with classical orchestras. It suits me.

'One thing I miss – and that's people dancing to the music. Jazz was meant to be danced to, and I've always thought that what I was playing was jazz. Just look at the programme for Carnegie Hall in 1938. It was full of jazz. I don't suppose we played more than three or four pop songs that day. At the time I didn't really enjoy the concert, and that was because we weren't playing for people to dance. I suppose I regard it differently now.

I asked him how he felt about playing his kind of music in an environment filled with the sounds of rock and what, for want of a better word, people call avant-garde jazz. 'I *hear* all that music, of course. Some of it I like – Blood, Sweat and Tears, for instance – and some of it I regard as today's kind of commercialism, but I don't get affected by it. I'm glad there's so much variety around, but I don't *feel* that way of playing.'

Hadn't near contemporaries like Woody Herman and Buddy Rich felt it enough, though, to lead bands today which were a mélange of jazz and rock sounds? 'Yeah, I've heard them – but I still don't think it's for me. My music is tradition, musicianship. A Fletcher Henderson chart is a Fletcher Henderson chart, and it has as much validity today as when he wrote it – and it's only a certain kind of musician who *feels* it. That's what I look for in the British musicians I play with over here. And in the States it's players like Zoot Sims and George Duvivier who feel it, so that's who I choose to play with.

'Youth must be served, and that's good – young people have always wanted to make their own kind of music that's different from what went before – but there'd be no sense in my trying to play like Coltrane. My tours are nothing to do with public taste, they're to do with Benny Goodman. Importing a rock rhythm section into my band wouldn't fit – they make too much noise for a clarinet player, anyway, don't they?'

He paused, cleaned up the fringe of mayonnaise around his lips, as if there wasn't much left to say. 'Okay,' he added, 'maybe I would like to hear how an avant-garde kind of soloist would fit into the band, but I know what the people who come to see me want to hear. It still *lives*, my music, you know.'

And that, I suppose, is fair enough. What Goodman plays now is music which is rooted in a certain stage of jazz history – but it's not just a feast of nostalgia (though nostalgia's all right too). The music is alive and even modern because Goodman and the musicians with him *feel* it; for him it's a case of doing what comes naturally – and that's what counts.

The point is worth making because it's become fashionable to question whether Goodman and his great band (or rather, bands, since personnel changed often) back in the 1930s and 1940s were 'truly' jazzmen or whether he took the jazz which came most naturally from black musicians and transmuted it into a commercially successful formula.

Some people have even dragged Nikita Khruschev into the equation. When Goodman took the first American jazz band ever into the Soviet Union in 1962, playing to almost two hundred thousand people, Mr K went to a concert in Moscow and is reputed to have said all sorts of things – including: 'It's not jazz, only dance music.' Well, apart from the fact that jazz *is* often (though not always) dance music, Goodman says that Mr K said no such thing. 'All he said was "Ho-ho. It's boom-boom-boom music".' Goodman seemed to wish the Russian leader had said more. 'I think,' added BG, 'it was the first jazz concert he'd ever been to.'

There's no doubting the fact that Goodman *did* make jazz, which in the way he played it came to be called swing, into a commercially successful product. Equally true, there were great black bands playing at the time – Jimmy Lunceford, for instance – who didn't get the credit they deserved because the publicity tended to be grabbed by the Goodmans, Artie Shaws, Glenn Millers, Tommy Dorseys and other white leaders. But such truths don't alter the fact that Goodman was a jazzman – and that jazz (like pop today) has many faces. I'm glad it has – that Ellington is different from Brubeck, Cecil Taylor from Oscar Peterson and Goodman from Basie. Only bores spend their time arguing what is *true* jazz and what isn't. The wise sit back and enjoy the fifty-seven varieties. *Vive la différence.*

Different in the 1930s Goodman certainly was. And it's because he was an innovator, both as a solo musician and in the kind of musical organizations he created, that he has established so commanding a place in the history of jazz.

His own clarinet style, which started out as rather imitative of Ben Pollack and Frank Teschemacher, became from around 1935 so personally definitive – full of clean lines and swing and soft cutting tone – that he influenced hundreds of jazz clarinettists thereafter. Almost alone he began a musical policy which transformed pop songs and standard riff tunes into a new style of hard-polished, brilliantly orchestrated, rhythmically exciting jazz called swing. The music dominated the late 1930s and early 1940s and created a social phenomenon of mass musical hysteria which drew crowd reaction for big bands later reserved for figures like Frank Sinatra and, later still, for The Beatles.

Goodman also did his bit for the brotherhood of man. When, in 1936, he took a black pianist (Teddy Wilson) on the road with him, he crashed through American racial barriers for the first time on a large scale. Many other black musicians – Lionel Hampton, Charlie Christian and Cootie Williams among them – came into the Goodman band after that historic shattering of the great American taboo.

Wilson and Hampton were also crucial figures in the Goodman combos which formed so superb a musical contrast to the roaring cascade of his big band. The various records made by the trio, quartet, quintet and sextet over a period of half-a-dozen years or so remain marvellous classics of the jazz small-group art.

Already we've mentioned quite a few stellar musicians. And nothing indicates more clearly how dominating, important and fascinating a figure Goodman has been in jazz history than to recall the men and women who have played with him – especially when one remembers that the story of the Goodman band is chiefly concentrated into a mere nine-year period, between 1935 and 1944.

On trumpet, Goodman used Harry James, Bunny Berigan, Ziggy Elman, Buck Clayton, Cootie Williams and Roy Eldridge at various times. Trombonists included Kai Winding, Joe Harris, Cutty Cutshall and Trummy Young. Among the saxists were Bud Freeman, Vido Musso, Wardell Gray, Stan Getz and Zoot Sims. Pianists ranged through Claude Thornhill, Fletcher Henderson, Mel Powell and Jess Stacy. Charlie Christian, of course, played guitar for him; behind the drums were Dave Tough, Gene Krupa, Sid Catlett and Louis Bellson; plucking the bass were Harry Goodman and Slam Stewart; and the vibes players are an especially strong list – Hampton, Red Norvo, Terry Gibbs and Teddy Charles. So are the singers: Martha Tilton, Peggy Lee, Patti Page and Dick Haymes.

This is no time either to try your patience with another list of names as long as that (which could easily be produced) or with too detailed a history of the life and times of Mr Goodman, but a certain minimum of basic information is essential. He was born in Chicago, Illinois, on May 30, 1909, and he's as archetypal of the American Dream – rags to riches, log cabin to White House – as you could imagine.

Eighth of the eleven children of an immigrant tailor, he got his first instrument at the age of nine from the local synagogue. The legend has it that he might have been a tuba player had he been a bit taller. But his older Brother, Harry – because he was bigger than Benny – was handed out the tuba. Another Goodman, Freddie, was given a trumpet. Benny got the clarinet.

He played his first significant stage date at the age of twelve, and the band leader who heard him then, Ben Pollack, later sent for him to join the band. His first recorded solo was in 1926, with Pollack, and in 1928 he made his only recorded solos on alto and baritone saxophone. Then he became a successful freelance in New York until he formed his first band in 1934. Almost from the start he was using the arrangements of Fletcher Henderson, and he got a regular radio series called 'Let's Dance'. The bandwagon was rolling – but it didn't go without hitches.

I refer to that marvellously informative book by George T. Simon, called *The Big Bands* (Collier-Macmillan Ltd), for an example of the hang-ups. Mr Simon is describing the Goodman band's first New York hotel engagement, which agent Willard Alexander had fixed for it, in May 1935:

> I faintly recall now that there weren't many people in the place the night I reviewed the band, so it's possible that the band might have satisfied all the varied ages who were there – all twelve customers. But so far as the manager of the hotel was concerned, the 'new-fangled swing band' was monstrous. 'Opening night.' Alexander recalls, 'they got their two weeks' notice.'

Later that year, at Denver, Colorado, people started asking for their money back on the opening night and the manager screamed at the band until it played waltzes. But, with enthusiastic support from John Hammond, the most influential jazz pusher around, who'd encouraged Goodman to go out as a bandleader in the first place, the breakthrough finally came at the Palomar Ballroom in Hollywood. The kids crowded the bandstand, screaming for more. Goodman went on to Chicago to play a three-week gig at the Congress Hotel. He stayed eight months. Swing was here (or perhaps there) to stay.

There are so many highlights after that, it's not possible to put them all in here. The historic Carnegie Hall concert in 1938 was one of them. The pairing of Harry James and Ziggy Elman in the trumpet section was another, swopping lead position and solo space. The combos were born, starting in 1935 with the trio (Goodman, Wilson and Krupa) and then steadily expanding as Hampton, Christian and Arthur Bernstein on bass joined in. Sidemen came and went – including Cootie Williams who, when he joined the band from Ellington's, inspired Raymond Scott to write a composition, 'When Cootie Left The Duke' – but nothing could shake the supremacy of Goodman in the swing field. He was top and stayed at the top until 1944 when he disbanded and took a long rest. In 1945 he picked a new band, with Kai Winding and Stan Getz, trying with no great success to be more modern, but by 1946 the great Goodman band was virtually at an end as a regular all-year-round outfit, like so many of the other big bands. An era was ending.

'I'm sick and tired of rehearsing,' Goodman could say late in 1946. 'I've had enough of that stuff. I guess I've just passed the stage where I want to knock myself out. For what? To get everything just the way I want it, I'd have to rehearse all the time, and even then I'm not sure I'd get it.'

That was twenty-five years ago, of course, and Goodman has kept on playing in a mass of different contexts, but never as a full-time bandleader. Sometimes he's had big bands who've played his old arrangements – well on occasions, with lack-lustre on others; sometimes it's been with small groups, usually very good; sometimes it's been with bop-style musicians, to whom he's not often related with any success. And he has, too, found a lot of satisfaction from a parallel classical career since 1938, playing most of the big classical works with all the great orchestras and doing unusual things like commissioning Bela Bartok, Paul Hindemith and Aaron Copland to compose major works for him to play.

He's travelled a lot, too, playing concerts in Europe and the Far East as well as Russia. At the royal palace in Bangkok he took part in a jam session with the jazz-bug monarch of Thailand, Phumipol Aduljej, in 1957. They made a movie, *The Benny Goodman Story*, about him in 1955, with Steve Allen playing the title role; and the only good thing about it was the sound of Goodman's clarinet. He made appearances himself in several other movies including *Stage Door Canteen* and *A Song is Born*.

A whole mountain of legend has grown up around him. He's always had the reputation of watching every dollar, and maybe that's natural when you're a self-made man. Perhaps, too, that's the way to stay whole and live long in show business. He's a stickler for perfection, and musicians who fell below his high standard were apt to get 'the Goodman ray', described by George Simon as 'a fish stare'. He's supposed to be absent-minded and the story goes that once he hailed a cab, opened the door, got in, sat back and asked the driver, 'How much do I owe you?' It's been a good life for him, it seems; a life of great achievement. He made it young and has stayed at the top or thereabouts ever since.

'Swing can thank Benny Goodman, and Benny Goodman can thank Swing,' George Simon once wrote. 'Swing can thank Benny Goodman for making possible its acceptance in a world which, before the advent of the King's reign, thought that the best swing hung between two trees in a back-yard and that a beat was reserved exclusively for cops and reporters.'

That was in 1946. And it's not a bad quote on which to rest one's case in 1971.

MJQ: the jeweller's touch

APRIL 1972

It is 1972. And the Modern Jazz Quartet is twenty years old. That is incredible enough in itself; ever since I came of age I seem to have been reading reports that they were about to dissolve. It is also unique.

There can surely be no other jazz band in history that has lived so long with only one change of membership, and that as long ago as 1955 when Kenny Clarke vacated the drum chair for Connie Kay. Even Duke Ellington and Count Basie and the other long runners have had to shuffle the pack as the years have gone by.

This makes the MJQ very special indeed. As an exercise in sheer human relationships it is special. For John Lewis, Milt Jackson, Percy Heath and Connie Kay to have *got on* so well during two turbulent decades is quite something, is it not? To have got on so well *musically* is equally remarkable.

As an act of creativity it is special, too. There are – must be – some limitations to the instrumentation of piano, vibraharp, bass and drums. The MJQ seem constantly to have been able to transcend them. Public acceptance of what they do, an acceptance which became heavily marked with understanding, appreciation and warmth, has also been one of the constants in a changing and often disintegrating jazz world during their history. So well understood are they that people have been doing impressions of them (in the sense that Peter Kavanagh, 'the voice of them all' and all that, used to do impressions) for years. I saw one earlier this year during a Benny Goodman concert, from his vibes player, Peter Appleyard. Audience recognition of Milt Jackson's careful style and mannerisms was instantaneous; and the laughter was full-blooded, but kind.

So – the MJQ are remarkable. To describe *how* they are remarkable is a more difficult task, not because their style defies description, but because we have grown so accustomed to their gifts and to writing about them that the words grow familiar. The MJQ are intricate but swinging; formal yet informal; sober yet witty; both tranquil and exciting; orderly yet relaxed. You know what I mean?

My favourite phrase about the MJQ comes from Whitney Balliett who is, I think, my favourite jazz writer anyway. They go at their instruments, he once said 'like jewellers intent upon their work'. Good, very good. Look at the way Milt Jackson attends to the tone and precision of *his* instrument; the shading is so delicate that the name of vibraharp (rather than the harsher sounding vibraphone) seems just right.

But if the phrase neatly sums up the care and precision of their music, it also embraces the intense concentration with which they listen to each other. That, too, is part of their quality, which enables them to play 'head' arrangements, or very lengthy improvisations, with the same air of perfection as surrounds their more closely-scored pieces.

Recently, listening to *Plastic Dreams*, their new LP for Atlantic, I was amazed again at the surprising quality of their improvisations and the freshness which they still manage to convey in many of their musical approaches after all those years of working together. One piece particularly, called 'Walkin' Stomp', is a minor miracle of togetherness – complex in texture and melody, swinging fantastically yet with no roars of drums (just the ching-ching of Kay's mini-cymbal), and with magical 'bent-note' (i.e slightly slurred) riffs from Heath's bass. It is to me a very summit of the MJQ's achievement in uncannily integrated improvisation.

There is another aspect to that record which should be mentioned. On two of the seven tracks, extra musicians are added: trumpets, trombone, French horn and tuba. That has been one of the ways in which the MJQ has tried to keep its freshness down the years – working out new ways of doing things. Survival in jazz, as in business or life, has to be one prime objective of any sensible human being.

The history of the MJQ is really a study in how to live with perfection. Mr Balliett put it this way: 'Unfortunately, philosophers and theologians, while urging the pursuit of perfection, do not tell us where to turn once that state is reached.' The MJQ achieved both recognition and a personal style so swiftly that creatively this problem of where to move next must have been a very real one for them. What have they done about it?

First, they have steadfastly continued to explore and re-explore the ground they've already dug over lightly. And often they've come up with gold, since they are such uncanny musicians. By way of illustration, listen to the difference between the several versions of 'Django' they have recorded, an exercise which is even more exciting if you have a good enough head to carry memories of their live performances around with you.

Second, they have from time to time – as on *Plastic Dreams* – added musicians on sessions to vary the pattern. These experiences have met with differing degrees of success. They swallowed Jimmy Giuffre and his clarinet whole; they were hard put to it to digest the angular tenor saxophone lines of Sonny Rollins; they were comfortable with the guitar of Laurindo Almeida, though a deal of what they played was not accepted by some people as jazz (whatever that is – in a few words, I mean: never mind, it was very good music). I'm not sure either that the brass on *Plastic Dreams* comes off in the way they wanted.

Third, the MJQ has branched away from jazz into other fields of music. John Lewis, who is the guiding light of the group – not because he is its leader, since it has none, but because he does most of the writing for it – has shown great enthusiasm during his career for what has come to be called 'Third Stream' music, which is a blending of jazz with European classical forms. He has made it very clear *why* he is.

He is, for one thing, a man who looks ahead; who sees that anything which stands still too long (apply this dictum to big business or to music or to any other human activity) ultimately grows moribund. He also has a fruitful imagination. And in an age when big jazz bands have found it hard to survive, he has looked at 'big bands' which *are* permanent, often because they're subsidized – I mean the symphony orchestras scattered around the United States and the rest of the world – and has wondered whether they couldn't be put to some jazz service.

'Third Stream music,' he said a long time ago, 'is the initial experiment in drawing the orchestras into the field of jazz. You see, I think of the

Quartet as a unit – almost as a solo voice – that needs the large foil of a big band for some of its music in the same way that a Parker or a Gillespie might. By working with these orchestras, perhaps we can pave the way for other musicians as well.

'This is my only reason for exploring Third Stream. Musically, I'm more than happy with the limits set by the Quartet. We haven't even approached those limits yet – if they exist. I still have a lot of things I want to do, but they all take time.'

So we have had the MJQ against a setting of string quartets, of orchestras, of Diahann Carrol's singing – but somehow they have never seemed so enjoyable, or so *right*, as when they have played themselves, pure and simple. Indeed in recent years, I detect that increasingly John Lewis has been content to allow the music of the MJQ to flow out freely without a great deal of assistance from him as arranger and/or composer. Their jazz has been more straightforward, with plenty of solo space.

Even so, one feels that John Lewis is the motive force behind the quartet. Billy Strayhorn's remark that Duke Ellington plays piano, but that his real instrument is the orchestra, works very well for Lewis. He is a pianist, too, but his real instrument is the Quartet. To put it another way: as the orchestra is an extension of Ellington, so the MJQ is an extension of John Lewis. In the last twenty years Lewis has got to know his partners inside out. You feel that he too anticipates the sound in his head, and has developed his great gifts as a composer through the three men who play with him.

The point is simply made by saying that if ever a member of the MJQ is ill and unable to appear, the concert is cancelled. These men know that the whole idea of what they are as a group just doesn't work if you subtract one element.

The quest for and achievement of perfection, as well as the imperturbable way the MJQ have gone on, unheeding of those who would tell them what to do, has reacted in one important way on their reputation. Success breeds its own reaction in the world that surveys it. The only kind of cows that are worth knocking are the sacred ones – and I suppose it is only human for people to get restive with perfection, impatient with it, wondering if it isn't all illusion. So the MJQ have had their share of that, too – the writers and the bar leaners and the bone pickers who have made almost a profession of trying to put them down.

I've referred already to that hardy annual of a story (though it's perhaps been less in evidence in recent years) which says that Milt Jackson is about to leave the group. This draws its substance from the obvious musical contrast between him and John Lewis – Jackson ebullient, passionate, full of blues feeling and jazz 'soul', and Lewis more restrained, more delicate, his jazz feeling tempered more obviously with a love of European classical forms. The contrast, though, is often painted in far more melodramatic terms, with Lewis cast in the role of cold, calculating villain holding back the overflowing talents of Milt the wild, romantic boy, a sort of latter-day Byron.

Well, Jackson may leave the MJQ one day. Nothing in this world goes on for ever. But after two decades, there is still no sign of his going. It's also as well to deal straightaway with that other hoary old drama which concerns Milt Jackson's numerous recordings away from the context of the MJQ. Excellent most of them are, too – vibes with sacks of 'soul', leaning always towards the blues. This side of Jackson is again depicted by some writers as Milt hurrying thankfully away from the Quartet's cloistered calm to play what he really wants to play.

The other way of looking at this, of course, is that here is another reason for the MJQ's survival – that the group exists without constraints on the freedom of any of its members to do something different from time to time.

The pattern of Jackson's musical life suggests that he enjoys being the wild boy on occasion – all blues and fire and blood – but that he also finds something deeply satisfying in what the MJQ creates. It may often be quieter and subtler, and certainly more a group effort, than are his out-of-school recordings, but this is one of Jackson's other faces. Isn't a jazzman allowed to have more than one? For that matter, isn't jazz allowed to stretch and flex its muscles, to extend its variety?

At the end of all argument, one can only say that though the MJQ have created a very special kind of music, which often offers attractions not usually associated with jazz, their work is still firmly jazz-rooted. Not that I would pay overmuch attention to the literal meaning of those words. The 1950s and early 1960s, when critics shook their lances at each other in ferocious arguments about what was and was not jazz, seem very distant now. Today's musical climate, in which people concentrate more on music than on labels, seems just right for the MJQ. Thank God for that.

Chapter Seven

Jazz: brief encounters

Jazz is many things; but it is usually night music, best heard after dark in intimate venues rather than in concert halls. In London, one club has dominated the scene – Ronnie Scott's – and for that reason many of these newspaper reviews resulted from performances heard there. Inevitably, they are usually thumb-nail sketches, but if they convey the rare flavour of some outstanding musicians and the abundant pleasure which they have given to me and their audiences, then length will seem irrelevant. All kinds of jazzmen are included – a gamut which runs from the old school of Hines and Hampton to innovators like Mike Gibbs, Mike Westbrook and Weather Report (who you could include under jazz or rock or neither – which is the way popular music has gone in recent years). The selection, however, can only represent a few soldiers from a mighty artistic army. For a music which is supposed to have expired several times since the 1950s, jazz has been remarkably alive in the 1960s and 1970s. It would be unrealistic, though, not to wonder what will happen to it in the next twenty years as more and more of its venerable performers cease to play. Its offshoots, its 'fusions', its contemporary styles will continue to evolve, of course; but its older styles have depended so much on the survival of individual musicians and on social contexts which have disappeared or are disappearing that the future is uncertain. Jazz *can* be scored; copyists *can* emerge. Whether the feeling, or the illusion of improvisation, or the personal touch upon which jazz has depended can be re-created is another question. I'm very glad to have been around in time to catch so many of those who started out in jazz decades ago, as well as to savour the sounds of those who succeeded them.

Kenton: pure if rarely simple

24 NOVEMBER 1963

Stan Kenton, in his third decade as a major band leader and now pursuing a thirty-concert tour of Britain, must be inured to the love-hate dichotomy he has always excited in the jazz set. The curse of the anti-'White Jazz' fundamentalists seems to have crunched almost exclusively upon his head, a tendency understandably encouraged by Kenton's weakness for verbal hyperbole; he calls his present tour 'The New Era in Modern American Music'.

Yet Kenton is as close in jazz stature, but not style, to Ellington – an early influence on him and the first notable big bandsman to reconcile technique and orchestral subtlety with basic jazz feeling – as he is distant from the jazz-emasculating school of Paul Whiteman. His opening Hammersmith concert last weekend, indeed, carried powerful overtones of Woody Herman: a Herman less earthy, but with richer instrumental colour and sophistication.

Jazz, fortunately, has many faces, and it is as nonsensical to suggest that Kenton's music is not one of them as to demand that every big band should reproduce the bounding blues-orientation of, say, Basie. He has elevated and inspired jazz technique and orchestration. He has provided a nursery for an army of players and composers – Mulligan, Getz, Russo and Rugolo among them. And although he has consistently experimented with neo-jazz concert music, he has always returned to the big jazz band pure, if rarely simple, for his most engaging work.

The present Kenton orchestra may not match his towering Konitz-Rosolino-Levey group of 1952–3, but it is outstandingly in the jazz mainstream. The element of sheer cerebral bravado is rarely stifling; the dynamic idiosyncratic brass figures, now texturally enhanced by the use of four mellophoniums (approximating to French horns), are still a stunning hallmark: the reeds continue to plot their moody, melancholic progressions; and there is ample improvisational space for soloists, notably 'Jig' Whigham (trombone) and Steve Marcus (tenor).

Yet there are flaws. The programme included much of his early work ('Peanut Vendor', 'Opus in Pastels', and others), and these well-worn battle hymns suggested that Kenton had not significantly advanced his jazz position since the forties, but only embellished it. There are striking similarities between his 'Artistry'-era themes and later orchestrations like 'Malaguena' and 'Maria', both in the tour repertoire and featured respectively on his two best LPs of recent years, *Adventures in Jazz* and *West Side Story* (Capitol).

There is, too, the ancient law (recalled lately by Desmond Shawe-Taylor apropos Benjamin Britten) that musical satisfaction chiefly springs from the balance between expectation and surprise. Kenton's constructions fulfil expectation, but surprise too seldom. His music has at times a terrible, and zest-killing, inevitability.

Hot, cool and Sonny

3 MAY 1964

Even in the often explosive terms of jazz performances, the alchemy unleashed by the American saxophonist Sonny Stitt in London late on Friday was remarkable.

He took the stand at Ronnie Scott's Club, where he is to play a month's season, in an atmosphere hushed as a temple. Within a minute his lifting, driving tenor was drawing from his audience clapping, stamping, whoops and beams as wide as the Thames. None of the great Americans visiting the Club has had an opening so relaxed, happy and auspicious.

Strangely he shares birthdays with the last, perhaps supreme, American visitor to Scott's, Stan Getz; but no comparison could confound astrology more. Getz creates the most intense moods, and is moody, appearing withdrawn and untouched by his listeners. Stitt is sunnily extrovert, responding to applause, with frenetic flurries of notes, delighted that he delights. Between solos he twists, talks to tables, jokes, shares a drink, and encourages his excellent accompanists, the Stan Tracey Trio.

He plays alto as well as tenor – and stylistically he can sound like two different men. That Charlie Parker, near death, told Stitt, 'Here are the keys,' is part of jazz legend. And alto Stitt, with his exciting cadence and searing sound, would be inconceivable without Parker. His finest alto piece was almost a lament for 'Bird' – a slow, intensely moving 'Lover Man', the tune which evoked from a sick Parker one of the tragic recording performances of jazz; fragmented, imperfect, yet of desperate beauty.

On tenor, Stitt has evolved a far more individual style which fuses Parker's wildness, Lester Young's cool lyricism and a strong dash of unsophisticated stomping. He played a lot of tenor blues on Friday, usually fast, with commanding invention, stamina and sense of dramatic climax.

Stitt sounds so fresh, it seems incredible that this elegant Bostonian, son of a college music professor, brother of a concert pianist, is forty – or that he won *Esquire*'s New Star award as far back as 1947. He may lack Getz's depth of feeling, but he swings with a breezy brilliance that should conquer London.

The Loneliest Plunk

14 MARCH 1965

He is something very special. His chameleon moods, his wanderings on stage, his mystic epigrams ('It's always night or we wouldn't need light') have made people suspect he is a special kind of joker.

But there is much more than that to Thelonious Monk, who last night opened a short tour at the Royal Festival Hall. Strip away the trimmings – like the black fur hat he wore at the piano last night – and you discover he is probably more the father of modern jazz than Charlie Parker or Dizzy Gillespie.

He has kept his strange dignity while the world has come round to accepting him for what he is; simply a musician playing what *he* wants to, unaffected by fashion. 'All you're supposed to do,' he says, 'is lay down the sounds and let the people pick up on them.'

His wife is said sometimes to mutter 'Melodious Thunk' at him. An LP of the fifties, which guyed his style, came up with 'The Loneliest Plunk'. Both jokes are apt, but the second is keener. He has gone his own way, almost making a philosophy out of being different.

Now, after the exciting forties, when he was the keystone of the bebop revolution, and the painful fifties, when he was largely ignored, Monk at forty-five thrives on acceptance. His angular, tangential piano playing, as last night's audience heard, is perhaps at its summit.

It was, usually, starkly simple, often beautiful – bizarre harmonic ideas in their nudest form, more like melodic epigrams than complete poems. But some of his compositions were so subtle that one felt only Monk could state the themes right, let alone improvise on them. The rhythms changed, beats were missed, odd chords collided, naivety was spiced with the sardonic.

Charlie Rouse (tenor sax), Ben Riley (drums) and Larry Gales (bass) glowed under his leadership. And following Monk isn't easy. He is, perhaps, inimitable. Still the loneliest even now that he has a crowd.

Postscript

21 MARCH 1965

The music of Thelonious Monk, even when the public spurned it, has consistently been all of a piece. Eminently and patiently logical; always surprising in its harmonies and rhythms; acidly beautiful. A week after his triumphant concerts at the Royal Festival Hall, one recalls above all that now it also radiates ease. The world has stopped kicking Monk and he seems not even marginally interested in kicking back.

This maturity, this lack of strain – though rarely of musical *tension*, which is the stamp of his work, as of most great jazz – has much to do with the men surrounding him. Charlie Rouse, the tenor saxist, has been half a dozen years with Monk and they have evolved the most fruitful partnership. Rouse, vibrato-less and flowing, is the straight man. He pours out pure sheets of sound often keeping (as in the classic 'Round Midnight') close to the melody. Monk, at piano, plays counterpoint – chopping up rhythms, shuffling notes, digging subtly into every harmonic possibility a tune offers. The tension is electric.

Monk sharpens the senses. He makes the most familiar work sound strangely new. In his hands 'Sweet and Lovely' came out unlush. Still handsome, but harsh; a touch of east wind in summer.

Apart from Rouse, there was Ben Riley, a drummer cool and musical, brushing melodies from his cymbals. Monk seemed utterly relaxed with these companions, playing for over an hour, returning for a solo encore, where in 1961 he stayed twenty minutes and abruptly vanished, leaving his audience teetering on the jagged edge of some painful harmonic precipice.

Herd again and again

22 JANUARY 1967

Only three men have a continuing history of large jazz orchestra leadership stretching from the 1930s to the present day: Duke Ellington, Count Basie and Woody Herman. This is not surprising. The raw edginess of the touring life, the icy facts of unsubsidized economics, the problems of temperament, the three-in-the-morning coach drives along endless highways – all coalesce into a murderous environment.

A man needs an obsession, or a friendly Arts Council, to run any orchestra, jazz or otherwise. Ellington, who comes to Britain next month, is inscrutably simple about it: 'The band is my life. It's holiday all the time.'

Herman, for whom Stravinsky wrote his Ebony Concerto ('The challenge for him was this bastard instrumentation of ours'), seems more aware of the gold reserves problem, but is just as obsessive. 'I lost 175,000 dollars I didn't have on that band,' he says of his so-called Second Herd, a classic jazz orchestra which broke up seventeen years ago. Yet he is now back in Britain, still the Herd leader. His renaissance since 1962, and his command of a young as well as middle-aged audience in America, are alike remarkable. So is his ability to keep on turning up splendid new musicians, to convert them instantly to the idiosyncratic style of his bands.

Herman's present Herd contains only three men – Sal Nistico and Bob Pierson among the saxophones, and Bill Byrne on trumpet – who came here last year. Yet the band plays with the same eager, surging and integrated power which has brand-marked every Herd. No other orchestra quite achieves the full-throated sound of a Herman ensemble – five-strong trumpet section blazing over the dark tones of saxophones and trombones; nor is propelled so dynamically by its drummer. Herman, of course, has discovered another power-house of a percussionist, by name Jim Gall.

The Herd made a kind of history when, as a prelude to the tour which started in Manchester last night, it became on Friday the first big band to perform at Ronnie Scott's Club. It plays Herman's always dazzling, sometimes reflective, orchestrations quite as well as the other Herds did, and in solo strength is the best of his latter-day bands.

Nistico still fizzes away like a demented jumping cracker. The trumpeter Richard Ruedebusch is a majestic find; a chameleon in his unusual range of styles and a great contrast to the stratospheric Lloyd Michael and the calmly lyrical John Crews. There's even an expatriate Englishman, Joe Temperley, in the saxophone section, and a pianist, Ken Ascher, with so sharp a feeling for big band blues that the departed Nat Pierce is scarcely missed. It's a cathartic experience.

Backwards and forwards

18 JUNE 1967

Nostalgia was as thick in the air as greying hairs and balding heads in the intimacy of London's new Purcell Room last Thursday. Teddy Wilson, whose dainty filigree work gave such bubbly sparkle to the Benny Goodman small groups of the thirties, was back in town, playing with as neat a British replica of the old mob as you ever did hear.

The thirties aura was overpowering. The musicians, in tuxedos, played behind a row of potted plants (not quite palms, but . . .) and there was a decorous hush about the place, with brushes unfailingly used in place of drumsticks. It was like BG making it again into Carnegie Hall.

It was as difficult not to enjoy what one heard, or not to be involved with the tight-packed audience's pleasure, as it was easy to remain fundamentally unmoved by what one heard – in the sense that a Miles Davis solo of the fifties or almost anything Ellingtonian can move one. Wilson is a masterful artist within his field: nimble, very lightly swinging, tuneful and a dazzling embroiderer of melodies. All this falls short of the summit of jazz experience, but it makes for very pretty pastures in the lowlands.

'Flying Home', 'Sweet Lorraine', 'After You've Gone' and the rest of the Goodman repertoire tumbled from Wilson's flying fingers, while the Dave Shepherd Quintet supported him nobly. Shepherd is a fine clarinet player in the BG manner, but the show was almost stolen by Ronnie Gleaves. He hammers at his vibes with all the panache that Lionel Hampton used to show.

Charles Lloyd, whose quartet gave its first British concert at the Queen Elizabeth Hall last night, is something else. He is looking forward, not back. If he resists an excess of gimmickry, he will be one of the great tenor players of the sixties, for he can already move one deeply as, sometimes, his teasing of tunes to a lingering death can move one smartly in the opposite direction.

His quartet is integrated to a remarkable degree, with especial empathy between Lloyd and the pianist, Keith Jarrett. On records, Lloyd reveals a rare range of tenor tone – softly beguiling as a Desmond or Getz at times, oblique as the latter-day Coltrane at others. Jarrett is so explosive (white-hot cascades of notes) that even the great non-phrase of the year, 'psychedelic jazz', gains meaning. It *is* just like being bombarded with all those lights.

Interestingly, Lloyd seems to have got through to the Jefferson Airplane set of California. He is clever, using avant-garde cadences quite naturally for occasional variety, not main statement. I am not surprised that he recently received a nine-minute ovation in Russia. Nor that he tells one, 'I'm running round laying all this love on people at a tremendous deficit.' Nor that he will be attacked as well as praised. His LP *Forest Flower* (Atlantic 1472) is, for adventurers, the best jazz buy of the month.

Death of a Liberator

23 JULY 1967

John Coltrane bestrode the last ten years in the history of tenor saxophone like a Titan. His death last week at forty makes the past twelve months, which has had so many deaths, from Henry Reed Allen to Billy Strayhorn, very melancholy for jazz.

Coltrane was like many African politicians. It was not possible to enjoy all that he did; but it was obvious that he was a liberator and a towering influence. In jazz development there are perhaps four key names on tenor: Coleman Hawkins, Lester Young, Sonny Rollins, and Coltrane. Each one burst bonds – and Coltrane was the man who showed young musicians some fascinating if often daunting further directions at a time when jazz seemed to have halted in the perfection of Charlie Parker's harmonic revolution.

'I'm trying,' he said last year, 'to work out a kind of writing that will allow for more plasticity, more viability, more room for improvisation in the statement of the melody itself before we go into solos. And I'd like that established point of departure to be freer rhythmically.'

Such words are like an archetypical statement from the jazz avant-garde, for whom Coltrane had by then become a god. He seemed only interested in finding new freedoms within his art, and it is an indication of the power and integrity of his music that he carried with him an enormous following however far he pushed the boundaries.

Coltrane dominated tenor saxophone polls during the 1960s. In 1965 he was placed, along with Hawkins and Young, in *Down Beat* magazine's Hall of Fame while his *A Love Supreme* LP was named Record of the Year. This was surprising for a record whose textures were so intense and whose sleeve note began 'Dear Listener, All praise be to God to Whom all praise is due'.

A Love Supreme remains, after many hearings, a most beautiful performance. Coltrane was not always a 'beautiful' player; but there was always a power and conviction to his work which put the listener in awe of him and emphasized his stature.

His periods with Miles Davis in the late 1950s are for many his crowning glory. But the impetus of the 1960s, when he discovered the soprano saxophone, and began enriching jazz with Eastern and African forms, may ultimately influence musicians as much as his rich, forceful tone has already done. For jazz, his loss is a grievous injury.

Lyttelton's twentieth

18 FEBRUARY 1968

They could scarcely be more dissimilar; one well-rounded, Kansas City out of Eton, looking wryly at life through quizzical eyes; the other younger, thinner, equally committed to his own kind of music, intense as a hunter who has just found the Scrolls.

But they are both, Humphrey Lyttelton and Mike Westbrook, in the British tradition of jazz, teachers and prophets.

They celebrated Humph's twenty years as a bandleader on BBC's *Jazz Club* last Wednesday. It was an uneven show, musically and otherwise, but Lyttelton's bold, assured trumpet thrust like a lance through the mists of feeble jokes and hollow laughter and even dispelled the memory of the unstarriest 'Stardust' in history, played, if I heard right, by the Red Onions Jazz Band of Australia, which I hope enjoys them.

We take Humph too much for granted. He is, in truth, a superb trumpeter, as firm of line and glowing in tone as Buck Clayton, whom he so admires. He has been a restless musician, refusing to stick in the trad groove where he began, experimenting all through the fifties (with West Indian flavoured bands among others), and ending up today with his best group – six or seven strong, playing mainstream music sometimes reminiscent of an Ellington small band, sometimes of Basie.

That band was easily the best thing about Wednesday night, with Tony Coe (tenor saxophone) and Chris Pyne (trombone) enjoying enormously the freedom the format gives them. British jazz is fortunate to have had so talented, dedicated and intelligent a man for its post-war father figure.

It's also typical of Humph's liberal bridge building that playing with him should have been John Surman, who must now be regarded as a baritone saxophonist on a level with Gerry Mulligan and Harry Carney. Surman is the bridge to Mike Westbrook, of whose bands he has been the cornerstone.

The rare appearances at The Old Place, Gerrard Street, of Westbrook's Concert Band, ten to fifteen strong, are real occasions. I heard his new work, *Releases*, which is played in two continuous sessions of an hour. It is an experience of immense excitement and beauty, bafflement and resolution.

What Westbrook does in *Releases* is to provide a firmly orchestrated map that consists of old swing tunes ('Flying Home' or 'Sugar') or folk songs or often pop, much of it written by himself in familiar styles. 'That way,' he says, 'people feel related to us.'

Between such signposts, lush and rich for reeds or breakneck and blistering for brass, Westbrook's soloists take over. The music is sometimes fiercely avant-garde (especially the altoist, Bernard Living) or very funny (Paul Rutherford, trombone) or brilliantly forthright and personal (Surman and Malcolm Griffiths, trombone). But always the players are striking sparks of new inspiration from each other; and there is a continuity and strength to the whole which is miraculous.

No one in his senses will miss Westbrook's *Marching Song* at the Euston Town Hall on 11 March. However that night turns out, Westbrook's men are creating the most positive and engaging jazz in Britain today.

Westbrook marching on

17 MARCH 1968

The work of Mike Westbrook epitomizes what twentieth-century popular music is about. It is recognizably jazz, but its content reflects, like a sun-soaked mirror, so much more. Its moods encompass military march and pop song, Ellington and hymn tunes, folk song and Debussy, requiem and, inevitably, the agonized turbulence through which modern musicians of all kinds have sought to break through the web of conventional harmonics.

Marching Song, the two-hour suite which his fifteen-piece Concert Band premièred during the Camden Festival last week, is not an unflawed work. Nor was it played in unflawed fashion. But overall it is the most moving, engaging and deeply satisfying extended jazz composition (and improvisation) ever to come out of this country. Stylistically it is not Ellingtonian; but this is the league in which Westbrook and his men are now playing. 'His men' are essential to the equation, for Westbrook without, say, John Surman, his soprano baritone saxophonist and co-composer, would be as unthinkable as Ellington without Johnny Hodges.

Not all of Westbrook is immediately palatable. He allows, for instance, the free form in-jokery of Paul Rutherford's trombone passages to be overdone, despite their technical bravura. But other areas of discord, which out of context would be repelling, are easily acceptable within the Westbrook framework. Of all the new musicians, he is the strongest on form; and thus he is able successfully to take outrageous chances with content. By working within a convention, he triumphantly brings off the unconventional.

Against the odds, *Marching Song* grows better and better over its long span. Surman, playing soprano saxophone in 'Other World' before the interval, created music of a beauty which jazz rarely hears – then exceeded when he was joined by Mike Osborne (alto) for the elegiac 'Tarnished' towards the end. Dave Holdsworth, whose flugelhorn powerfully recalled the Miles Davis-Gil Evans collaborations, and Malcolm Griffiths, a trombonist of dazzling wit and invention, were other outstanding soloists – but it was the all-round *orchestral* performance, majestically propelled by the two-bass, two-drummer engine room, which made the evening memorable.

Even Buddy Rich's declamatory and beautifully arranged version of the *West Side Story* suite seems tame after Westbrook. But his band, now touring with Tony Bennett, is efficient enough. It is, I suspect, as good as last year's swinging outfit – excellent in ensemble passages, if short on solo strength – but the effect is blurred because this time it plays only one half of the show on its own. Thus Rich's frequent demonstrations of his world-beating skills on drums loom larger, and the orchestra's performance diminishes in proportion. But, to judge from the tumultous reception, Rich's sorcery was what the people had come for – and Mr Bennett evoked even wilder acclaim.

He is a master professional, pleasing to hear, a commander of audiences. But craftmanship is not all. He lacked, for me, sufficient variety of approach – which his smooth saunter through nineteen songs pointedly exposed – as well as that dynamic flair which transforms everything Sinatra touches.

Don Ellis flexes himself

4 AUGUST 1968

The Don Ellis Orchestra, rumoured for some time to be the greatest thing in California since talking pictures, played two nights at Ronnie Scott's Club last week en route from Antibes. For the jazz bigot, it must be at first sight (and first sound, too) the ultimate deterrent.

Its members, doublet-clad, looked like refugees from a medieval movie lot. Novelty band uniforms? Didn't they go out in the forties? 'That's what the hip people out West are wearing,' says Ellis. Non-Reagan voters, you bet.

They tune up, all nineteen of them, including three percussionists and two bassists, one hiding his sitar in a prayer mat, with the gravitas of a symphony. Ellis, always announcing the exotic time signatures he uses – 'this is like 2, 3½ and 5' – sports a four-valve trumpet made to produce quarter tones and often projects it through an echo device, so that he plays harmonies with himself. Personal amplification is everywhere. When the five flautists stand, each trailing flex from flute, the prospect threatens mutual strangulation.

Do not, despite all, tune out. This marvellously disciplined, yet free-as-air orchestra is almost all it's cracked up to be. Ellis' music is daring, exciting, intriguing, completely personal, yet very much of its time. The contemporaneity is really the point. Though there are, for instance, shades of

Woody Herman in the breakers of sound which flood from the brass, or of Kenton in certain studied harmonies, what Ellis has created for the first time is a big band founded in the dual pop-and-jazz tradition which so many of the best young musicians today understand. This is a splendid and natural evolution.

Open minds and resilient spirits will find Ellis' artistry resplendent with wonders, despite a narcissistic tendency to spin out strange effects and thus to dissipate tension. The churning beat of the percussionists is as uplifting as good pop, but infinitely more cunning in its internal rhythms. There are fine soloists, especially Pete Robinson on assorted keyboards. The section work is dauntingly good, yet the band explodes with improvisation. The sight may be gone; the sound can still be well sampled on Ellis' LP, *Electric Bath* (CBS 63230, at 36s 8d).

Promises from Mike Gibbs

6 DECEMBER 1970

The most imaginative and exuberant popular music in Britain is, I swear, being fashioned on those too few occasions when Mike Gibbs is able to find a place for his fifteen-piece band to play. His concert for the Jazz Centre Society at Notre Dame Hall, off Leicester Square, on Friday was a masterpiece created for one evening only, triumphantly acclaimed by a large audience, and sadly left unrecorded.

Despite the claims of the other very fine London bands, like Westbrook's and Collier's and McGregor's, Gibbs at present is king, an improbable Rhodesian with frizzy hair, kindly face and a regular job (such is the musical life) playing in the pit orchestra for Bacharach's wonderful 'Promises, Promises'. There is nothing coming out of America to match him either, though Quincy Jones on his new A and M album, *Gula Matari*, has something of the same feeling.

Gibbs bring off this rare trick of combining various popular styles, and especially modern jazz and rock, whilst avoiding any sensation that the music is contrived. His writing has structural strength enough to support a cathedral, yet gives all his musicians a heady freedom in both solo and ensemble passages. He seems able to adapt his scores to gravity (the 'Canticle' he wrote for Canterbury Cathedral is a gem), or up-beat joy (his riotous 'Five for England'), or nodding tongue-in-cheek at folksy America (his adaptation of Gary Burton's 'Country Roads').

The bedrock of the band is the thunderous rhythm section of two drummers (John Marshall and Clive Thacker), with Frank Ricotti on tuned percussion and a brilliant bass guitarist, Roy Babbington. Against this backcloth, nine horns blow, with superb counterpoint from Chris Spedding on electric guitar and Mike Pyne on electric piano. Their dynamics, their tonal contrasts, and the virtuosity of their solos – Spedding was especially conquering on Friday, as was the silver-toned Henry Lowther on trumpet – form a total sound which seems to me the work of genius. Even in its more solemn moments, this is music which overflows with joy.

Some of the Gibbs' current repertoire will be released on a Deram album early next year. Meantime, his first LP on the same label, called simply *Michael Gibbs*, is still around – and for comparison, the Quincy Jones album mentioned earlier is interesting. The track called 'Hummin' is the closest to Gibbs in style, featuring the extra bonus of bassist Major Holley singing in unison with his instrument and Toots Thielemans whistling similarly to his guitar.

Kenton at sixty

13 FEBRUARY 1972

Stan Kenton is sixty next Friday, and that seems ridiculous. He is not grouped in my mind with classic jazz figures like Ellington or Goodman. To me, he is still that dapper Californian who came roaring out post-war playing a brassy, highly sophisticated music called Progressive Jazz with titles like 'Artistry in Rhythm'. Yet, almost by stealth, he has achieved a special historical status.

Musically, Kenton remains a controversial figure, for he has always seemed impatient with jazz's conventional borders. He has consistently involved himself in 'symphonic' jazz. He places such importance on composition and orchestration that it has been easy for ascetic aficionados to call his music pretentious, lacking spontaneity.

They miss the point. Some Kenton music *is* overblown. But the swinging scores once written for him by Bill Holman, Shorty Rogers and Gerry Mulligan assure his jazz status. So does the glittering list of Kenton sidemen during his thirty years as bandleader – Art Pepper, Bud Shank, Zoot Sims, Maynard Ferguson and Lee Konitz among them. For the rest, he has vastly enlarged the jazz vocabulary, using splendid composers like Pete Rugolo. He has, too, been an ardent jazz proselytizer.

During the 1960s he was out of fashion. The big bands were mostly finished, although Kenton was still touring his bands in limited seasons. Capitol Records issued few of his albums.

Kenton, however, was seeking a new power base. He was out in America's schools and universities, teaching and winning converts. Now he has a new army of young followers. For the past eighteen months he has led a full-time orchestra, and although he benefits from the general big band revival in jazz, he follows a particular path. He plays, above all, the American university circuit; and everywhere, he *educates*. Back in Britain last week, his first visit since 1963, Kenton explained. 'The kids are growing up, seeking more sophistication in music. Look at bands like Blood Sweat and Tears, and Chicago – marvellous bands. They're playing jazz, but the kids *thought* it was rock. My own band opens up a whole new world for college kids. They hear guys playing music they thought was impossible. They get ambitious!

'Rock is music for children. I have no regard for it, nor for so-called folk music. There's no dimension to it musically. It's adolescent. Simon and Garfunkel are simply doing what they did around camp fires during the Gold Rush. When you hear a pitiful piece like "Bridge Over Troubled Water", well . . .'

Two years ago Kenton formed Creative World Inc. It is a fan club, but more importantly it is a record company, conducting a crucial experiment in musical business, by-passing radio and television and other mass media. At each concert, Kenton asks for names and addresses. Those who oblige (and the mailing list is already an international sixty thousand) receive news of the band and its records. Kenton is issuing old albums and new – and they're *selling*.

Kenton says his present band is the best he's led. It probably is. At Ronnie Scott's Club on Friday, un-amplified, it gave a memorable performance, with passion, discipline and imagination most beautifully blended. Among this brilliant collection of young musicians, all in Kenton's tradition yet possessing personal flair, John von Ohlen on drums was quite remarkable. He whipped the band along without drama, sensitively shading his work to match the varied soloists, extracting an incredible range of tone from his drums.

The trombone section, rich and subtle in colouring, had an outstanding soloist in Dick Shearer. The trumpets were scalding, whilst of the saxophone soloists Quin Davis (alto) was bitingly of the Art Pepper school. They played new orchestrations chiefly by Ken Hanna and old warhorses like 'Intermission Riff', and they received a standing ovation for music that was beyond category, beyond price.

Melly comes back

17 JUNE 1973

George Melly is memory, almost a venerable institution: all those nights of the 1950s when he roamed the revivalist trad-jazz halls, drinking and rip-roaring and punting his improbable blues songs with Mick Mulligan's band. Melly is the recall of sweaty summer evenings in grotty suburban pubs and clubs in Wood Green and Wythenshawe, beer glasses slopping, heels clicking on wood or stone floors jiving in pairs, short haircuts and earnest spectacles and shellac 78 numbers briskly traded, fumblings in car parks.

He captured the period vividly in his immensely readable autobiography, *Owning Up* (Weidenfeld & Nicolson), but he dropped all (or nearly all) of that in 1962 to concentrate on writing and balloon filling for the Flook strip. Now, unlikely circumstance, he's headlining at Ronnie Scott's Club, which would have been almost unthinkable in that temple of modernism a few years ago, but in the present eclectic climate is somehow unsurprising.

High camp is in fashion; so is shaming and genteel outrageousness; and Derek Taylor, once Beatles PRO, has worked hard at refurbishing his new protégé's image. Melly fits the bill, and sedulously works at the image – suit as datedly crumpled as his marvellously wicked face, imbibing cigar and booze between choruses, mouthing graffiti jokes.

It would be very easy not to enjoy Melly. His style is totally derivative – born so closely of sedulous study of Bessie Smith, Fats Waller, Lonnie Johnson and company, with a touch of the Al Jolsons thrown in, that he's almost an impersonator. Intellectually, one rejects his capers because he hasn't lived the experience which made the music – and black blues is essentially autobiographical and idiosyncratic to its creators. His innuendos have the impact of a schoolboy saying 'knickers'.

Yet in the end, arid rationalism fails because Melly is, in the club context and with John Chilton's empathetic trumpet to obbligato him, richly entertaining. He works very hard; he has punch and panache; his fruity songs remind us of a rich heritage, even though lacking much of the feeling; and sometimes, as with Jelly Roll Morton's lamentful 'Michigan Water', he moves the heart.

It's unnerving, the way he succeeds. Explaining a blues, he says: 'That's to add a cultural gloss to an evening of smut.' Yet it's more than that. The drollness, camp, blues, swagger come together, make sense, make entertainment. It's like trad's answer to Alice Cooper.

Opposite him, Ronnie Scott himself was playing superbly, deputizing for

Frank Rosolino, trombone hero of the cool-jazz fifties, and that somehow seemed right, for every note awakened more memories – this time of Gerrard Street and Frith Street days when Tubby Hayes bestrode the Scott Club like a colossus.

Hayes' untimely death last weekend, aged only thirty-eight, robs us of a remarkable artist. 'The best jazz musician Britain has produced, and quite probably the best it will ever produce,' said Scott. Few will disagree.

Tubby won every British poll worth winning. On tenor sax, he could hold his own with any American, recorded with the likes of Clark Terry, James Moody and Roland Kirk, and once memorably (and uniquely) substituted for Paul Gonsalves in Duke Ellington's band. He added flute, soprano sax, vibraphone to his range with consummate ease.

Artistically, his work fell into three periods. First, the 1950s and early 1960s when, surely and with inspiration, he played with small groups like the Jazz Couriers (alongside Ronnie Scott) and his own quintet. Then, he became more and more daring, dazzling (sometimes blinding) the listener with bucketing pyrotechnics. His big bands, too, were joyous.

Finally, after long illnesses, his style grew more spare. He had had his problems – with marriages, with drugs and, at the last, with his heart, the ultimate cause of his death – but never did it dampen his spirit, his optimism, his cheerful niceness. 'Latterly, because he was short of breath, he had to pare his playing down to essentials,' said Ronnie Scott. 'I liked that bare style best of all. His finest work was still to come.' Tubby is probably irreplaceable; certainly unforgettable.

Dizzy, West Side and pictures

29 JULY 1973

John Birks Gillespie, alias Dizzy, creator with Charlie Parker and a few others of modern jazz, is preaching the true word at Ronnie Scott's Club now. As a trumpeter he remains dazzling, carving the smoke with uptilted horn, filling the ears with happiness.

But he's so much more. After all those joyless modernists who plink and plunk and look grave or angry or curl the lip and say nothing, what a pleasure it is to see someone who comes on like a human being. He *is* a preacher, in a way: telling his listeners humorously how jazz happened, laying on the anecdotes – about, say, the French Rivvyairya or gypsies who whupped it to him – like a mad artist. He's Falstaff, though, as well, with girth now matching the prodigious bulge of his cheeks, a man who at fifty-five enjoys life and wants everyone to enjoy it with him.

This is his first season in a British club and he's brought over a sparkling quintet, especially the driving drummer, Mickey Roker, and a superb new guitarist, Alexander Gafa. Gafa plays straight jazz guitar (often like Wes Montgomery), or rock guitar, or flamenco with equal ease. In one number, described by Dizzy as a sonnet ('that's what me and Shakey always wrote') dedicated to a group of gypsies, Gafa produced five minutes' worth of Manitas da Plata and then romped into varieties of *bossa nova* and Afro-Cuban for the next five. He's a find.

That sonnet was marvellous, with Dizzy sounding at times like the muted Miles Davis of *Sketches of Spain* (now, alas, defunct), and at others shouting away as he did with his big band. His dynamics are always impressive, especially when he skips softly through a theme at speed, and his style is masterfully many-coloured. But it's still the Afro-Cuban mode that remains his touchstone; he himself plays around on congas and jingle-sticks these days. Not to be missed.

The club was packed tighter than it's been for years, with a younger than usual audience, too, the night I went. The youth of the audience is also noticeable at the revival of *West Side Story* (Collegiate Theatre) which, in the age of the new, gives a reassuring feeling that at least some of the great artists and part of the great repertoire of this century's popular music are not going to perish from neglect.

The artists of the new *West Side Story* have been adequately reviewed already; what struck me all over again was the triumphant strength of Leonard Bernstein's score and the remarkable fit and wit of Stephen Sondheim's lyrics. The point-counterpoint of words and music – clever, witty, true – in 'America' and 'Gee, Officer Krupke' remains a marvel; the only element which slightly jars, fifteen years later, is the sentimentality of parts of the second half.

Not the least reason for my conviction about the music's lasting qualities was the whipcrack performance given by the pit orchestra, spurred and inspired by an American conductor, Ed Coleman. Everyone should give themselves the pleasure of hearing it.

Nor are Dizzy and Bernstein the only revivalists currently demonstrating themselves to be still life-enhancing. Jazz itself is having quite a time. There's the season of Jazz in the Movies at the National Film Theatre at which tonight, for example, there are shorts featuring Duke Ellington, Stan Kenton, Louis Prima, Cab Calloway, Nat Gonella, Stephane Grappelli and George Shearing among others – what a bill! Next Saturday's marathon all-nighter has *Pete Kelly's Blues* plus the Glenn Miller, Benny Goodman and Gene Krupa stories (well, you can watch 'n' sleep).

There's the exhibition of Valerie Wilmer's photographs, *Jazz Seen – the face of Black Music* at the Victoria and Albert Museum, which must be a rare (if not unique) collection to have been created by a Briton. Very rare, because in terms of commitment to her subject, in her range, and in her lack of clichés – she usually presents people straight and true, not in the smoky glitter and distortions of club and studio scenes so beloved of jazz photographers – Miss Wilmer's viewpoint is powerfully and personally her own.

Big band surprise

2 SEPTEMBER 1973

There is nothing surprising about the quality of the Mel Lewis-Thad Jones Big Band; it has musicians, arrangements, ideas enough to keep it comfortably in the world's top half dozen. What is making it so attractive during its season at Ronnie Scott's Club is the quality of its surprise.

Just how ignorant we in Britain still are of so much good popular music in America – due to distance, the sad nature of music's agitprop machine, and the topsy-turvy policy on album releases – was indicated by the performance of Dee Dee Bridgewater.

Thad Jones announced the band's singer. The crowded club almost discernibly evinced disinterest. Then Miss Bridgewater appeared, stunningly beautiful, sounding somewhere between vintage Sarah Vaughan and Norma Winstone. She was marvellous, riding the big band surf triumphantly, putting together alarmingly creative reconstructions of standards like 'By The Time I Get To Phoenix' with wit, grace and a sweetly husky voice that was always part of the band.

Her husband, Cecil Bridgewater, is in the trumpet section, his brother, Ronald, in the reeds; just two musicians in a splendid ensemble. The band is cunning. It plays relaxed bounce for the first ten minutes, with just the rhythm section and off-bursts of, say, a flugelhorn (Jones) and baritone sax (Pepper Adams) duet. But the muscle is there – not least because of Mel Lewis' drumming; it's a band that hasn't to show off.

Its joys include a superb trombone section, hingeing around the fluid Jimmy Knepper; a succession of fine soloists, including a stratospheric trumpet section leader, Jon Faddis, and Jerry Dodgion on saxes and flute; and ever-changing textures within the ensemble. Above all, it has humour. Roland Hanna (piano) is its prince of jokers, flipping in and out of sly impressions, from Erroll Garner to Fats Waller.

A delight, yes. So too was Tony Crombie. Leading a trio as contrast to such a big band can't be an easy chore. He made it seem so. Is there any drummer today who by mere tickles of cymbals can imply beat so firmly? Neat, dynamic, fuss-free. He makes pretentious free-formists sound like phoneys. Still (with John Marshall) our best jazz drummer.

Tracey's progress

25 NOVEMBER 1973

Stan Tracey started younger than most of our middle-aged jazz statesmen – around sixteen, as a piano accordionist – but it still seems ridiculous that last week's full-house celebration for him at the Queen Elizabeth Hall should mark a thirty-year span in the music.

It feels like only yesterday he was the *enfant terrible* of smoky jazz cellars. He looks younger than he is. And, most importantly, he remains astonishingly youthful in his music. He has listened to the new jazz sounds and, artistically, absorbed them. He has become even more adventurous in piano style than in his long period at Ronnie Scott's Club. Yet he is, as always, the most instantly recognizable artist in British jazz.

So it was Tracey as soloist who became the focal point of the evening. And immediately after a mixed first half, he produced, for fifteen minutes, a spontaneous improvisation whose surprising audacity left me gasping. His grasp of structure and harmony, consonant or dissonant, was the secret, whilst his range of musical ideas suggested two dozen names – Ellington and a far-out Gershwin among them, but above all Tracey.

Then he was joined by alto saxist Mike Osborne for a most satisfying duet before, finally, playing a set with his new quartet, Open Circle. If any group could persuade the doubters that there *is* something to the often pretentious, often boring free jazz of recent years, then Open Circle is it. The bass of Danny Thompson especially, strong and singing, was a blinding revelation of superb modern musicianship.

That first half: well, a different quartet was led by Tracey through parts of his outstanding *Under Milk Wood* suite, one of eleven albums by him now unobtainable. It was pleasant, faithfully done, but lacked the spark of the original album. Tracey's big band then displayed his orchestral talents – beautiful ensemble work, reminding me (heretically?) of Kenton as well as Ellington, and dashing solos from Ronnie Scott, Ronnie Ross, Malcolm Griffiths and David Horler. But, oh, how cruelly the indifferent amplification and acoustics marred the performance!

A great evening, though, in retrospect. Tracey has given to British music with a wealth that the musical world has scarcely even begun to return to him.

Burton meets Gibbs

24 MARCH 1974

Modern music has produced few partnerships so rewarding and innovative as that between Gary Burton and Mike Gibbs, whose qualities were for the first time fully revealed on stage and on record last week. The shock of pleasure I experienced was similar to that when, long ago, I first heard Gil Evans' many-splendoured orchestral settings for another great soloist, Miles Davis.

Burton, unequalled as a vibraphone virtuoso, and Gibbs, the Rhodesian-born composer, met in 1960 at the Berklee School of Music in Boston. Since then Gibbs has often composed for Burton's small groups and for Stan Getz. All that, however, was only a prelude for last week's revelations.

Even unsubtle amplification at their Rainbow Theatre concert could not disguise the glories of the music. Burton was cast as the main soloist with a large jazz band, but it was when he played *within* the band that the magic really worked. His fluent, hypnotic sound, with continual sprays of notes lightening the texture of Gibbs' orchestrations, created an effect unique in jazz.

There were soloists other than Burton – notably Kenny Wheeler on flugelhorn, Stan Sulzman on alto saxophone and Steve Swallow and Chris Lawrence with their contrasting bass styles – but all of them were only facets of the ensemble. It was Gibbs as orchestral writer who was on show, and superb he proved to be.

Glowing tone colours from him we expect: rich combinations of brass and reeds and electric pianos, with tuba and, on this occasion, three double-basses to add unusual depth. Even more astonishing, though, is his ability to unify idioms. A piece which first states a typically haunting, oddly-shaped theme ends up as roaring rock-and-roll with, en route, incursions into free improvisation as well as hints of both Ellington and Kenton. The transitions and the blend seem totally natural; and that is the essence of Gibbs' genius.

A short solo set by Burton; a gloriously-paced drum passage by Bob Moses; and a perfect performance of 'Dance: Blue', originally written for Graham Jones's ballet, *Totems*, were other particular highlights of a fine concert. Much of the music played is on *In The Public Interest* (Polydor £2.50), the first Gibbs-Burton LP, just released.

This is a major modern jazz album by any standards, performed by an American band, however, and not the Anglo-American aggregation I heard last week. Mike Gibbs, whose music has suited both The Goodies and

Canterbury Cathedral, will be sorely missed when he leaves London after nine years to spend at least twelve months as composer in residence at Berklee.

Hampton high-flyer

19 MAY 1974

A not inconsiderable piece of jazz history came gloriously and joyously alive last week when Lionel Hampton brought his stomping band and his own dazzling instrumental skills to Ronnie Scott's Club. For excitement, audacious showmanship and swing, Hampton, in his sixty-first year, remains unparalleled.

His background is worth recalling. He was playing drums with Louis Armstrong when he was sixteen. He pioneered the vibraphone as a jazz instrument, recording a solo on it with Louis forty-four years ago. He became, in 1936, a member of the Benny Goodman Quartet – and, with Teddy Wilson, helped to break down the barriers which at that time prevented black and white musicians playing together.

At Scott's, and doubtless elsewhere on his British tour, he behaved with all the zest and enthusiasm of a man thirty years younger. He plainly still loves the music he plays. He adores performing. And the rapport established with his audience could have been achieved by only a handful of artists in the world.

Musically, he was fascinating. No other vibes player can swing like Hampton. This is a matter of timing; for example, he holds off striking a note just that fraction long enough to set up the special tension and surprise so essential to jazz. He is full of contrasts. Some tunes he treats very barely, with economy in ornamentation; with others, he sprays notes around like a mad machine-gunner, each one perfectly struck and timed.

Skills of this kind he thrust into compositions which ranged from modern Latin-rock, through old-time swingers like 'Hamp's Boogie' and Goodman quartet favourites such as 'Moonglow' and 'Avalon', to camped-up versions of Jewish folk sagas, with lyrics in the language of origin. His arrangements were excellent – with, surprisingly, a stunning treatment of the *2001* movie theme – and his ten-piece band not only played them vigorously but included several fine soloists, especially the flautist, Milt Heisler.

Finally, his showmanship. He laughed, he roared, he told jokes, he leaped around the stage and on three occasions sat at the drums to play thunderous solos during which he juggled magically with sticks (sometimes four sticks at a time) whilst a strobe light flickered away to create a numbing visual display. Popular music today is many things, but entertainment is one of its fundamentals. Hampton as entertainer and musician was an experience anyone who saw him at this, his first British club appearance, will never forget.

Free Kirk

22 SEPTEMBER 1974

It was more than a decade ago that Roland Kirk, jazz showman extraordinary, came whooping on to the scene with his aggressive and extraordinary style, his manzello and stritch and nose flute and all those other breathtaking instruments which became his hallmark.

But beneath the surface exoticism, which laid him open to charges of gimmickry, there remained a splendid jazz soloist. And at Ronnie Scott's Club currently, without abating one whit his exuberant commitment to being an entertainer, it's his musical virtues which strike home most tellingly.

He is now, of course, Rahsaan Roland Kirk. Incense burns merrily as he performs. His garb is orientally minstrellish. He stomps around the audience playing a New Orleans clarinet piece, cunningly guided by the sound of tambourines. And he still uses a bewildering variety of reed and woodwind instruments, gongs, bells, whistles, conch-shells and clappers.

And yet . . . I have never heard him produce better jazz. Now, when he plays two or three reed instruments simultaneously, the orchestration is superbly precise. He doesn't actually do that three-in-one act very often these days, content to lay it out only when the need for contrast is there. Instead he plays tenor saxophone beautifully in the Sonny Rollins manner. He offers flute solos which are at times crystal clear and at others utilize all those effects of pizzicato finger-stopping, voice-over and general mayhem which have made him a unique stylist on the instrument. And in everything he does – from affectionate caressing of Erroll Garner's 'Misty' to riotous Scottish reel with bagpipey horns – he commands his audience as few jazzmen today can.

Such an audience, too. Never has Scott's been so crowded as it was last Tuesday, or with so young-toned a congregation. I don't know whether Kirk alone drew them, or Kirk plus Tom Scott's LA Express (who were playing a short season whilst over for the Joni Mitchell Wembley concert), but the whole affair was transformed by the music and the excited reaction to it into one of those nights not easily forgotten.

It should also be said that Kirk's accompanying group play well and might – despite Kirk's own thrilling contribution – be heard more, especially the excellent pianist Hilton Ruiz. Tom Scott's men weren't overshadowed either. I've recommended them before; a sparkling and inventive jazz-rock quintet with fabulous interplay between Scott's horns, the electric piano and the truly inspired guitar of Robin Ford. Their imaginative music obviously appeals to a wide audience, for their tune 'Strut Your Stuff' recently achieved minor-hit status in the American *Cashbox* charts.

Ardley at Camden

6 OCTOBER 1974

Last Tuesday evening, at the Round House, two girl cellists played unaccompanied for twenty minutes a most attractive composition of Neil Ardley consisting of variations, almost entirely scored, inspired by a simple Balinese tone-scale.

It was neither an interlude in a symphony concert, nor yet the festival of some new Eastern sect. It was part of the magnificent Camden Jazz Festival which for the past week has been demonstrating that in the realm of good modern music Britain presently has little to learn, or even to fear, from America, where modern popular music was born.

Demonstrated, too, has been the total inadequacy of the old musical terminology to describe what now goes on in that limitless treasure house which is called conveniently (yet so misleadingly) 'popular music', within which I would include 'jazz'.

'Jazz' itself has, indeed, become so loose a word as to be meaningless. Most people will understand it in the context of Count Basie's orchestra or a trad band aping the ancient New Orleans masters. But it wouldn't lead them to envisage Ardley and his music – nor even that of, say, Mike Gibbs or Mike Westbrook.

These three composers most often use jazz instrumentation, of course. Their music has rhythms, improvisation, colourations familiar in older jazz. But they use rhythms taken from rock music, too. And aren't there also many rock bands who improvise, which was once the hallmark of jazz?

The plain truth is that 'popular music' now contains within itself so many styles, variations and sources of inspiration as to be indescribable except as 'music'. Its range stretches from songs as simple as folk ballads once were all the way through to symphonies more complex than, and just as terrifyingly grand as, Beethoven's.

The analogy grows even more ironic – for the works of Westbrook and Ardley (and of Americans like Gil Evans) show them to be inheritors of the

Western 'classical tradition'. They employ far more orthodox compositional devices, as practised from Bach to Britten, than do contemporary 'serious' (?) practitioners like Cage or Stockhausen.

Forgive me this discursion. But the word 'jazz' could not, if understood with its customary overtones, begin to describe the awesome calibre of some of the music played at the Camden Festival.

The first concert last Sunday, for example, was by Mike Westbrook. His splendid orchestra, which could cut to pieces anything I've heard out of America recently, played his new work, *Citadel Room 315*, as well as his *Electric Fanfare* and *Love Dream and Variations*. Among the highlights was a poignantly elegiac section for clarinet and two bass clarinets; a sombre duet for French horn and bass clarinet; a very pretty ballad for flugelhorn and reeds. Scorings like these adumbrate Westbrook's sophistication.

So panoramic is his style, so many his influences, that one moment I was reminded of Bach, then of Ellington, then of Kenton. Westbrook has absorbed just about everything good in American music this century and, spicing it with his own idiosyncracies, produces swinging, zestful, imaginative scores seized upon with joy by his musicians.

John Surman, improvising with virtuosic bravado on baritone and soprano saxophones and bass clarinet, was the star of the orchestra. But so many were the good things from Henry Lowther (trumpet), Malcolm Griffiths (trombone), Stan Sulzman (saxophones) and others, it seems hard not to mention every musician.

The Neil Ardley evening began with him conducting an hour-long composition by Barbara Thompson, *The Awakening*. This mingled the sounds of synthesizers and the human voice (Norma Winstone's) with the usual 'jazz' ensemble of saxophones, brass and rhythm, with the addition, too, of complicated percussion and vibraphone scorings.

It was a fascinating exercise, less obviously 'jazzy' than Westbrook's work, bursting with strange tone colourations and surprising themes.

Ardley's own second half was *Biformal from Bali* – first the cellists, and then the full orchestra playing their set of variations upon the Balinese theme. Elegant and beautiful were the sounds, in the tradition of his superb *Symphony of Amaranths* (1971). Jon Hiseman's drumming was, throughout, a supple, subtle and dynamic wonder.

Of course, the Camden Festival has not been all symphonies or all British. 'Classical' jazz has been represented, too (Bobby Hackett, and a recreation of Paul Whiteman's music), as has small-group work (Stan Tracey's *Under Milk Wood*) and many other facets of contemporary music. Its rich variety has been its strength and its justification.

Pass the guitar

20 OCTOBER 1974

'It's weird when you just kinda die out at the end,' observes Joe Pass after finishing a guitar improvisation on 'Spring is Here' so dazzlingly complex that a booming final chord would seem an embarrassing impertinence. It isn't weird at all; rather is it completely right in the context of that particular song, and those who have been enjoying Mr Pass' artistry at Ronnie Scott's Club will suspect that he knows it.

He's a wry, witty and thoroughly engaging man, Joe Pass, who made a lot of people realize what they had been missing when he blossomed recently as Ella Fitzgerald's partner on a memorable album. Now, at Scott's, where he continues this week, he's enhancing his reputation.

By no means is he precisely an American Django Reinhart, but his style certainly has some of the French genius' romanticism, with more than a touch of flamenco. The extra element is his orchestral inclinations. So fast is his fingering, so sure his grasp of harmonics, it's hard to believe that so many effects are being created by a single guitar. His performance is truly virtuoso, beautifully satisfying to the ear.

It's possible, of course, to judge his artful symphonies rather too rich, the ornateness sometimes overpowering the sense of swing. I was too entranced to worry much about such dry pedantry. And as soon as he invited Tony Crombie (drums) and Lenny Bush (bass) to join him after a solo set, he thundered away rhythmically just to show he could do it.

There isn't anything he *can't* do on the guitar, indeed, including those octave runs in the style of the late Wes Montgomery. He virtually distils the history of jazz guitar so far into a luxuriant personal style, good enough to put him among the best three guitarists in the world today.

Ronnie Scott's has, by the way, just passed its fifteenth anniversary, a rare event in the world of jazz clubs these days, and it seemed very appropriate that opposite Pass was a band led by drummer Tony Kinsey playing straight old-fashioned bebop – the sort Scott's existed on in its early days. The melodies, often stated by alto and tenor saxophones in unison, were clean and true, the improvisation spun without tonal distortion, the beat rock-steady.

Not the least of these good sounds was Pete King's alto, his fluency as remarkable as it was a decade ago, whilst Kinsey pulled out a drum solo crisp enough to impress even Buddy Rich, who was sitting out front repaying the compliment to Ronnie Scott, a recent successful debutant before audiences including Benny Goodman and Woody Herman in Rich's New York club.

Joe Pass as soloist is lovingly captured on *Virtuoso* (Pablo, the Norman Granz label, £2.46) and as partner on Ella Fitzgerald's *Take Love Easy* (Pablo, £2.46) both recorded in 1973. Ronnie Scott himself has a fine – and long overdue – album just out, playing in the trio (Mike Carr, organ, and Bobby Giens, drums) which recently stirred them at Carnegie Hall. It's called *Scott at Ronnie's* (RCA, £2.44).

Zoot and friends

2 FEBRUARY 1975

Exhilarating it can be to explore the new horizons and imaginings of today's best popular music. But equally enjoyable is to rediscover an old faithful who hammered out his style years ago, who continually refurbishes it. Such is Zoot Sims.

It's almost thirty years ago that he was in the classic Woody Herman 'Four Brothers' saxophone team, and around half that time since he became the first American to appear at Ronnie Scott's original club in Gerrard Street. Now he's back at the new Scott's, playing a season of deeply satisfying quality.

He hasn't changed much. He's an attractive big bear of a man with a face that's always looked lived in – like his saxophone. And his sound is marvellous.

Sims swings, sets your foot tapping. He moves through endless cadences without panic or melodrama. He never strives for an effect like lesser honking and squealing mortals. With easeful artistry he lays down infectious and entertaining improvisations, cunningly timed and possessing a grace which disguises the muscular discipline within.

His tone is crucial. It is sometimes strong, sometimes silky, but never angular. Listen to his lower register. Where others rasp, he produces a well-rounded sound, as if he were playing in a large resonant vault. He's excellently supported by a British trio (Alan Branscombe, Ron Matthewson, Martin Drew) and he makes even those familiar Jobim bossa novas sound fresh. Hear him. There aren't many of him left.

The other act, Jackie Cain and Roy Kral, are refreshingly different too. They sing, and he also plays piano, along with another splendid British threesome led by Frank Ricotti on vibraphone.

Their overall musicianship is unquestionable – neat, cool harmonies, which used to be called 'hip' in the Kerouac era, with lots of vocalese and occasionally (an admitted prejudice of mine) whistling plus voice in unison.

The songs are interesting too: their own, Don Sebesky's, Alec Wilder's, André Previn's, Bach's, Bernstein's.

It's enjoyable, impeccable. But what they lack is more of Zoot Sims' kind of muscularity. The sound is sometimes like stripped-down Sergio Mendes. I welcome, however, their skills and taste.

Count-down to Scott's

9 NOVEMBER 1975

'We've been trying to get into this place a long time,' observed William 'Count' Basie last Wednesday as his band limbered up for the first frontal assault at Ronnie Scott's Club. It does, indeed, seem ironic that the most distinguished living leader of a jazz orchestra should have had to wait until his seventy-second year to appear in the world's most distinguished living jazz venue.

Still, it was worth the wait. Basie himself defied stories that he might retire soon by taking longer piano intros than for some time; striding away as in younger days; and the band, despite the absence of familiar faces, was magnificent.

Basie's sound has this distinctive mark: the band swings – oh, does it swing! – and it can bite, but the uniquely enjoyable tension it creates in listeners is because it rarely overstates. Rather does it sport the implication of tremendous unloosed power. The horns wail, but are seldom uncouth. Like a big cat, it is: the sheen is on the coat, but the muscles rippling beneath are what really count.

One further trait. Basie's ensemble sounds are utterly magical. For a bandleader whose reputation is for swinging blues, Basie creates the most exquisite voicings for saxophones (often leavened with flutes) and brass, with whom the use of mutes is crucial.

Listen to the classic 'Li'l Darlin'' to hear Basie's virtues. The beat is laid back and relaxed: the brass shuffles behind bucket mutes, mingling lazily with the saxes. The colouring is as distinctive as Ellington's.

Standards like 'Darlin'', several Sam Nestico originals, and inevitably blues aplenty, were on Basie's programme. Of the older guard, Bobby Plater played gorgeous Hodges-like alto and trombonists Al Grey and Curtis Fuller were tremendous, with Grey especially witty in his use of plunger mute. The only question mark was against a tenor sax version of 'Body and Soul', unpleasant in tone and far too full of quotes, from 'Trees' to 'Cocktails for Two'.

The new guard, however, were impressive too. The youngish trumpet section glittered, and the drummer, Butch Miles, is one of the finds of the decade – a catapulting inspirer and dazzling technician.

Maybe it's the young men who have charged up the sound. It is undeniably Basie, and the longer the band plays the more Basie-like it is. But there's a touch of other big bands – updated Rich and Herman – in there, too. No band, not even Count's, is an island.

This week the majestic Basie moves to the Palladium to back Frank Sinatra and Sarah Vaughan for their historic season. How apt that the theatre where Duke Ellington played in 1933 should remind us now that jazz is still a vital part of the multi-faceted popular music mainstream.

Weather Report – sunny

30 NOVEMBER 1975

Josef Zawinul and Wayne Shorter, who are the heart and soul of Weather Report, are not jazzmen. Neither are they rockers. They are musicians. The wondrous variety of sounds and moods which this incredibly integrated band creates – from the 1970s equivalent of Chopin *études* to zipping rhythmic thunderstorms which make most disco soul singles taste like last week's cold cuts – is the essence of what has happened to good modern music.

It is rooted in jazz, for the illusion of improvisation remains the key to Weather Report, and it was jazz which first taught all kinds of popular musicians that art. But see how Zawinul and company have developed, diversified and enlivened jazz.

The band is, for one thing, dramatically presented. When it came to a sold-out New Victoria Theatre last Thursday, riding on the wings of being voted number one in America by *Downbeat*, the musicians entered to electronic sounds of space winds. Infernal lights burned and flickered. Then, behind batteries of keyboards and percussion, they plunged into an unbroken set of over two hours which displayed all their arts.

Vienna-born Zawinul, who like Shorter has a long history of sidemanship with renowned jazz combos, culminating in the jazz-rock cauldron of Miles Davis' bands, is an absolute master of every keyboard – electric and acoustic piano, synthesizer, organ, all of them attuned to his tonal demands.

Shorter, whether on soprano or tenor saxophone, or electric clarinet, or mouth-whistling through the synthesizer – a brilliant effect, this – spawns powerful riffs and inventive improvisations with continuous brilliance. The various tones he gets on soprano are remarkable. The two percussionists create a drive which is probably unmatched today, and the bassist also uses electronics to create unique shadings from his instrument.

Overall, an enchanting, exciting and memorable concert. More ideas, more ravishing tones and melodies, more rhythmic excitements than you'd get in a month of other more bruited bands, as their latest album, *Tale Spinnin'* (CBS £2.79) demonstrates. The Weather Report outlook: definitely sunny.

Tracey and Thomas

29 FEBRUARY 1976

I have, unsurprisingly, always considered Dylan Thomas' *Under Milk Wood* a minor masterpiece. The jazz suite which Stan Tracey wrote ten years ago, inspired by Thomas' work, has been likewise hailed. Put the two together, though, and you have a transcending experience of triumphant delight, both moving and joyous.

Donald Houston and the Tracey Quartet, featuring Art Themen in Bobby Wellins' original tenor sax role, performed the marriage of words and music at the New London Theatre last Tuesday and it was sad that so few people heard one of the year's artistic coups. Rarely have jazz and lyrics been so enlightening of each other.

Tracey's suite is marvellous in itself, but Houston's sensitive readings explained everything. 'Eastern music undoes him in a Japanese minute' leads slyly into the spiky tune of 'No Good Boyo'; the verbal romance of Miss Price and Mogg Edwards heralds 'Pen Pals'; the deliciously ironic 'Praise God We Are A Musical Nation' glides towards Tracey's jaunty 'Cockle Row'.

Sometimes it was all music, with Themen and Tracey incredibly empathetic. Music, perfect in tone and volume, often enhanced Houston's musical voice. At other points – Houston softly speaking the sadness of 'Wee Willie Wee' – there were, rightly, only the words.

Perfect, all of it; a superb production, which deserves an album of its own.

Toots in the foreground

22 JANUARY 1978

Not too many people other than his tight-knit corps of fans will know much about Jean 'Toots' Thielemans. He is, relatively, one of the background men of popular music, whose sound rather than his name or charisma is his hallmark.

Yet he is unique in his achievement as a modern jazz soloist on harmonica and, probably, in his neat effect of whistling edgily in unison with exquisite guitar improvisions. You'll have heard him (without knowing him) on many film scores, especially those by Quincy Jones, as you may also have listened to his catchy classic 'Bluesette' without realizing its name or composer. His arrival to play at Ronnie Scott's Club is the most delightful première for a long time.

Few musicians have paid their dues more comprehensively. Born in Brussels fifty-six years ago, he endured the German occupation, learning in an attic from fragments of Django and Duke. Since then he's been largely American-based, playing with Goodman, Shearing, Quincy Jones and studio orchestras, leading his own groups all over, including the USSR.

The depth and richness of tone he achieves from the chromatic harmonica at Scott's is wonderful to hear. It is profound, dark, appealing and, when he turns to impressionistic ballads by Ray Brown or Joanne Brackeen, this solidly-built bespectacled genius in blue can make the simple old mouth organ weep.

The group he's brought with him match perfectly the sense of swing (and the gentle humour) which seems inborn in Thielemans. There is a particularly inventive electric pianist from Holland, Rob Franken, and a ringing-toned bassist, James Leary, who like the drummer, Eddie Marshall, is a San Franciscan.

Not that Thielemans needs them all the time, good as they are. In a moving tribute to Ellington, he played with gentle touch and deft fingering magnificently understated versions of 'The Mooche' and 'Black Beauty'. He pulled, finally, a stunning stroke where, as it were, he half needed support. Confessing he'd always dreamed of playing guitar and harmonica together, he posed a riddle. Bluesmen answer the riddle, of course, by strumming away whilst vamping straightforwardly on a simple mouth harp supported by a rigid harness. But how can you work it with a chromatic harmonica, the one with the push-button which achieves semitones?

Thielemans showed us how. Fingering the guitar with his left hand, and holding harmonica to mouth with his right, he got Marshall to strum the guitar through a sophisticated version of Stevie Wonder's 'Isn't She Lovely?' The audience, already overflowing with goodwill, exploded after that feat, as it deserved.

The belting Earl

16 APRIL 1978

He is called 'Fatha'. And father Earl Hines assuredly is, the progenitor of all modern jazz playing, from Teddy Wilson to Oscar Peterson and beyond – innovator, blessed performer and ebullient entertainer.

When he ran his big bands back in the hustling thirties and the twitching forties, he had this trick of wearing a large glittering ring on his right hand which, as the curtain rose, was entrapped in a narrow spotlight beam. The theatricality went with his expensive style and expansive personality; and so did the sparkle.

Hines today is an artistic miracle. At Ronnie Scott's Club where he has one week still to play during a rare visit, the ring is still twinkling, the artistry still as overwhelming – and that, by all normal standards, is absurd.

You survey this man of seventy-two, urbane and broadly smiling, so sophisticated and pleasant, looking like fifty and playing piano like forty, and the questions explode. Can this really be the young genius who made it with Louis Armstrong in '28, who survived for years at the Capone-dominated Grand Terrace in Chicago, who lured Charlie Parker, Dizzy Gillespie and Sarah Vaughan into the first bop-tinged big band of '42?

He's had his ups and downs since then. He told me once he was always meeting people who thought he was dead. At Scott's, Earl Kenneth Hines has never been more gloriously alive, and for all kinds of reasons.

First, his own playing. He starts his ninety-minute sets solo, which with Hines is all you really need. He is his own rhythm section and horns as, with bounding single finger or octaves, flashing arpeggios and boggling stretch of hands he cascades through tunes old and new.

All that, however, for those who love him is obvious virtue. He has so much more to offer. To begin with, he has surrounded himself with four superb musicians. The reeds player is heard first adding a clarinet coda to a Hines piece from the middle of the club. When he hits the stage he plays alto, tenor and clarinet with a swinging mix of bop and mainstream which brought a standing ovation. The bassist, Wesley Brown, is no slouch either, whilst the drummer, Ed Graham, turns on a solo spectacular at the end which, with a finale of illuminated drumsticks and strobe flicker, rivals

Emerson, Lake and Palmer and has the customers jumping up and down as if on trampolines.

Greatness in art (or anything else) resides in having no fear of competition. Taste in jazz resides partly in who you pick to play with you. Hines has brought us the best here, and he lets these young lions upstage him all through, sitting the while with a broad beam of satisfied wonderment like the den-father he is.

The final stroke is his singer, Marva Josie, a beautiful slim tigress who, stretching for lows and highs with true jazz feeling (mixed with a touch of opera), brings a dynamism rarely seen to all she does.

Jazz, as someone once said, means Hines. Do not miss him. It is magic, solid gold magic, whose like you will seldom know again.

Oscar's orchestra

19 NOVEMBER 1978

Oscar Peterson lives dangerously. He has in recent years made his talents so freely available – in concerts, in clubs, on record, on television – that he ought, by normal standards, to have been taken for granted long ago. But then, he defies normality. His gifts are so immense and so varied that he will go on winning the kind of ecstatic reception he earned at Ronnie Scott's Club last week for as long as he cares to play.

Oddly, though, his gifts have become double-edged. It is amazing how ready smaller men have been to turn his most remarkable strengths against him. He is, to begin with, the most complete technician ever heard on jazz piano, rivalled only by Art Tatum, his idol. A pianist friend (no slouch himself) once told me he had no idea how Peterson escaped from some of the harmonic mazes he plunged into; it was all done at such speed, the naked ear couldn't keep up.

Yet Peterson's detractors continually cudgel him for his dazzling skill, seeming to assume that technique must always be the enemy of imagination or feeling. Not so. With Peterson, it is the ability to attempt what no others dare which gives his expansive imagination such exciting expressions. There have also been times, beginning in the 1960s, when those who seem to treat jazz as a political statement have accused him of archaism. I daresay he doesn't mind standing for music rather than manifestos. He treats all the bits and pieces of the pianist's trade, from lush arpeggios to walking bass boogie, as if they were a treasure-house made to his customized specification.

Later still, in this decade, the attackers have sniffed at his television series. Maybe they're the same kind of people who thought Louis Armstrong should have tagged along with King Oliver for ever. Peterson (like Satchmo) has reached out to wider audiences, breaking down barriers of musical prejudice, stimulating curiosity about jazz and music generally – an activity to welcome rather than censure.

Thoughts like these, however, come strictly *after* a Peterson performance. While he is playing, you are so in thrall to the music, so uplifted by it, there's no time to ponder critical grouches. Last Wednesday, Peterson was producing again his remarkable distillation of jazz piano history. The striding power of Willie the Lion Smith was echoed, the nimble right-hand lines which Earl Hines taught the world, Tatum's beguiling audacity and Fats Waller's wit. And not only *jazz* history. His beautiful rhapsodic introductions are European, Peterson again refusing to conform to category, a means by which a simple Dizzy Gillespie theme like 'Con Alma' is miraculously transformed, and other promising vehicles too, many of which one caught: 'People', Newley's 'Who Can I Turn To' and 'Nature Boy', as well as a sly quotation – he never overdoes quotations – from 'Buttons and Bows'.

Peterson mostly played in a trio and nobly was he served by John Heard (bass) and his frequent British partner, Martin Drew (drums). But totally solo playing is still his glory, revealing most strikingly his exquisite rhythmic drive and command of dynamics. After all, when he is so orchestral, who needs additional orchestration?

Chapter Eight

Singers of Songs

Thousands of performers sing popular songs – or shout or croak or grunt them. Only a few, however, do so with such style, authority or rare power of personality that they transcend any category but their own. Ella Fitzgerald may be labelled 'jazz', Joni Mitchell 'rock', Mabel Mercer 'cabaret'. For me, they are simply singers, valuing music *and* words, creating unique works of art, sometimes from the most banal and unpromising material. So there is no stylistic unity to the work of the artists who are reviewed and, occasionally, interviewed in this chapter. Crosby and Sinatra stand with Aznavour and Minnelli, Diamond and Dietrich, Simone and Garland. Some of them, of course, are more than singers; they are actors, actresses, composers, legends, institutions. Some have died; some have become tragic symbols; several seem larger than life. The review of Judy Garland in 1969 had especial meaning for me in retrospect, for it was written only a few months before her death. I count myself very fortunate, too, to have enjoyed many hours with Bing Crosby in Mexico and London during the last two years of his life. For the rest, the words that follow are explanation enough; they reflect some of the most memorable people and performances I have encountered.

Lena by torchlight

12 APRIL 1964

One word, from the thesaurus she demands, is inevitable: intensity. She may not belt out songs with the classic brashness of Merman, nor re-create them as magically as Ella, nor sweet-and-sour them like Peggy Lee. But no singer of popular music so dominates a song, stamps it with so distinct and vivid a character, charges the most banal phrase with such histrionic glitter. With Lena Horne you feel the authentic electricity at the nape of the neck.

She opened her Palladium season last week with a sixteen-song performance of unswerving passion. At forty-seven she retains all her riveting beauty, her lithe grace, her imperious poise, as well as her ability to ensnare her audience with the slightest gesture. She scarcely moves at the microphone, simmering with the external quiescence of an atomic pile.

She could, predictably, make 'Mother Macree' sound like a torch song. With her the art of the sexy becomes almost a science; every minimal pout, crouch, slouch, scowl, shrug, arm-crook, headshake, hip-flick, knee-thrust, indrawing of breath, crumpling of cheek, baring of teeth, fracturing of vowel seems precisely calculated. Yet, oddly, there is no sense of confidence trick; the artistry and the compulsion of the ritual are too hypnotic.

But if her singing were only a celebration of the sexual it would soon become a bore. It is not. Her voice ranges widely in mood and colour. 'I Wanna Be Evil' may lacerate, but in 'Accustomed To His Face' she achieves a moving tenderness, in 'Let Us Out' tomboy humour, and, at other times, a swing so innate you almost believe she was born to sing jazz. A great and singular artist, brilliantly set off in the orchestrations her husband, Lennie Hayton, has created for her; the persistence of her talk about retirement is saddening.

Minnelli, rough diamond

15 MAY 1966

Well no, it is neither pop nor jazz. It is Liza Minnelli, who has, turning today's wizened cliché rump upwards, almost become an 'all-round entertainer' before she has learned to sing. Well, not exactly *sing*; to use her voice would convey my meaning better.

This is intended not unkindly. It is a long time since The Talk of the Town has presented an act which is such rich value; part-gold, part-embarrassment, and all of it, even the avalanches of decibels, grandiosely fascinating. We are watching a considerable artist, halfway developed. Rough, but definitely diamond.

Who are these people who say she isn't like Judy Garland? Of course she is. The reflection of her mother at around the same age of twenty is agonizing. There is the gawkiness, emphasized by her size and the short, schoolgirly dress; this seems a little too contrived. There is the dramatic quality of voice, the belting and too frequent fortissimo, even the shrill vibrato. Everything she does is several touches too much.

But what she will have to offer when she cools it is obviously immense. She approached the full sum in the Aznavour classic 'You've Let Yourself Go'. For the first time she took a song, explored it, wrung its meaning, instead of trying to kick it over the housetops. She must do this more often. Aside from singing she dances wonderfully, with two hilarious men, one fat, one thin, in the best routine in town. For students of form this is one not to be missed, despite the gaucheries.

Aznavour: any poor devil

7 AUGUST 1966

'I am saying what they are thinking without daring to say themselves,' explained Charles Aznavour, in English. 'In every song is a problem that touches somebody in the audience. Said by me, they accept it. I have not the face to hurt them. I am not a handsome, talented man. My voice is froggy, everything about me is common. They identify with me.'

Time magazine picked up the same line. 'His words are the plea of any poor devil, sung in any poor devil's voice.'

The poor devil is now forty-two. He is five feet four, with a body whippy and fatless, a crumpled face and a receding hairline. He appears insignificant, with brown, melancholy eyes; one of nature's victims.

His success – and he must be much more than a millionaire – has come in the last half-dozen years. In the 1950s he was booed off the stage in Paris. He is a singer and composer of songs which deal wryly, realistically and often brutally with the business of love, death, drink and women. He is also a movie actor, producer, and, latterly, writer. The veneration with which he is treated in France has been accorded to no one else since the war, except perhaps de Gaulle.

It is a safe bet that most Britons have never heard of him. Which demonstrates that in terms of taste, the English Channel can be twenty thousand miles wide. Aznavour has already subdued most of the West: Europe, North and South America, even the Middle East.

Earlier this year he went on a two-month tour of Canada, the Caribbean, Argentina, Uruguay, Brazil, Morocco and Spain. In Argentina no record had ever sold more than sixty thousand copies; Aznavour's 'Venice Blue' promptly sold two hundred thousand. His total world sales are of the order of tens of millions. Only The Beatles, Presley and maybe a couple more names among artists who have emerged in the past ten years are in this league.

Soon Britain will have its first live taste of him: a solitary concert at the Albert Hall. His neglect of these islands has an explanation. He refuses to take part in TV variety shows. 'I cannot,' he says, 'explain myself in five songs.' An Aznavour performance is all or nothing at all – maybe thirty songs, each one with words or music, or both, written by him.

He plans his excursions carefully. It took him over ten years to pummel French taste into accepting what he had to say. Only now, he believes, is Britain becoming ready for it.

In that old faded dressing-gown,
Your hair in curlers hanging down,
What could I have been thinking of?
Was it with you I fell in love?

This is typical Aznavour, although the effect in English, and without his projection, is muted. The middle-aged husband, viciously honest, is talking to his wife in a song called 'You've Let Yourself Go . . .'

I gaze at you in sheer despair,
And see your mother standing there.

The stock-in-trade of his lyrics is the physical pleasure and bitterness of love, cynicism, wifely nagging, nostalgia, defiance, despairs and the fears of middle-aged males about their virility. 'Bonne Anniversaire' deals with a wedding anniversary: the wife's hair is not combed, the dress comes late, the zipper is stuck, the theatre is shut. *Who?* is the worried monologue of a man in love with a girl twenty years younger . . .

Who will take your mouth?
Who will fill your bed?
And bury me for a second time?

The programme for Aznavour's last American tour announced that he was singing songs of 'love and other sorrows'. He does not wrap up love in soft tissue and call it 'romance'. He often celebrates the body, but not as a pornographer does. He promises no thrills, no delicious seductions, no honeyed flesh. He is concerned with the sadness of existence, out of which all the other poor devils must try to wring some sense.

He is, however, not as *un*sentimental as he would have us believe. His harshest songs sometimes go soft at the end. 'I couldn't hate you if I tried, I always want you by my side,' says 'You've Let Yourself Go'. The cynicism collapses into life-is-bloody-but-we-have-each-other. Thus he maintains a tension between sentiment and reality.

Aznavour has written around seven hundred songs, mainly of this kind, since he was eighteen. 'For me, love and death are mixed. When someone is in love, he is near death. He has this feeling that he is going to die if something bad happens.'

He has no false modesty. 'I brought a new approach to the song business. If you think something, why not sing about it? There are nudes in painting, why not in songs? If Lolita is in a book, why not Lolita in a song? The difference of age between a man and woman in love is often. I write many songs about this. Yet for years my work was regarded as immoral. Until 1960, sixty percent of my songs were banned from the French radio. But now, all is accepted.'

Aznavour writes in French. He speaks competent English-American; also fluent Spanish, Italian, German. He sings in all five. Many of his songs have been carefully, and freely, translated into English by Herbert Kretzmer, musical writer and dramatic critic of the *Daily Express*, and Marcel Stellman of Decca. But this is not easy. Aznavour's words are often closer to poetry than twentieth-century popular song; and they must be made singable. On the printed page, they can seem banal. They have also sometimes been judged too honest for English ears. So much for swinging London.

'Après L'Amour' deals with the reactions of a man when the act of love is over. 'I am saying my hand is on your body, your body is naked,' explains Aznavour. 'It is a risky idea, but it is not a risky song.' In English the meaning of this song (retitled 'Don't Say a Word') has been much softened, though the locale is obviously bed.

Aznavour has had a new translation made for this country. 'It is right for England now. Of course, it is going to be banned on the air, but I was banned so long in France that I have the habit.'

Aznavour has extended the moral frontiers of popular song. In today's social climate this perhaps is not surprising. That he should, with his unheroic physical equipment, have become a hero is also not unprecedented. He has the appeal of the underdog, the little man – the role he usually takes in his films. Chaplin, Charlie Drake, Norman Wisdom have played the same game. 'It is the force of the weak,' he says.

But this is by no means all. The size of his record sales, and the composition of his audience at halls like the Olympia in Paris, indicate that he appeals to both the young and the middle-aged, men as well as women. The music that goes with the words may partly explain this unusual feat. His melodies mix many elements: French music hall songs, Gershwinese, rock 'n' roll, blues, Latin-American rhythms, marches. There is in his music something for everyone.

This is reflected in public reaction to Aznavour. To follow him around Paris is a surprising experience. Everyone smiles on seeing him. He is always stopping and speaking. A girl of perhaps seventeen offers him a grubby newspaper parcel. He unwraps it to reveal a small religious medallion. Gravely he embraces her, kisses her on both cheeks. A workman in blue overalls is cleaning windows. 'Charles,' he cries, crossing the street and hugging Aznavour. They talk for five minutes and shake hands. 'No,' says Aznavour, 'I have never seen him before.'

This goes on all the time. Yet every encounter is an affair of great dignity. He is never mobbed. 'They respect my wishes. I like to cook, to shop, to go and see if the tomatoes are good. I will not be the slave of my popularity, I must be a free man.'

Aznavour is as dramatic out of the theatre as inside it. During a stage performance he turns his back, growls, clenches his fists, reels drunkenly, sings in darkness, points accusingly, shouts, whispers, pleads, thrusts hands in pockets. He may appear to some Anglo-Saxon eyes and ears to *over*act. He is a grown-up act for grown, or growing, people.

Despite all this virtuosity, though, there remains the matter of his voice. It has been described as being filtered through Gauloises or dragged through a Parisian gutter. If elastic could be rusty, that might describe its timbre. Yet the act comes off. This fact is not explicable. He has a quality of voice which is, for some reason, instantly acceptable to audiences no matter what its limitation of technique or range. This happens with only a very few singers.

His voice has a hypnotic quality, too. It is akin to the keening sound known in Middle Eastern countries. This is a fact that *is* explicable.

Aznavour was born in the Latin Quarter of Paris of Armenian parents shortly after they had fled the Turkish massacre of 1922. His sister Aida, a young-looking handsome woman, was born sixteen months before him in Greece while his parents were still wandering exiles.

The sense of family is all-pervasive with him. When he uses the word, which is often, it means friends, associates, pets as well as relatives. He stands at the centre of a tight-knit group of people. They live near him, move around with him. 'If he weren't Armenian,' said one friend, 'he would have to be Jewish.'

Aznavour seems very kind, very straight, very trusting. He has not, as is common with showbusiness, changed his friends with the size of his billing. The *gouvernante* of his house in the village of Galluis, thirty miles from Paris, he has known since childhood. His secretary, Eddie Kazarian, is the son of an old Armenian actor-friend. His accountant has been with him fourteen years; his sound-and-light man, Danny Brunet, for a dozen; his manager, Jean-Louis Marquet, for twenty-two. He has just built a house for his parents next to his own. His sister and her Armenian husband, Georges Garvarentz, also live nearby, as do two friends from the mid-1940s, Fred Mella, lead singer of the Compagnons de la Chanson, and Mella's Canadian-born wife Suzanne.

It is a clan, encouraged to exist, and sustained quite deliberately, by Aznavour. 'It is important to have your friends near you,' he says. 'One must prepare for the future – the bad future.' Of his retinue of assistants, he adds: 'We do everything together. My way of working is a kind of socialism.'

All this is not dissimilar to the way Frank Sinatra cushions himself with people. The relationship between the two men is quite close. Aznavour records for Sinatra's label, Reprise; he always carries Sinatra records in his suitcase when he travels; Sammy Davis, of Sinatra's clan, introduced Aznavour's stage show in America.

Like Sinatra's, Aznavour's childhood was poor. His father was a singer, his mother an actress, but they had to be cook and needlewoman respectively to earn a living.

At nine, Aznavour and his parents agreed he should go on the stage. At eleven he left school to concentrate on acting and singing. He was sixteen when the war began. He doesn't talk much about the Occupation. 'I sold newspapers, swept streets, things like this, there were a few singing jobs too.' Then he teamed up with an actor called Pierre Roche. For eight years, till 1950, they had a double-act, and Aznavour began writing some songs for Mistinguett, Edith Piaf and Maurice Chevalier.

Piaf was a tremendous influence. She encouraged him to go solo, to interpret his own songs. This he did in 1950, and then the hard, ten-year war for recognition began. Only in 1959 did he make star billing at the Alhambra in Paris. In the same year came his first big-selling disc and the start of six years of international success, including nearly a score of films made with directors like Truffaut (*Shoot the Pianist*), Cayette (*Crossing of the Rhine*) and René Clair. He never sings in his films. This year he both starred in and produced *Convoy to Dien Bien Phu*, a colour movie made on location in Cambodia, a more expensive job than is usual with French films.

'I did it for France,' says Aznavour. 'I could do films for Hollywood, but this is the country that made me. I demand to be free, but a man must have somewhere to hang his suit. For me, it is France.'

'Free' is the word Aznavour uses most often. He must be free; his children must be free; his animals (he has five dogs and many caged birds) must be free; his friends must be free.

But Aznavour's 'freedom' means the freedom to work. This is his first obsession. He usually works an eighteen-hour day. 'I know my life is a flop – as a father, as a human man. You must make a choice: a successful life as a man, or showbusiness. I have chosen showbusiness.' He shrugged. 'Now it is too late even to make a choice. I belong to the public, or to my pride. My only salvation is to become a greater artist.'

Aznavour has two children. Patricia, aged nineteen, is a plump, jolly girl who obviously adores him. She travels a lot with him and wants to be a singer. 'I take her to see Streisand, Minnelli – all of them. This education is more important than the baccalaureat.' Patrick, aged fifteen, is away at school.

He has been twice married, twice divorced. 'My first wife, I was young and poor. Patricia is our daughter. One day you find you are growing up mentally, and the wife is staying in the same place. In the end, you part. My second wife I prefer not to speak about. Patrick is the child of neither wife. He was born to a chorus girl I had a love affair with in Paris, for just two days.'

It is tempting to see Aznavour's songs as partly autobiographical. But this he denies. 'They come from watching people, that is all. My only enjoyment in life is to look at people, to examine them, to talk, to argue. Everywhere, in nightclubs, in restaurants, in the streets, I watch. I guess what they think, what is their life. I am watching you. What is your hope? Have you ambitions? Are you happy?'

If Aznavour's songs do not mirror his life, though, his life might sometimes be seen as mirroring his songs. He has a Swedish girl-friend called Ulla, who is about twenty years younger than he: this situation is the preoccupation of many of his songs. 'She is my quiet girl. She has the same kind of power as my sister for knowing about people. I cannot live without a woman's company. Whether I will marry her, I don't know. I think maybe I am not the marrying kind. With me, work is all. It is the quality of the work that can give real joy.'

We spent around thirty-six hours moving around Paris with Aznavour. In Paris he recorded five songs for a new EP disc in one hour forty minutes, leaping around, doing impersonations, grimacing, joking against himself, mock-marching, like a man plugged into an electricity socket. Aznavour crackles most of the time. He shepherded Liza Minnelli before, during and after her first appearance at the Olympia. He looked at contracts, cheques, translations. He spoke with perhaps two thousand people. He showed his new film to distributors – and sold it. He looked after us with great kindness.

It was surprising to find him using so modest a car as a Vanden Plas 1100. 'He had a Rolls three years ago,' said one of his friends. 'But it was too big. It wasn't *him*. I said to him it was a bit much. So he sold it.

'That's one of the likeable things. His concern for what *others* feel. That, and the fact that he's a fighter. Like now, he's determined to make an American career as big as in France. He'll go on till it's done.' Aznavour was walking down the ramp to the plane, alone. 'Well, he could have turned out far worse, couldn't he?'

Nina Simone, performer

18 APRIL 1967

The last, and only, time Nina Simone had a season in England, she performed in a *boîte* seating perhaps a hundred people. This time it's the Albert Hall, with its capacity of about seven thousand, and other major arenas.

Her life's been rather like that. So is her musical style. Contrastful. She played (when she was plain Eunice Kathleen Wayman) for the first time publicly at the organ of the Methodist Church in Tryon, North Carolina, where her mother was a minister. Later she was at the Juilliard School of Music in New York, hoping to be a concert pianist.

Then she got a job accompanying vocal students in Philadelphia and gave piano lessons. In 1954 she started working in a club in Atlantic City, thus succumbing to the temptation, long felt, to play notes other than those someone else had written down for her. She also needed the $90 a week the job paid.

This progression gave her that sinful feeling. One publicity hand-out says (being publicly attuned to the dolly-dominated, teen-spending sixties) she 'was very surprised to find that she was going down well with the audience, made up primarily of college students and young people.' But she has said: 'It was the kind of bar where the drunks sleep at the back. It was a dive. I felt wicked.' She changed her name to Nina Simone so that her mother, and the mothers of her pupils, wouldn't know.

She was working a shift from midnight till 6 a.m. playing the usual kind of piano drowned by the crunching of cocktail crisps, the sloshing of rye whisky into glasses, and chat. Pop songs, some jazz, even a little Bach. She was asked to sing, too. She sang.

It would be misleading to say she never looked back. There is one story that a Philadelphian disc jockey telephoned her record company a couple of years later to report that her superb version of Gershwin's 'I Love You Porgy' was being heavily requested. 'Forget it – it's a local rumble,' said the voice on the phone. It was not. It sold well over a million copies. But it indicated that Miss Simone did not convince everybody. She was not an overnight, packaged, computerized success.

What was she, in fact? This is the crunch, and the trouble. Some people (those who write columns entitled 'Music' or 'Jazz' or 'Pop' – or those who don't write but who think that way) grow disturbed when artists don't fit neatly into categories. Miss Simone does not, and thereby aligns herself with Duke Ellington who says, 'that's my great big juicy argument – against categories.' Simone, like Ellington, simply performs music. Both of them (and the analogy should be pushed no farther) also perform music with a highly charged dramatic content.

A performance by her *is* a performance. She dresses for effect – a liking for a white dress on her powerful body, chandelier earrings framing her imperious face. Her piano playing, and the playing of the two or three carefully chosen musicians who accompany her, is full of theatrical *coups*, of light and shade.

So is her singing. Her unusually flexible and vibrant voice leaps from blues holler to smooth huskiness to sulky whine. It mates with her material, and these songs provide a rare panorama of American Negro music this century.

A typical programme by her mixes (and contrasts) field chants, church and gospel music, folk songs ancient and modern, blues, jazz, 'standards' by Cole Porter or Aznavour or even A. Newley and L. Bricusse. Sometimes one is even uncertain exactly where to place her songs. One of them, 'Be My Husband', done to a whiplash cymbal rhythm, could be meant as a quasi-chant of the slave era or a dubious celebration of flagellation.

She can, of course, be a jazz singer. She swings often, and she has the gift of fashioning words and tunes as if she were composing them herself at that moment. This, surely, is what jazz is about. But to call her simply a jazz singer is inadequate.

She is now thirty-three, married to a former detective sergeant of the New York police, called Andy Stroud, who is also her manager and writes many of her songs. She was the sixth of eight children. She says that her parents were 'the poorest of the poor'. She believes that if they hadn't discovered at the age of three she had perfect pitch, she might not have got the money (raised by a local music teacher) to begin and continue her musical studies. She has been through the mill.

These experiences make her a devastatingly dramatic, positive woman off-stage as well as on. She fixes her eyes on one from a great height.

She is given to declarations like: 'I hated those snotty night clubs with a passion. Those rich people hovering over you and making you sing those silly requests. People go to night clubs to drink and press somebody – you're just part of the furniture.'

That, as they say, is show business. Now she can have Carnegie Hall (she has) or the Albert Hall or most anywhere she chooses.

Judy on the brink

5 JANUARY 1969

No logic, no analysis, no judgment in the world can completely explain the phenomenon of Judy Garland's performance at the Talk of the Town. She walks the rim of the volcano each second. Miraculously she keeps her balance. It is a triumph of the utmost improbability.

Time has ravaged her singing voice. Within a certain range of scale, tone and volume it survives – most beautifully in a downbeat arrangement of 'Just In Time'. Outside that range, the vibrato is wild and uncontrolled, the pitch uncertain. At times she needs to sing very artfully indeed to disguise the flaws.

But the singing is not so important as the tension and the compulsive gamble of the entertainment. For an hour she conducts a ritual whose contrasts would unhinge most performances. She moves around endlessly, with quick nervous gestures, darting uncertainly to her musical director or the glass on the piano. She bathes the ringside in schmaltz, kissing her admirers, dropping names, tempting applause to dry up. She mixes sharp cracks – 'I'm going to do something extraordinary. Not only am I going to appear . . .' (uproar) '. . . but I'm going to sing a new song' – with indistinct mumblings. Pert professionalism collides with urchin gaucherie.

That her first-night audience, even discounting its preponderantly show-biz nature, gave her so rapturous a reception is still not completely susceptible of explanation, but I will try.

She is a legend, and legends are revered. Yet her secret is partly that she makes fun of the legend – the songs, herself and her image, even the audience. Somehow, too, she has never grown up. Her body, slim and supple in a trouser suit of bronze, is frail and girlish. Yet when she sits in a spotlight to sing 'Over The Rainbow' she is not only Dorothy on the way to Oz, but also a woman in her middle forties whom life has pummelled. The pathos is terrifying.

Above all, she stands for the immaculate nostalgia of a whole generation – Andy Hardy, Odeons on steamy afternoons, records of Glenn Miller and early Sinatra, girls next door. They don't write life like that any more, and Judy Garland evokes it for all those who wish that someone would.

How like a movie script of the forties it is that half of her music was lost before the opening. But it was all right. Bandleader Burt Rhodes listened to her records and produced sparkling orchestrations inside forty-eight hours. They don't make many musicians like that any more either.

Sweet and smoky Ella

7 APRIL 1974

It has perhaps not escaped your notice that Ella Fitzgerald's performances at Ronnie Scott's Club, now (alas) concluded, were by common consensus a triumph. I concur. She was magnificent.

After hearing her perform last Wednesday, the immediate effect – apart, that is, from playing more of her ravishing records – was to make me listen in swift succession to the voices of Sarah Vaughan, Anita O'Day and Morgana King. The intention was to see if the afterglow of tasting her artistry in a club lasted against the challenge of a few rivals. The result was simply to confirm Ella's ascendancy. As an interpreter, a seeker-out of music's subtleties and, above all, as a singer who could inject rhythm into a heap of damp corduroy, she remains without equal.

She has, of course, done almost forty years' singing since she made her first record with Chick Webb's band in 1935. But the pounding her vocal chords have taken shows surprisingly little. True, her voice has lost a little sweetness; it has more smokiness now. She has, indeed, almost two voices. During her masterly long version of 'The Man I Love', for example, she was all honey-softness for the first chorus; then she switched to rough-and-smoky, scat-singing her way through variation after variation.

The years have also given her more vibrato and a slight inability to sustain length of note. But such foibles seem of no importance against the impeccable timing, control, swing and poise of this popular genius. And more. She can move an audience emotionally today as never before. There can scarcely have been a version of 'A Foggy Day' as affecting as that which Ella is currently offering, *in extenso*, with Joe Pass backing her on guitar. Mr Pass' blindingly nimble work was another highlight of the evening, along with Tommy Flanagan's driving piano in an all-star accompanying group.

From the Middle Ages

29 SEPTEMBER 1974

The combined ages of Sammy Cahn, Ethel Merman and Marlene Dietrich make around two hundred, and the songs they sing have nothing to do with rocking around any clocks. After a week when they dominated various London stages, my mind is intoxicatingly awash with Porter, Gershwin and Berlin (not forgetting Cahn) and the continuing vitality of the Middle Ages of twentieth-century popular music has been triumphantly affirmed.

Especially, and unexpectedly, through the humour, words and conquering joy of Sammy Cahn, whose *Songbook* entertainment (New London Theatre) is quite splendid. He is perhaps the most successful practitioner still extant of that dying breed, the professional Tin Pan Alley lyric writer. Sometimes he has written at the corny moon-June level; but at his best, the witty rhymes snap, crackle and explode.

Back in the 1930s he produced 'Bei Mir Bist du Schon' with Saul Chaplin. Collaborating with Jule Styne he wrote those early Sinatra blockbusters, 'I'll Walk Alone' and 'Saturday Night is the Loneliest Night of the Week' among them. Then, with composers including Jimmy van Heusen, came reams of award-winning movie songs, including 'Three Coins in the Fountain', and the 1950s–1960s wave of 'Come Fly With Me' Sinatra hits. It's impossible (as another of his songs says) to list his scores of hits without exhausting my space.

So, these are Cahn's credentials – but what does he *do* for two hours on stage? He delivers, with the timing and manner of a Groucho Marx, hilarious anecdotes about his craft. He explains the unglamorous facts of the hit business. He sings a lot, with Richard Leonard's dazzling piano playing, and has others sing his work too – very well in the case of Lorna Dallas.

His subtle presence holds the show superbly together. 'If it moved, we wrote for it,' he says of his vaudeville clients in the early days. Or again, 'Since we were at the studio, they had first refusal – so they refused it first.' He explains that he doesn't need to feel romantic to write a ballad: 'You write ballads when you're hired to write ballads.' And again, gleefully recalling that 20th Century Fox forgot to write a contract for *Three Coins in the Fountain*. 'So we let them have fifty per cent of it, and remember whenever you hear "Make it mine, make it mine, make it mine", half is ours!'

It's very tart, very American, very good – like a walking-talking *New Yorker*. He also sings parodies of his own and others' songs. 'It's impossible – to make love in a Toyota, it's impossible' is perhaps the most printable. He's the best one-man band in town.

Where Mr Cahn is slyly surprising and unsentimental, Ethel Merman (Palladium) is full-frontally showbizzy, a formidable matron who tells you precisely what you're going to get. 'You wouldn't see me as Mimi in Bohee-meee. They say my voice is pure brass.'

So it is. She belts her way as she has been happily doing for decades, since *Annie Get Your Gun* and earlier, through twenty songs, mostly identified with herself. The audience were warm. The show was zippy, professional and totally predictable. A little of Miss Merman's lusty lung-power goes a fair way.

So, too, with Marlene Dietrich's unchanging repertoire and monumental poses, which were again laid out in London last week (Grosvenor House). She is a living legend, as they say. She still creates chilling moods with anti-war songs like 'Where Have All The Flowers Gone' but the artifice, rather than the art, now shows through. The voice weakens, supported increasingly by Burt Bacharach's brilliant arrangements. Those who love Marlene will love it. For those who think the legend somewhat inflated, the magic is fading.

Bing: The Long Long Road

2 MAY 1976

Bing Crosby, whose voice has been heard more often by more people than that of any mortal in history, sings less for the world than he used to. But that, like the style in which he lives, is through choice rather than necessity.

'It's no more effort to sing today than it was. I don't *practise* any more, except in the week before a show, but I sing for myself everywhere. I can't help it – when I'm shaving, when I'm walking, when I'm writing letters, but never on the golf course. That would be conspicuous. At golf, I only allow myself to whistle.'

There's a house on the outskirts of Guadalajara (pop. 1,200,000) in Mexico whose walls are regularly washed by the gentle Crosby tones – usually, he confesses, the songs of John McCormack, rather than 'White Christmas' – since that is where, for two months each year, he quietly takes his ease. It's a desirable situation, on a small private estate where Pablo Casals bought the first property, overlooking cliff-hanging highways, spiky hills and the emerald fairways of the San Isidro Country Club.

Yet there's nothing grandiose about it. In San Francisco, his home base, he has forty rooms and an English butler. In Guadalajara there's one storey, three bedrooms, a sitting room plump with souvenirs, and a daily woman who comes in to keep the dust down. Bing is often there alone, since his teenaged second family and his wife, Kathryn, are hotfoot about their own careers, a development of which he is properly proud.

A lot of people in Guadalajara know him, and he's much involved in supporting good causes there as elsewhere, but it's not easy to get to him. The house has no telephone. You reach him by calling Houston (Texas), New York or Los Angeles, and in time your hotel telephone rings and by way of Mr Gonzales, the local golf pro (who else?), you are discreetly driven to the man.

All this is of a piece with Bing, his art and what he has made of his life. The trouble with Crosby, and the Parthenon or Everest, or the British Museum, is that they've been around for so long they get taken for granted. We forget what life might have been like without them. Without Bing Crosby, less tuneful, less funny, less benign.

Despite the unparalleled four hundred million records sold and the fifty or more movies – that's easily one for every year since he became a star – he's a low-profile man. In retrospect, he seems to have pursued the role shrewdly. He has been a family man and stuck to average-man hobbies – baseball, football, horses, fishing, as well as golf. His famous quote about anybody believing they can sing as well as he, especially in the bathroom shower, has even encouraged the world to accept, misguidedly, that he has an average-man voice. To entitle his autobiography *Call Me Lucky* completed the deceptive depiction of himself as just an ordinary Joe.

The only thing obviously flamboyant about Crosby is his clothes, and these – his cool blue eyes being colour blind – are accidental. At our first meeting in Guadalajara he wore a plain blue sports shirt, yellow socks, yellow cardigan, red-white-and-blue check trousers and a green golf hat, back of head, and it was so true to legend it seemed to make him less conspicuous than ever.

The legend, however, disguises as much as it reveals, and after fifty years it's time for owning up. Bing Crosby – just in case longevity, his knack of unobtrusiveness and sheer familiarity have obscured the fact – is arguably the most influential singer of our century and probably (since pop is the most practised art form) its most single influential artist in any category. He created a new, personal vocal idiom which is still being copied.

To achieve this, he had his share of luck; but he also managed, in the first twenty-five years of his career especially, a ferocious work rate which carried him through the recording of four thousand songs. Even today he works one third of every year which, 'at seventy-one, ain't exactly retired'.

His famous cool is only part of the man. In Guadalajara, his continuing fascination with music made him enthusiastic, bubbling. He was constantly disappearing to bring in new tapes he'd made. He'd play them and ask whether they would be right for his London appearances. Then, maybe, he would sing a few bars to show his pipes were in order – which they were, his voice deep, strong and virtually unimpaired.

'My voice hasn't changed at all that I know. I've come down a bit in the keys I choose, otherwise I'd be straining for notes and sounding bad. That's all. One of the things I do is a forty-five minute medley, thirty-two songs with at least eight bars of each, and that's no problem.'

Bing is similarly direct and uncomplicated on most subjects, a man who has never shouted on social and political issues, but whose views are not colourlessly cool. He enjoys life. He doesn't, however, think much of modern living.

'Come on, when you get down to it, the family is the basis of everything – of the community, and the community's the base for the state, the state for international government. That's where it's all gone wrong. I deplore the permissiveness of our society. Freedom has become licence, and how can anyone in his right mind deny that the courts are too lenient? Violence hasn't grown only because of that, but it has to be a factor. I notice there are no bombings and no hijackings in Russia, and don't tell me about the courts there.

'Let's be realistic. My children are going to see rough times. You and me, we've had the best of it. Do you go to the movies? I walk out on them a lot. There are good movies – I saw *The Man Who Would Be King* the other day, great, and things like *The Sting* and *Butch Cassidy*. I saw Al Pacino in *Dog Day Afternoon* and he was very foul-mouthed, I don't mind that, because the movie was good. But all these heavy heavings and pantings and gropings you get today – awful! Did you see *Shampoo?* This guy on a motorcycle covering dames on the circuit. There wasn't *anything* they didn't do, including an affair on a toilet seat. It's all too dirty for me, just disgusting.'

On music, he's just as consistent. 'Sure, there are great songs, great artists today. Jimmy Webb, James Taylor, Neil Diamond, Carole King, Bacharach, Sondheim, Mancini. I could go on all day. And there are many more great groups by a hundredfold than there were – and they're *better* too. Modulation, harmony, it's above everything we ever did. But why does rock have to be so much hammer-hammer, so much volume? It gets awful monotonous, and you can't hear the words. There was one of your British groups here recently with the biggest build-up I've ever seen – The Bay City Rollers – and they were just *terrible*.

'Of course, being my age I do look back. To people like Satchmo and Teagarden and Duke, who was the greatest musician of them all and the nicest guy, such geniuses. The most talented woman I ever knew was Judy Garland. She was a great great comedienne and she could do more things than any girl I ever knew. Act, sing, dance, make you laugh. She was everything. I had a great affection for her. Such a tragedy. Too much work, too much pressure, the wrong kind of people as husbands.

'I'll tell you who are my three best male singers. They sing a song like it was written – intonation, phrasing, tune. Buddy Clark – he died in 1949 in an aircraft accident – Matt Munro and Barry Manilow.'

I looked surprised at the names. Bing added Nat King Cole ('an amiable nice fellow'), Frank Sinatra, Tony Bennett and Mel Tormé ('more musicianly than anyone else') without flicking a muscle.

Of himself, he says he's not a singer but a phraser. 'I don't think of a song in terms of notes. I try to think of what it purports to say lyrically. That way it sounds more natural, and anything natural is more listenable.'

He was an elocutionist as well as a singer at his Jesuit school in Spokane, Washington. 'I took those eloquent lines in my teeth and shook them as a terrier shakes a bone,' he says of melodramatic epics like Robert W. Service's *The Shooting of Dan McGrew*. Well, it was fine training. You don't miss a word if Bing sings. He developed almost a fetish about diction when, with the jazzy 1920s blooming, he dropped law at Gonzaga University, Washington, and took to the road as a musician.

'I used to listen to those trained singers, really forcing for volume and high notes and I just couldn't understand what they were *saying*. I sure hated that. I wanted to sing conversationally, to reach people with the meaning.'

There was nothing lucky about that decision; it was a matter of taste. His luck resided almost totally in timing, for he was in his twenties just as the revolutionary explosion of Afro-American music – compounded of black and white musical styles, of blues, gospel, rags, foxtrot and much more and, ultimately, given the name of jazz – was about to sweep the Western world and become, in one form or another, its accepted popular idiom.

The microphone and the radio were also on the horizon, removing the need for singers to bellow, to strive for tone and volume at the expense of lyrical meaning. The mike was to be Bing's instrument, the one he taught the world to use. His style pointed the way for Sinatra, Como, Bassey, Andy Williams, Tony Bennett, or whoever else you care to name, including Tom Jones, Elvis and the rock-and-rollers too. They may not all have copied him, but he showed all of them what could be done.

Inevitably, it seems now, he joined in 1926 the band of Paul Whiteman, 'the King of Jazz', whose smoothly orchestrated approach made the new music acceptable to a mass audience. He had long since ceased to be Harry Crosby: it was Bing because of his youthful fascination with a comic strip called The Bingville Bugle and its hero, Bingo. Whiteman's orchestra contained so many magnificent musicians – the Dorsey Brothers, Jimmy and Tommy; Bix Beiderbecke; Joe Venuti; Eddie Lang; Frankie Trumbauer – that Bing breathed in the slurs and surprising cadences of jazz phrasing as freely as air. His singing reproduced that bounce and relaxation, and although many others, including Al Jolson and Bessie Smith, were innovating too, often earlier than he, it was through Bing's voice that everyone learned the tricks and liked them.

'For phrasing, for taste, jazz was the start of me,' he says now. 'When I went out with Whiteman and ended up as one of the Rhythm Boys, well, I could sing every note of those Tram (Trumbauer) and Bix choruses. That's where I learned to be easy – jazz solos, especially slow, are like a kind of conversation.

'They taught me so much more, too. I roomed with Bix a long time and he was a wonderful man, with a wry sense of humour – quite a gentleman. He drank away too much, everyone knows that, but did he work! And did he move it all on. Stravinsky, Ravel, Debussy, he was always playing these records. I didn't know what he was talking about at first, but it all rubbed off.

'We were like the rock-and-rollers in their early days. Everybody said they were terrible. They said that about us, too, called us swooners and crooners. Even the musicians teased us. It was Tommy Dorsey who first called me the Groaner, would you believe?' Singers were so little regarded they had to sit in the band with an instrument even if they couldn't play one. Crosby was given a peckhorn, like a flugelhorn, till he played some sour notes during *Rhapsody in Blue* and Whiteman, observing that he was lousing up the band, gave him a violin with rubber strings.

It's usually been accepted that in the Whiteman days he was a rake-heller. 'Wine, women and song in that order' is one newspaper quote attributed to him and (during Prohibition) he was jailed thirty days for drinking.

Today he says he didn't raise much hell. 'Sure I drank, but I never missed a job because of it – well, almost. Life was just one big jam session in those days. I'd gamble, play golf, go to Mexico, that kind of thing. But too much has been made of all that. I was just an average guy, really, and I was strongly religious, still am.'

Average guy, certainly; but in the 1920s and 1930s, so many average guys were rebels. Bing included. See this, however, strictly in terms of the revolt of his generation, which spurned the restraining conventions of the pre-1914 social order. It was a cheeky, comparatively light-hearted rebellion, very unlike the sullen heavy-toned dissent of the rock age. These rebels wanted not to overthrow society, but to enliven and amend it. Their weapons weren't demos, politics, pot and doomful Dylan battle hymns, but slang, dancing cheek to cheek, raccoon coats, and jazz. That debonair jauntiness has never deserted Bing, not even in his later phase when he became, by inclination, a conformist ordinary symbol of middle-class America.

Again, the timing was exactly right and lucky, for Bing's mixture of talent and ordinariness arrived just when the Western world started wanting heroes it could relate to rather than flamboyant untouchables. Bing was one of the first anti-heroes. 'He has emerged as a figure that is often affectionately regarded as the ideal American male,' Whitney Balliett wrote in 1953. 'If, in a larger sense, the bigger-than-life common man is a new figure to the world and is the century's hero, Bing may also be one of the first of the Universal Common Men.'

None of this was to become apparent, though, until Crosby left Whiteman in 1930 and began playing the club and vaudeville circuit as a soloist. His capacity for work was astonishing. 'There were no mikes until 1930, so you had to belt it out to audiences of up to maybe two thousand. One week in New York I played eight shows a day, rushing between the Brooklyn and the mid-town Paramount theatres courtesy of the subway, getting on at 42nd Street. I couldn't sing for a week after that.

'I'd stand in the wings a lot watching the comedians work. Frank Fay, Jack Benny, Burns and Allen, people like that, and I'd suck in their timing. That was great for singing. It's timing with a song just like it is with a gag.'

Soon after he went solo, an unknown, Bing married his first wife, Dixie Lee. WELLKNOWN FOX MOVIE STAR MARRIES BING CROVENY, one Hollywood headline stated. It's tempting to think that marriage sobered him. Certainly the relationship worked, he had four sons, and in time most of his family became enmeshed in the many successful businesses – oilfields, race tracks and horses, an orange juice factory, a cattle ranch, gold and uranium interests, baseball team ownership – which have made him very rich. 'He doesn't pay taxes,' as Bob Hope quipped. 'He just calls up the Treasury and asks them how much they need.'

Music, however, was the foundation of wealth, and the man who massaged the incipient Crosby talent in the 1930s was a businessman – Jack Kapp, boss of Decca Records – who encouraged Bing to become the singer reflecting all possible musical tastes.

'He got me to do everything in those ten years or so – blues, ballads, patriotic, country and western, hymns Protestant and Catholic, recitations, Strauss waltzes. And the people I got together with, too. You know, duets with Jolson and Judy Garland and Satchmo; too many to remember. Singing with the Mormon Choir. Chaliapin on my radio show. Jack even pulled in Jascha Heifitz to record with me – "Where My Caravan Has

Rested" – can you imagine that? Today I don't even remember the tune.'

He la-la'd a bit in his Guadalajara sitting room, and so did I, since Bing doesn't mind who he sings with, and then we laughed because we couldn't either of us recall the melody. Not that such forgetfulness is typical. It was in the Kapp days he got the nickname 'One-take Crosby'. He doesn't read music, so he used to have the band play a song through once and then record it straight off.

He needed that knack. Once early recordings like 'I Surrender Dear' and 'Stardust' broke the ice, he was from 1931 the first solo singer to front a regular radio show. It made him a national idol very quickly, and the run of movies helped – from comedy shorts directed by Mack Sennett, through musicals, to the seven classic *Road To* comedies, co-starring Bob Hope and Dorothy Lamour, and, in the 1940s, relatively straight parts like the priest in *Going My Way* which earned him Oscars.

His hits became the eloquent medium of the hopes, nightmares and fantasies of the years he lived through. The love songs have been the accompaniments to courting, marriage, farewells, reunions, deaths of damn near everyone in the English-speaking world over forty. 'White Christmas', with all-time record sales of over thirty million, turned accidentally into the greatest nostalgic anthem of one major war and then, unendingly, of the peace and smaller wars which followed it. 'Buddy, Can You Spare A Dime?' was as much a mirror of the 1930s Depression as was Bob Dylan's 'Blowin' In The Wind' of the agitated, fragmenting '60s.

Today, Bing doesn't miss hit-making or the movies.

'I'd only get bit parts now in movies. But there might be another *Road*' (the last, *Road to Hong Kong*, was in 1962). 'A fellow brought a script, and Hope and I quite liked it. It suited our age. Hope wants it to be more like Monty Python, so maybe . . . But apart from that, I get better exposure on the tube.'

When he isn't working, Bing gets up at seven and breakfasts with his two teenage boys; his first wife died in 1953, and in 1957 he married Kathryn, a former beauty queen who now runs a daily TV chat show, and has usually departed for the studios by the time he surfaces. He reads the papers or books a lot. It takes him two hours to deal with his mail – he's involved in writing for many environmental and health causes. 'I want to save ducks and salmon – and cure arthritis, all that kind of thing. I may make a TV promo in the morning at home for cancer. I lunch in town, hit a few golf balls, maybe see a movie.

'I do exercises every day, five or ten minutes to fight bursitis. But it's walking I'm a fan of. A long brisk walk every day for two or three miles. Up where I live you don't get mugged. You see the street scenes, keep in touch.'

He still, however, prefers to do most of his walking on golf courses, even when he's taking a beating from his fourteen-year-old son, Nathaniel (handicap two, against Bing's nine). His golfing demeanour, cheerful and relaxed, has often seemed a mirror of the man, indeed.

There's also this wonderful true story about Jack Nicklaus, when Jack was at his twenty-second birthday, making his way on the top circuit, very well-behaved, nice, but rather tense whilst playing the Bing Crosby Tournament at Pebble Beach. After a hairy day, Nicklaus was dining quietly with his wife, wanting to be alone, when an urgent telephone call for him was paged. Unwillingly Nicklaus went to the phone, and there was some guy on the line singing 'Happy Birthday' to him. Nicklaus waited, increasingly impatient and managed to say thanks, despite his edginess.

'But who is this?' he asked.

'Bing Crosby,' said the man.

'Oh,' said Nicklaus, 'I'm sorry. I didn't recognize the voice.'

To continue performing, on stage or fairway, Bing has had to watch his diet as much as his exercise. 'I eat everything, but the golden rule is small helpings. I've been 152 pounds for thirty years, except when I had surgery two years ago.'

That's all he says about his operation, which was to remove a grapefruit-sized non-malignant fungus from his left lung. For him to be singing again much as he's done for approaching half a century is astonishing. About all the operation did was to make him stop smoking that symbolic pipe; 'the doctor didn't say I should, but it didn't taste so good anyway.' He still looks little more than fifty, and in his warm unspoiled fashion acts precisely as you'd expect of a man about whom a fine critic, Henry Pleasants, wrote: 'When we hear Bing Crosby, we hear the voice of an old and treasured friend.'

It is absurd, of course, that he is only now making his London debut at the Palladium: we can't count the incident during the bombing of London in the war when the police, worried about the crowd outside a Soho restaurant, asked him to sing to persuade them to disperse. He gave them 'Pennies From Heaven'.

No engagement has been so important to him in his whole life, he says, as this Palladium fortnight, and it's as believable – not just showbiz interview chat – as his statement that London is his favourite city. 'What other city can possibly compare? It's unmatched anywhere for its theatres, its galleries, its music and, I happen to think, for its people. Besides that I can get to racecourses and superb golf courses by the dozen from London in no time at all.'

He reflected a bit more, his mind back on the show. 'I think I ought to come on right at the start of the show, don't you? It's a real pain for people waiting through the whole first half to see the guy they've come to see.'

Thoroughly nice Julie

13 JUNE 1976

The orchestra, forty-strong, were hushed; in the auditorium breaths were held, handkerchiefs crushed in damp hands. Off-stage, the pure cream of the voice perfectly sang the phrase 'All I Want is a Room Somewhere'. And then she spring-heeled into view, the front rows rose in unison to their feet, and seventeen years and a whole Hollywood fairy tale later, Julie Andrews was triumphantly back on a London stage, smooth of face and loosely clad in symbolic Givenchy white.

Nothing can possibly destroy the pleasure which her hour-long wander at the Palladium through the thoroughly ancient but deliciously tuneful world of *Mary Poppins, My Fair Lady* and *Camelot* gave to her admirers. Julie is a legend, indestructible: the ordinary girl from Walton-on-Thames with the extraordinary four-octave voice who started in a family variety act at eighteen, was transported to Broadway stardom in *The Boy Friend*, and created theatrical history after she opened as Eliza Doolittle in 1956.

She is also an image: thoroughly nice, decent, safe, unsexy, ready to show a leg briefly but then sure apologetically to button herself up again. So different, she is, from all that tougher, more abrasive world of pop which has happened since, in the same year of 1956, Elvis Presley also exploded. There's even a chauvinistic brush-stroke to complete the picture. 'She has that terribly British strength that makes you wonder how they ever lost India,' her director, Moss Hart, observed when she battled through her early Eliza problems.

Her image she preserves with religious care, and who can blame her when so faithful a following don't want one hair of it changed? Yet one is allowed to grieve that so little – except a bland unchanging stream of clear sound – has come from the early promise of that remarkable voice.

Singing is about beautiful sound; but popular singing is also about passion, wit, meaning. The songs she still chooses to shelter within encourage the dearth of emotion. She cheated a little, promising to sing songs she hadn't normally had the chance to do, but then limiting herself to a little slight music from Stephen Sondheim and Paul Williams.

It could have been a deliberate display to tantalize us with what might have been, a piece of self-mockery, a careless brush with the passion she has spurned. Who knows? I wish, however, that into this superbly-orchestrated, brilliantly-danced, too-sweet chocolate box of a show she could have injected something unknown, sour, astonishing. She might have surprised herself as well as us.

After Crosby, Tormé

27 JUNE 1976

Crosby on Tormé: 'The most musicianly of singers, and the finest singing entertainer.' Tormé on Crosby: 'Probably the greatest popular singer of all time; certainly the greatest influence on me and everyone else.'

How profligate that, when some weeks are so thin, these two remarkable artists should have opened simultaneously last week. Crosby had never done a theatre season in London; Tormé hadn't performed a supper-room date here for nine years. Both are currently stunning their packed audiences into various states of disbelief.

Bing Crosby, who has a week to run at the Palladium, first. His show has surprises, but the biggest is that that he is here at all, at seventy-two, being in so many ways so true to himself and the art he almost founded. The revelation, the mastery of phrases and cadence, the intimate way are just as you imagined they would be.

Every singer for half a century has, we know, learned from him. And everything he taught is still intact with him except, perhaps, that the range of true tone is a little narrower and the breath doesn't quite last out on final notes. But what compensations he brings us.

Who else, young or old, would be on stage for most of two-and-a-half hours, starting at the start, ending at the end? Who else would sing excerpts from, or sing entire, well over fifty songs? He does almost forty in his personal medley, from 'I Surrender Dear' to 'Mississippi Mud'; his handsome family of four sing-a-long for another ten; he solos on newer ones like 'Send In The Clowns'; he duets with Rosemary Clooney, Ted Rogers and his children.

The opening is brilliant, by the way; an old Movietone News clip of Bing and Astaire at the wartime Stage Door Canteen. From then on it isn't only tearful nostalgia, although hearts and eyes are moved, and the tumultuous standing ovation at the end is an instinctive salute to the daddy of them all. The songs (banal and beautiful), the orchestration, the gorgeous warmth of Rosemary Clooney, Ted Rogers' hard-hitting jokes and the swinging Joe Bushkin Quartet make this an entertainment so memorably bountiful that its few imperfections seem unimportant and most other evenings shrivel beside it.

He swings still, our old and treasured friend. He laughs at himself with dignity. As one curious passer-by inquired of him; 'Didn't you used to be Bing Crosby?' Now we know he is, he is.

Mel Tormé's light, airy and wide-ranging voice is totally intact. He's as relaxed as Bing, as funny and even more dynamic. A further fortnight he has at the Talk of the Town and, if a Crosby ticket is unavailable, at least go hammer at the Talk's portals and insist you see this great entertainer.

He sings a lot of songs, too – a dozen MGM oldies in his *That's Entertainment* sequence; an updated 'Mountain Greenery' with Blood, Sweat and Tears, 'Spinning Wheel' in counterpoint; an exquisitely arranged 'Nightingale Sang in Berkeley Square' that will crack your heart.

But it's his jazz flavour which blows up the storm. He drums à la Gene Krupa, and then launches into a big-band tribute where he scat-sings like Ella and vocalizes all those Basie and Woody Herman riffs like a man possessed with living ghosts. Supreme singing artistry, it is. When he finished, the ecstatic audience jumped to its feet as if they stood on springs.

Diamond: behind the glitter

26 JUNE 1977

Ira Gershwin got it so right when, three years ago, he inscribed a theatre programme of *Porgy and Bess* with these words: 'For Neil Diamond, who sparkles with plenty of plenty.'

Diamond's hallmark is, indeed, abundance. He has, since the 1960s, composed a hoard of idosyncratic songs, some of them excellent. The variety of his subjects and melodies is more interesting than that of most of his contemporaries. As a performer, he charges into battle with conquering enthusiasm and spontaneity. Above all, he unfurls the banner of surprise.

This last quality was especially evident at the Palladium on Friday. The previous evening he had sung, as expected, for around two hours without a break. On Friday he suddenly stopped after ninety minutes, proclaimed an interval, and returned to perform with equal intensity for a further one-and-a-half hours. The audience would plainly have liked him to stay even longer.

His rapport with those listeners was striking. They continually responded to Diamond's moods, sitting enthralled or standing to sing as he commanded them, yet never threatening to overstep the bounds of propriety. No stage-storming seemed likely, not even when he invited one or two people up to join him. Few other popular singers could make themselves so available, yet remain so unscathed.

For this expansive and expensive phenomenon, there is no complete explanation – but the spell his music casts must be part of it. Diamond has, in essence, produced a crafty fusion of modern sounds: rock, reggae, jazz, country, ballad and Broadway are among the elements. He spans the chasms of category.

Not every song he writes is golden. But the conviction with which he interprets his material (even the overblown *Jonathan Livingston Seagull* saga) is awesome. And when he fashions music from the hard experience of his early years in New York – especially the sequence from his *Beautiful Noise* album – the quality of the songs matches the dynamism of the performance.

This was undoubtedly the most artistically satisfying part of the concert. From that *Beautiful Noise* album, he sang the title song, together with 'Street Life', 'Stargazer', 'Surviving the Life', 'Lady-Oh' and the sparkling 'If You Know What I Mean'.

Before and after the break, he ranged through material from all periods of his career, with occasional songs by other hands. The obvious pieces were there, like 'Morningside' and 'Song Sung Blue'. But 'Longfellow Serenade' (a delightful acknowledgement of the American poet) demonstrated more firmly his individuality among modern songwriters.

The production is finally what makes a Diamond concert so special. His band is very talented and completely empathetic. Every note is meticulously in character.

The lighting and stage effects match his musical extravagance. They vary from the glowing Manhattan skyline which is set behind *Beautiful Noise* to the gigantic looking-glass panels in which the whole theatre is mirrored towards the remarkable conclusion of a remarkable entertainment.

The art of Mabel Mercer

10 JULY 1977

One of the major differences between London and New York is supper rooms, those Manhattan pleasure palaces both large and small where the art of intimate cabaret and music survives so lustily. London post-war has had little feeling for them, which perhaps explains why Mabel Mercer has taken forty-one years to come back here from America to perform.

Her name is little known in this country of her birth. She has never had a hit record. She stands apart from most contemporary forms of popular music. She is seventy-seven years young. She is a remarkable and unique artist, one of the great interpreters and guardians of popular song – especially that of Cole Porter's generation, but not excluding Joni Mitchell's.

She is also massively influential. Frank Sinatra has said that singers (himself included) have learned untold lessons from her phrasing and diction. Billie Holiday was among that army.

Mabel Mercer has other heavy armour firing for her – colourful tributes from Leonard Bernstein, Johnny Mathis, Leontyne Price, *et al*; purple passages from a dozen American columnists; capsule descriptions like 'high priestess' and 'Queen of the supper clubs'.

If all this makes her sound too good to be true, then her opening at the Playboy Club, London last week dispelled distrust. She was magnificent, sitting in her usual elegant chair to perform, acting out songs sad and funny in a half-speaking, half-singing voice which she herself has called a basso profundo that sometimes hits the right notes on a good night.

To say she transforms songs into works of art and communicates with her audience in warmly personal terms is accurate, yet maybe deterring. An education she is, but painlessly so. She is naturally entertaining, a born actress, an ageless communicator of joys and sorrows. She sang two dozen songs from a repertoire of around one thousand. At first they were Gershwin, Cy Coleman, Lerner-Loewe pieces, with rhyme schemes neat and classic ('my nights were sour, spent with Schopenhauer').

A superb version of Joni Mitchell's 'Both Sides Now' marked an important change of style: Mabel Mercer picks up good songs whatever their vintage. Then she returned to pieces from her past, 'Chase Me Charlie' and 'It Was Worth It' among them, the witty rhyme schemes still crackling away and her pianist, Jimmy Lyon, providing flowing counterpoint.

That Mabel Mercer is a singer's singer, mainly dealing in the rather unreal world of sophisticated fantasy favoured by the best popular songwriters in the period 1920–50, will be a recommendation for some listeners, if not for others. But her mature artistry, born from a lifetime of performing, touches all her subjects, trite or tart, with a particular sorcery.

The daughter of a black American jazz musician and a white British vaudeville artist, convent-educated in Manchester, she was touring music halls in the First World War. After London shows, a long stay in Paris in the 1930s, and her final emigration to the Bahamas and America, Mabel Mercer's career is finishing in a pop age of gigantic arenas and blockbusting electronics.

The quieter art and elegance of popular song as laid out so sumptuously by her is an experience to be savoured whilst it survives. She is appearing for three more weeks in the Playmate Grill, which is an adequate if not perfect room for her.

Joni Mitchell's masterwork

5 FEBRUARY 1978

January has brought us at least one album in the popular field (to use the conventional phrase) which is unlikely to be bettered this year or to be displaced from its residence in 1978's best twenty. It is unique, magical, adventurous and, since perfection in pop would defy its nature, humanly fallible.

This wonder is Joni Mitchell's ninth album, *Don Juan's Reckless Daughter* (Asylum K63003, £5.49) and it consists of four sides, of which the third for me is largely dispensable; but the other three are manna.

Miss Mitchell, folksy from Canada, raised in classy pop, able to be bitter, yet more often posing as someone hesitant in commitment, especially emotionally, takes with this double album her most decisive step yet towards the music which might one day be her Everest. She has, long since, paid her dues in the once-off *popular* pop song – shortish, strong on melody, light on depth; she has also done the linked song sequence.

Now, she presents songs without particular sequence or especially catchy phrases, but whose musical interest and subtleties will keep them spinning for months on turntables. She has, too, produced one epic which is half-poem, half-concerto, a work of sixteen minutes entitled *Paprika Plains*, evoking her home town in Canada.

This, surely, is her masterwork. The poetic imagery is powerful, quivering, mysterious; never was her voice more sure and appealing. Her piano playing is more than adequate, and the orchestration by an old hero of the British scene, Michael Gibbs, exquisite. Throughout – as, indeed, for much of the whole album – the singing bass-playing of Jaco Pastorious and, less often, the saxophone of his Weather Report companion, Wayne Shorter, lend beauty and distinction to the enterprise.

Paprika Plains, however, is only a part of the riches which blend folk, jazz, rock and symphony admirably. Every song – but especially 'Cotton Avenue', 'Off-Night Backstreet' and the title number – has so much to commend it. Musically and verbally, this is material of immense attraction and sophistication.

The reservations (flaws seems too hard a word) centre on two aspects. Each side is short on time, too short, I think. Artistically, Miss Mitchell has moved so far in enigmatic verbal symbolism and cleverness, she sometimes has problems in maintaining the balance between the demands of the lyrics and the structure of the music. Thank God some popular artists have such problems!

Heartbreak hall

23 JULY 1978

The Pagliacci tradition – smiling bravely through on stage while your heart is breaking – has never afflicted this century's popular music. From blues to rock, many artists have consumed us with their suffering set to music. This art lives too close to life to be inhibited.

The question, then, has never been one of principle, only of degree, of taste, of artistic effectiveness. And rarely has the question been posed more sharply than at the Festival Hall last Tuesday, as Nina Simone, whose musical achievements are immense, went through an anguished, unforgettable evening which began in triumph but which ultimately disintegrated, her passionate art becoming uncontrolled harangue.

The history of this great singer, whose dramatic gifts and musical range make her unique, has rarely been untroubled. Fiercely proud, a civil rights campaigner in the 1960s, she has lived stormily with the commercial world of pop. She claims to have been frozen out, boycotted.

Four years ago, disenchanted, she abandoned performances. Apart from one London concert and a triumphant visit to Israel, she had virtually disappeared. Then, recently, a magnificent album (*Baltimore*, CTI label) was issued, her first for years. Many in the packed and loving hall on Tuesday assumed she was restored and ready to sing.

From the start, uneasy disquiet flooded from the stage. Her demeanour was mournfully regal. She sang superbly at times, but overlaying her performance was a sense of lament, almost of doom. Lines like 'I feel discouraged, I think my work's in vain' and, in particular, a vast improvisation during the already sad July Collins song, 'My Father', in which she referred to 'bearing up my coffin', came through as if she were in agony, artistically sustained but terrifyingly real.

During the interval, fans left notes on her piano. One, obviously asking how she was, snapped her restraint totally. For several minutes she conducted a private dialogue with one stage-storming exhibitionist. The rest of the evening was part-music, part-pleading as Miss Simone recited her problems – lack of money; assaults upon her person or integrity; loneliness.

'Give me love, give me attention, give me money,' she sang at last before, inevitably, referring to Judy Garland and Billie Holiday. She claimed to be not of this world, 'commanded' the audience to leave 'phone numbers to help her through depressions, and suffered a person allegedly representing 'Women Against Rape' to seize the microphone and lecture those who believed they had come to hear music.

Music of unmatchable quality they had heard too – at times. For admirers of Miss Simone's artistry; however, this final shambles was a sadness – as also was the incitement to some moronic onlookers to scream that they would kill whoever harmed her.

Interviews are interviews; concerts should be concerts. That Miss Simone's artistry merits rich rewards is obvious from her new album which – oddest thing of all, considering its splendour – she says was recorded under conditions she found almost unbearable.

Sinatra and the generation grip

17 SEPTEMBER 1978

To talk about Frank Sinatra, whose week-long festival at the London hall of that name has now concluded, is scarcely to talk about music alone. With Sinatra, voice slowly rusting as his seventh decade rolls inexorably on, we are discussing the uncanny power which particular masterpieces of popular song, uniquely interpreted, can exert over the mass consciousness of a whole generation.

So, all the clatter there has been about the decline of the voice (relatively marginal, anyway, these past five years) seems almost irrelevant. Of course his voice is going. The range is not so comprehensive; he pitches it lower; the breath doesn't consistently survive longer lines; and there are times when the husky patina crumbles into gravel as he descends the scree of a Gershwin cadence.

All true, and to this can be added other qualifications about his concerts according to taste – including their bizarrely idolatrous nature and Sinatra's excessive tendency to amend other people's lyrics with personal phraseology which sometimes works, but which too often includes synonyms as ugly as 'broad' for 'woman'. But, as Ché observes in *Evita*, that's not the point, my friend.

Sinatra's grip on a generation, from the time he came out with Tommy Dorsey in the 1940s and then immortalized *Nancy* and other songs with Axel Stordhal, never rested upon his vocal quality. It sprang from his way with a song. He could, for example, reshape any melody into a unique reading. He enhanced that gift with the equally jazz-like attribute of swing, a talent especially unfolded in his 'Swinging Lovers' interpretations. Along with this went his diction, clear and crisp.

At the Festival Hall, these qualities have still burned brightly. His mastery of melodic pace and phrasing dominate, for example, the old anthem, 'The Lady Is A Tramp'. Add to this his almost infallible choice of songs and the class of his arrangements – how he loves to recite the litany of great modern composers, and the arrangers he uses, dominantly Don Costa and Nelson Riddle – and the ultimate secret is closer.

For all these elements coalesce into one illusion. The heart of his performances last week lay in a group of songs, some old some new, which he sang with a sumptuous thirty-two-strong string section, and in a medley where he sat in the half-light, cigarette glowing, telling us (from *The Girl Who Got Away*) that 'the road gets rougher, it's lonelier and tougher', that 'suddenly you're older'.

And with those sudden strings, those bleak words, he opened up the cave of nostalgia for the generation who mostly formed his audience. He made them recall what they'd done or failed to do, where they'd been proud or ashamed, how they'd laughed or wept – time destroyed then recreated by one man's style. Like it or not – and this can happen in popular music as in no other art form – Sinatra is the keeper of a multitude's memories.

He entered, one should add, with no musical introduction, as if his presence were enough. He introduced some new songs from an album to come, of which Elton John's 'Remember' had a memorable cellos-and-basses introduction, Costa-scored. He made a gaffe with a sickly quasi-religious piece about father and son. He departed with ritual gifts, chunky, unabashed and velvet-haired. History has him.

Sarah still divine

12 NOVEMBER 1978

After all these years – around thirty at the top for her – there ought to be few surprises left from Sarah Vaughan. Yet each time you see her, the audacity of her talent confounds you. However repetitive is her stage 'business', she always finds something new to do with the music.

She brought off several such coups at Ronnie Scott's Club during her autumnal visitation last week. 'East of the Sun' was one – a superb reading of a pleasant song, her voice entwined with Walter Booker's bass fiddle lines. It wasn't the first time this duo had done it, of course, but the illusion of spontaneity was intense.

She had another triumphant marriage of voice and arrangement with Ellington's 'I Got It Bad'. Subtly, the simple slow beat behind her shifted into a loping 'Western' metre reminiscent of Ferde Grofe's 'On The Trail'. That almost jokey move shook the song up, and us along with it. By such gestures she ensures that the legacy of classical popular song endures in the memory, since she continually reminds us of the right compositions, brilliant or banal, by refashioning them.

This is the jazz in her, partly innate, but also absorbed down the years in clubs and concert hall, playing with fine musicians from Charlie Parker to her present pianist, Carlton Schroeder. She is one of the great daring improvisers of the century. But no one could succeed so well purely by rephrasing a lyric or a melody. There is much more.

First, the voice and its many colours. Smoky clubs and wearing travel have marked it, but the range of emotion, pitch and colour remains remarkable, from darkest contralto depths to piping peaks, and always full of emotional conviction. She could easily have made an opera singer.

Second, the band and its many talents. How well Miss Vaughan understands the need to have inspiring musicians playing with her. Her usual superb trio of Schroeder, Booker and drummer, Jimmy Cobb, is complemented currently by her new husband, Waymon Reed, playing soft flugelhorn counterpoint. With her voice often used as an instrument, it's a marvellous quintet. There's a time, too, when she sits at the piano and plays for herself; remember, it was as second pianist that she got her great chance with Earl Hines in 1943.

With these formidable assets she conquers, but in truth there are other aspects of the act which have become rather less compelling, including the lengthy and banal dialogues she conducts with the audience. There is now a ritualistic air to her criticisms of the sound system, her asking customers if the microphone stands bother them and requests for face tissues. But then, ritual is of the essence with many great artists. Perhaps it helps to reassure us, before the magic takes effect, that they're only human.

Chapter Nine

Off-stage People

Composers, impresarios, producers, directors. They, too, form part of the pattern of popular music and a few of them – not necessarily the obvious ones – are represented in this chapter. Some were written about because they stood at a particular milestone in their careers – Norman Granz with the twenty-fifth anniversary of his invention, Jazz At The Philharmonic; Hal Prince as he waited to launch *Cabaret* on London. But both, of course, had a glittering decade still to come, for Granz continued to present great artists and to record them on his Pablo label, while Prince kept on staging musical theatre hits all the way to *Evita* in the late seventies. Other subjects were interesting to me because of what they stood for (Irving Berlin as, perhaps, the pre-eminent mainstream composer of the century) or because of what they had to say, which was certainly true of Jeffrey Kruger, who projected in surprising ways some of the more unexpected aspects of the pop music business.

Hal Prince: 'You've got to hustle'

11 FEBRUARY 1968

'For me as a director, *Cabaret* has been the most important show I've ever done. Before it opened I'd had a couple of flops. I had this feeling I'd been losing too much of other people's money. There were questions about me as a creative person. It *had* to be a success.'

Harold Prince, also known as Hal Prince or Prince Hal, is talking about his show whose London production opens in a fortnight's time. On Broadway it is a hit, now in the second year of its run. Artistically, the conception and execution of this musical about Berlin in the thirties, based on Van Druten and Isherwood, are totally brilliant. Financially, Prince's backers have, as so often, had reason to rejoice. It's odd to find him so concerned about flops and losing money. For in the tough business of the Broadway theatre he has, very swiftly, made himself a millionaire and enriched an army of angels.

His reputation has, to his chagrin, been built as producer rather than director. This month, plump and ruddy of face, sideburned and slightly balding, he has been bouncing in and out of London preparing Judi Dench, Peter Sallis, Lila Kedrova and the rest of the cast for the *Cabaret* opening. February is quite a month for him, with *Fiddler on the Roof* opening in Hamburg (the thirteenth production around the world) and *West Side Story* in Vienna.

Musicals have been his money-makers, and not only for artistic reasons. Because they are so costly to stage, they paradoxically offer the greatest scope for economies. And to a field where budgets tend to be supremely elastic, Prince has brought both artistic flair and the extra, crucial element of sound business methods.

'I don't like to waste money, that's my neurosis. I cost everything down to the last button. The *Cabaret* fabrics I got in second-hand shops – no *haute couture*. I modelled the set on a sordid little club I used to hang around in Stuttgart when I was in the army in 1951. I *hate* paying anybody $8,000 a week. So I don't like the single big-star show. I like plots which involve four or five people equally. That also happens to please me better as an artist.'

The going price for staging a Broadway musical is now around $500,000. Prince squeezed the *Cabaret* bill down to $400,000, yet it has not inhibited him as a director. In its Broadway version, *Cabaret* seems a lavish, abundant show, bizarre and beautiful. *Fiddler on the Roof* appears to cut no corners either, but its 150 investors had only to find $375,000 to put the show on the road. Their profit already approaches 1,000 per cent.

In a sense, indeed, Prince is the very model of a hard-selling American business man. He got his first show, *The Pajama Game*, moving in 1955 by holding auditions in the drawing-rooms of friends. The composers and a few chorus girls would belt out the songs while Prince recited the story line and passed round Scotch to prospective investors. Before he moved on to the next audition, he carefully poured back unfinished drinks into the bottle. 'I wasn't the brightest guy in my class,' he says, 'but that's an advantage. You know then you've got to hustle.'

Prince hustled his way through college – 'I knew exactly what I wanted: to be a writer and director. Until I was thirty I never slept more than four hours a night' – and on to an apprenticeship with the illustrious Broadway director, George Abbott. Then he teamed up with the late Robert Griffith for *The Pajama Game*.

'We were so busy stage-managing that show, we never saw it from the front till six months after it opened. That was my problem. I got landed with this producer image – the man with the big fat cigar. I hated it. It took me ten years as a producer before I *directed* anything.'

By the time that happened, Prince had enjoyed five hit shows in a row, endured his first two flops and met his wife, Judy, in Paris. They married in October, 1962. 'I'd been a bachelor a very long time and I thought marriage would eliminate this neurotic demand I have to keep busy, but it hasn't.

'I can't wait to move on to the *next* show. You get to hate a hit very quickly, because the fun goes out of it. There's only the terrible problem of keeping the standard up. I get very restless when I'm not busy.'

At forty, Prince takes his success and his money coolly. His Manhattan house is modest, a rumpled lived-in place. There he is planning a movie and two new musicals – *Zorba The Greek* and *Billy Liar*.

'Spending money isn't equatable with the good life. It makes me uncomfortable. The so-called rewards of success, the Rolls-Royce, the house in the country, don't interest me at all. I'm a worrier, I'd get a prize for that. It's not difficult right now to have terrible long periods of the blackest depression. I have them about my work, about America, everything.

'The greatest happiness I can know will be when guys like you write "Mr Prince, director" instead of "Mr Prince, producer-director".'

Norman Granz: JATP is twenty-five

21 APRIL 1968

'I don't believe in a stamp-collecting attitude – these people who want one of *every* period. At first I bought madly, but now I know which two or three pictures contain the essence of this man for me. These I am keeping. I've balanced my portfolio.'

Thus Norman Granz explains his decision to unleash twenty-five Picassos on the market, at Sotheby's, on Tuesday. Though he is arguably the most important impresario-producer jazz has known, his attitude to records is similar. He has a hundred or so only. 'To keep stacks of them it's physically impossible to listen to would be foolish. A couple of LPs can capture the genius of any great musician.'

This year is the twenty-fifth anniversary of Granz's invention, Jazz At The Philharmonic. These overwhelming presentations, which had on one bill more big names than any touring shows before or since, were fascinating in themselves, if not always artistically successful. They brought together musicians of differing styles and backgrounds and let them react against each other in jam sessions.

Granz's tours also ensured that millions of Americans who happened not to live on either coast, or in Chicago, got to hear great jazz artists in the flesh, and by bringing JATP to the Continent in 1951, he opened the way for the landslide of jazz concerts which similar numbers of Europeans have enjoyed since the mid-1950s.

Granz ran his shows because, obviously, he liked jazz. He also wanted to make money, which he did – one of the few men to become very rich indeed through jazz. There was a third and crucial reason. He was combating racial prejudice.

'Billie Holiday came crying to me – it was 1941, I was just a college boy –

because her friends couldn't go into this club in Los Angeles to hear her. So I went to the owner and said why didn't he let me take over the place on the day he was closed and run a jam session. I did it and I completely desegregated the house. I had Nat Cole's Trio and Lester Young and some of Duke's musicians. It was very successful and the clubowner didn't worry about black and white once he saw the green. He could make a lot of money. There was nothing illegal about desegregation, see, it was just the custom. That was the pattern I followed, with Jazz At The Philharmonic and everything. To concentrate on breaking down custom by giving a carrot to promoters. It worked.'

In today's situation, such tactics seem, like so much else in white America's approach to civil rights, too little and too slow. But in the context of the time they were almost revolutionary. Granz smashed segregation in club after club on the West coast. In one ballroom which refused to allow Count Basie in to hear Harry James, Granz threatened to produce ten white witnesses who would say that admission was refused after tickets had been bought. 'The owner thought it would work out cheaper to let us in.'

Once Granz launched JATP, it became a nation-roving spearhead for desegregation, earning him the National Negro Publishers' Association award in 1949. 'I kicked off in 1943, with just a single concert. The big auditorium in LA was the Philharmonic. I designed a bill which said "Jazz Concert at the Philharmonic", but it wouldn't fit the type-size I wanted. So I dropped the word 'concert'. That's how the title happened.

'In 1945, the first national tour was a disaster. But in 1946, with Lester Young and Coleman Hawkins, it was a hit. For the next eleven years we did two ten-week tours a year, covering about fifty or sixty towns each time. We never played a segregated concert – not even in New Orleans. We staged the first lunch counter sitdown too, at Jackson, Michigan, around 1947. The musicians waited behind the counter stools, sitting down as they became empty. We were half an hour late for the concert and we still hadn't eaten – but we made our point.

'I smile when I hear that well-worn line about JATP just doing rabble-rousing, showy stuff. The tapes of those concerts prove we didn't. Critics would hear one honking blues by Illinois Jacquet and damn the whole show. They forget all the ballads, the MJQ, the Ella and the rest. Other artists seem to get away with it more easily. Like today The Beatles are respectable and the days of the teeny-boppers are forgotten.'

Since 1957 Granz has put together JATP tours only seldom. Star musicians, he says, tended to have their own groups by then and didn't want to jam. 'I had no interest in simply presenting ready-made shows. Being an impresario isn't a very profound occupation. It just needs judgment of pricing and audience. With JATP I could *produce* the thing creatively.'

In 1959 he sold his splendid jazz label, Verve – and, increasingly uneasy with America, moved to Europe, where he now lives, wheeling between Geneva and London and New York. Today he presents a few artists in whose work he fervently believes – Ella, Duke (though a failure between them to agree on terms has doused hopes of an Ellington tour this year), Oscar Peterson, Ray Charles.

He is not bored with jazz, but with the business of presenting it. He wants (as with his Picassos) to move on. 'Maybe I'll produce Hochhuth's *The Soldiers* in America. And I want to make a very political movie about Vietnam. Don't smile. I was an editor with MGM long before I took up the jazz business.'

Irving Berlin: salute at eighty

12 MAY 1968

Irving Berlin's secret, says Bing Crosby, is very simple. He writes songs that are eminently singable. Crosby's bank balance proves it. In twenty-five years, the easy, sentimental lilt of Berlin's 'White Christmas' has harvested several million dollars for Crosby and the composer. This is the most lucrative pop song ever known. Over four hundred artists have recorded it. Disc sales approach one hundred million.

'I am a ham,' Berlin himself once said, 'I think to be a good song-writer you've got to be a kind of ham.' He means, I take it, that his songs are simple, that they deal sentimentally with the preoccupations of Western mass society – love, home, happiness, self-pity, and giving people what they have *wanted* to hear before they realized it themselves.

The Niagara flow of his music began with *Alexander's Ragtime Band* in 1911. Then came the big musicals of the 1910s and 1920s – the Ziegfield Follies and Music Box revues – and sheaves of lasting ballads such as 'Always', 'What'll I Do?', 'The Song Is Ended' and the rest. The great movie musicals of the 1930s were his, especially *Top Hat* and *Follow The Fleet* for Fred Astaire and Ginger Rogers. In the last war there were the long-running show *This Is The Army* and dominating songs of optimism like 'It's A Lovely Day Tomorrow', which he sent to Britain before Pearl Harbour. He followed it with buoyant musicals (*Annie Get Your Gun*, *Call Me Madam*) which were the hallmark of an era until rock 'n' roll broke up the pop music scene.

He is arguably the pre-eminent American popular composer of the century. Jerome Kern was perhaps the more beautiful melodist, Cole Porter more sophisticated, Gershwin more musically ambitious. But no one has quite caught the American spirit like Berlin – the optimism, brashness, energy and sentimentality of its people.

Alexander's Ragtime Band is the cornerstone of twentieth-century American pop music, which has become the pop of the Western world. Before Berlin wrote it, pop had been sweet ballads and waltzes and polkas and music-hall or musical-comedy songs. With *Alexander*, the syncopation of Negro jazz was first used to shape a commercial Tin Pan Alley hit. The ragtime craze swept the West, made fortunes for ballroom owners, and has ignited virtually every development in pop music since.

Berlin's songs have reflected more than the exploding America of those years. 'God Bless America' (1938) was soft-sell patriotism three years before the Japanese attacked. He has given the country the hymns of its frontier dream (*Annie Get Your Gun*) and written the musical background to war. *Call Me Madam* symbolizes American folksiness caught up in the nation's post-war world responsibilities. His lack of significant activity in recent years perhaps reflects the way in which the American dream has been steadily encroached upon by the nightmare.

If his music can be equated with that American dream, so can his life. He was born Israel Baline in Southern Russia, on May 11, 1888, youngest of the eight children of a rabbi. When the family emigrated, Berlin was four, and New York soon drew forth those qualities which Americans seek in their folk-heroes.

He was sturdily independent. In his teens he worked around clubs and vaudeville theatres as a singing waiter. There was tragedy – his first wife died in 1913 soon after their honeymoon – and novelette romance when, in 1926, he secretly married Ellin Mackay, daughter of a communications multi-millionaire.

He never learnt to read or write music (another fashion he has given to pop composers) and he knows only one key, F sharp major. He works on a special piano with a lever which can transpose his melodies. He attributes his melodic simplicity to his lack of technical knowledge, and the straightforwardness of his lyrics to the fact that American is not his native tongue.

'Irving Berlin is the greatest American song composer,' said George Gershwin. 'He has vitality which never seems to lose its freshness. His songs are exquisite cameos of perfection. Each one is as beautiful as its neighbours. Irving Berlin is America's Franz Schubert.'

John Green: time running out

22 SEPTEMBER 1968

'If anyone had told me in 1965 that I'd spend two years as Lionel Bart's arranger,' said John Green, 'I'd have said he had rocks in his head.' Mr Green, musical director, orchestrator, choral arranger, part-composer of the movie *Oliver!*, which opens in London on Thursday, intends no detraction – he adds, indeed, that he wouldn't have missed a minute of it. But you can see what he means.

Before the English creator of *Oliver!* was born, Mr Green, then called Johnny, had composed songs which (unlike Mr Bart's) have become part of the permanent jazz-pop repertoire: 'Body and Soul', 'I Cover The Waterfront', 'Out of Nowhere', 'Coquette', 'I'm Yours'. He has written concert works. He has won four Oscars, either as composer or musical director or both, during three decades of movie work ranging from *The Great Caruso* to *West Side Story*. He has written stage musicals. He has led dance bands and conducted every kind of orchestra from pit to symphony.

Last year, when he was in the midst of his labours on *Oliver!*, was his first absence from the well known Hollywood Bowl concerts in eighteen consecutive seasons. He is one of those supremely versatile American professionals, like Leonard Bernstein and André Previn, who move between musical categories in a free and fluent way which seems impossible in Britain.

Such chameleon variety may appear an enviably fulfilling career pattern in music. Yet in his late fifties, John Green, whose physiognomy and carnation buttonholes aptly suggest both Malcolm Sargent and Noel Coward, is far from fulfilled.

'Versality has undermined my career as a composer. What I really want to do is to write a great stage musical or a musical that's intended specifically for the screen, like *Gigi*, or a symphony that means something. All my life I've been sidetracked.'

He was born into a rich New York banking family. At eight he wrote his first serious work, a tone poem called *Washington Crossing the Delaware*. But his father believed he was born to be an administrator. 'I remember his telling me, "You can be a pretty good banker or merchant or doctor and still hold your head up in community, but there's no bum like a pretty good artist – and I think you're pretty good."'

Apparently compounding his problem, Green took an economics degree at Harvard and also wrote his first big song *Coquette*. After college, he even tried working in a Wall Street bond house, but quit after six months to become Gertrude Lawrence's accompanist.

For her, in 1930, he wrote *Body and Soul.* It was one of a package of four songs for which she paid $250 outright, but when it became a hit, she returned eighty per cent of the copyright to Green and his lyric writer.

He became a rehearsal pianist, then orchestrator, then conductor for Paramount. Commissions began to flow in. For Paul Whiteman he wrote the *Night Club* suite of six impressions for three pianos and orchestra, and when Jack Buchanan brought him to London in 1933 to compose the score of a musical (*Mr Whittington*) he also recorded with Carroll Gibbons and wrote a BBC musical with Jimmy Dyrenforth. Back in America he plunged into a long series of radio shows.

The first Broadway show he composed (*Here Goes The Bride*) flopped and he was tempted to form a dance band – Johnny Green, His Piano and His Orchestra. He was very successful – not least in his enduring recordings with Fred Astaire, including 'Just The Way You Look Tonight' and 'Pick Yourself Up' (one of the first pop records with a genuine fugue inbuilt) – but in 1940 he impulsively paid off his band and tried again to barnstorm Broadway. For a second time his show (*Hi-ya Gentlemen*) flopped and, with his money running low, he became musical director for *By Jupiter!*, the last Rodgers and Hart show, and was suddenly successful again. The reviews wrote about him at length; 'he moulded the people on stage,' one said. He wrote his third Broadway show *Beat The Band* for George Abbott – the first failure George ever had – but when MGM pressed him with big money offers, he bought his way out of a deal to conduct the new Rodgers and Hammerstein show *Oklahoma*, and went to Hollywood.

California has been his base thereafter. His first Oscar, for *Easter Parade*, came in 1947. In 1949 he became MGM's Director of Music – administrator and creator once more – and in the same year conducted the Los Angeles Philharmonic for the first time at the Hollywood Bowl. Since then, movies and conducting have filled his days. 'I've never found time to do the one thing I really want to do.'

In these terms, *Oliver!* is just one more distraction, although Mr Green would doubtless dispute the choice of word. 'It's turned out to be a two-year job, because the scoring of a motion picture is an engineering job based on precise techniques. There were forty-one minutes of difficult background music to compose for *Oliver!* and fourteen songs to be orchestrated. If you want to know why that takes so long, I'll tell you. You go into Chappells and buy a piece of sheet music and later, much later, you wind up with a completely orchestrated and choreographed number maybe ten minutes long.

'All this I enjoy – in fact *Oliver!* is the most rewarding thing in its genre

I've ever dealt with. Dramaturgically Bart's tunes work whether they're standards or not. But I still want more. Frankly I've been through a period of complete and utter disdain for contemporary music – not only pop and The Beatles, but serious music too, from *musique concrète* onwards. I've revised my opinions somewhat, I've less of a closed mind, but I can't escape my idolatry of professionalism. I've hated this golden age of the amateur. I simply don't believe that *anybody* can write a song or play a guitar. That's one big reason for my involvement with *Oliver*! It's been a literate, fascinating challenge, something really worthwhile.

'I know that time is beginning to run out. I'm about to write a serious choral work based on the Book of Job. I need ten years I haven't got to develop my symphonic repertoire as a conductor. Above all I want to do what Leonard Bernstein has been able to do – compose serious music when that was the right thing, and light music when that was right. I suppose it's strange to sound as if one has yet to begin as one approaches sixty.'

Henry Mancini: against the deadlines

25 OCTOBER 1970

Perhaps only a few among the audience who will ultimately see the movie thriller, *Salem Come to Supper*, produced by Mel Ferrer, will feel sick. But it's already happened to studio musicians who played Henry Mancini's score. They rested before continuing.

The film wasn't to blame, but the sounds they themselves created. Writing for the odd line-up of five keyboards and seven woodwinds, Mancini eerily tunes one harp and one piano to a quarter-tone down. 'It gives you vertigo to listen because the Western ear just isn't attuned to it. In Persia and Japan they *think* quarter tones. They sing naturally in the cracks – we don't.'

Mancini, a very prestigious movie composer indeed – *Charade, Shot in the Dark, Breakfast at Tiffany's* and more, plus the hit tunes like 'Moon River' that went with them – is in town to conduct at the first Filmharmonic concert at the Albert Hall. He has surprising views on many matters musical.

Movie music: 'I don't feel constricted. You play the rules – like playing within the confines of a football field – and you weave patterns freely once you accept that. That's one game. A Broadway musical, which will eventualize eventually, is another game, but I'm not in awe of Broadway. I play the concert game too – I've just recorded my first suite with the Philadelphia Orchestra.'

Composition: 'I write most things at home on a rented piano, but I don't *need* a piano. What comes out at the end of the pencil is in my head.'

Rock and jazz: 'Some rock musicians are very indulgent. They once saw Ravi Shankar take half an hour to tune up and they think that's for always. I've seen Segovia do it in one minute. Musicianship, though, is up one thousand per cent on five years ago. Blood Sweat and Tears – brilliant. They're almost as big as the original Benny Goodman band, and with overlays they're bigger. So the big band sound is back, isn't it? Creedence Clearwater – a marvellous honesty about them. Johnny Cash – one of the great jazz singers; an honest directness about him, like Armstrong. And Miles Davis. Well, someone had to set down the guidelines as to how far rock and jazz can be fused. With *Bitches Brew* he's put it all together for the next ten years.'

The past: 'My wife had sung with Mel Tormé's Meltones, and I was in awe of that music. But now I don't look back to any golden age. It's the future that's golden.'

Pressures: 'I'm a creature of assignment. I work best against a deadline. Is there any other way to write music?'

Jeffrey Kruger: hit record roulette

26 NOVEMBER 1972

The Beatles, Stones, Simons, Garfunkels, Led Zeppelins, Osmonds and Slades will perhaps not believe it, but the *New Musical Express* says that the biggest-selling album of the last decade in Britain was *Little Drummer Boy* by the Harry Simeone Chorale. *The Sound of Music* album will probably overtake Drummer Boy's 13·5 million sales by end-1972, but the statistic reveals the plump midriff of pop music's profile.

Mr Jeffrey Kruger will not be surprised. *Little Drummer Boy* was on his record label, Ember, and after two decades in the music business he has grown used to turning over a useful penny in areas not especially fashionable.

He calls himself a television addict; and throughout the day at his luxurious, antique-heavy office in Belgravia, the colour TV flickers soundlessly before his eyes. In 1968, in Las Vegas, he saw a then unknown singer-guitarist on TV in his hotel room. He got second rights in the musician, Glen Campbell, from Capitol Records and put out six albums on the Ember label. All made the album charts.

He met Liberace just as fortuitously. Kruger switched from the Panam New York flight to TWA at the booking counter at Heathrow because he'd seen the movie Panam were showing. Liberace was on TWA too. Within six hours, Kruger had persuaded Liberace to record with him – and, following his recent visit, Liberace's name is re-established in Britain.

Few people outside the business will know of Kruger. But he has shown remarkable staying power; and his sharp commonsense has arguably done more than any other man's both to reflect and to shape popular music taste here.

In November, 1953, when he was selling 'shorts and Superman' for Columbia Pictures and playing club piano spare-time, he opened the Flamingo Club, first at the old Mapleton Hotel, later in Wardour Street. It's perhaps the longest-running popular music club anywhere and has uncannily reflected pop vogue.

It began as a jazz club. Later, it specialized in rhythm-and-blues, becoming a major breeding house for talent. Jimi Hendrix, Georgie Fame and Desmond Dekker broke through there. More recently, it's been a progressive rock centre.

'If I'd wanted to develop a mad empire, I could have signed and exploited many more people,' says Kruger modestly. 'But too many people get too greedy in our business. I work only with people I like.'

Even by that criterion, he hasn't exactly wasted his time. After seeing *Rock Around The Clock* in America in the mid-1950s he pulled back Tony Crombie from a jazz tour in Israel, formed a new band, got them to learn the seven tunes from the film, and when rock 'n' roll mania hit Britain had Tony Crombie and the Rockettes (and four more groups) ready to leap on to vaudeville stages.

'Crombie took £3,500 in the first six days at Portsmouth Empire. It was the best week of my life.' Kruger also produced the first British rock 'n' roll film, *Rock You Sinners*, with once-trendy artists like Terry Dene.

He sees more growth, indeed, in the concert field than in any other. 'The public are so fickle, you see. More than ever. And most artists only want you when they're climbing. Then they knife you when they've made it.

'Look at the charts. Six months or so ago, if you'd tried to re-release old records, the DJs would never have played them. The charts were full of progressive pop. Now, you get a couple of Osmonds, a couple of progressive, a couple of freaks, a couple of reissues – and that's the charts. There's no loyalty to artists, no criterion on talent.'

The telephone rings; Kruger lifts an American cigar ('Cuban makes me ill') from his square brown face and asks an airline PRO to be very nice to Gladys Knight on her flight home. 'D'you know,' he adds, 'you've as much chance playing roulette of getting lucky as you have trying to pick a hit record today. I'll stick to bread-and-butter albums – jazz, country and western and Liberace. Those I know I can sell.'

Chapter Ten

Times Past

Popular music has always been marked by continual vogues, fads and shifts of fashion. Few people tried to sell yesterday's music, except in specialist areas like jazz and blues, until the 1960s. Then, the so-called 'nostalgia' bandwagon began to roll. Some bands aped the music of past decades. Record companies ransacked their archives, pushing out compilations of everything from old crooners and vaudeville artists to (by the 1970s) early rock 'n' rollers. A stream of books on popular music people and periods followed the acceptance of 'pop' as a subject for critical writing within the columns of newspapers both serious and frivolous. 'Nostalgia' records and bands reflected, in part, the rejection by one generation of their offspring's music – pre-Elvis versus post-Elvis – and of divisions *within* generations too. But this surge of interest in the past also signalled a growing widening of taste, together with a realization that popular music forms a vibrant and inescapable counterpoint to twentieth-century life.

The two long pieces here, both written in the 1960s, show my own fascination with the musical past and the interplay of music with history. *Sound of the Forties* was part of a survey of that decade's general history published in the *Sunday Times Magazine*. From the same publication comes *Lilli Marlene*, part of a series called *Alamein and the Desert War*.

Sound of the Forties

3 JANUARY 1965

In 1945 Gertrude Stein heard a Paris concert by a section of the American Band of the Allied Expeditionary Forces which Glenn Miller had originally formed. 'Jazz,' she said afterwards, 'is tenderness and violence.'

Today, looking back to the early 1940s when he played in an RAF swing band called the Squadronaires and was Britain's finest jazz trombonist, George Chisholm says: 'There was this edgy feeling with the people we played for – not knowing what would happen tomorrow. The more frantic the sound, the better they liked it after a few beers. The only other kind of music they wanted was when they were dreaming of peace or their girl and crying into their beer. Everything was very fast two-beat rhythm or else slow ballad – nothing in between.'

'Music became too important,' says bandleader Woody Herman. 'Half the bands and singers wouldn't have made it but for wartime hysteria. There were pressures on people looking for release and escape and they'd pay for anything – just to have a ball and spend the money they'd earned in defence plants or the Services. We were playing Broadway eight or ten weeks at a time, five shows a day, always queues round the theatre. It was ridiculous. We just weren't that good.'

The forties were a most important period of revolutionary change and trend setting. Perhaps no ten years before or since has produced so many good popular songs or so many bad.

During the decade the big dance bands, covering an immense range of jazz and pop styles, reached their peak and then went into decline. One of them, Glenn Miller's AEF Band, set so perfectly polished a standard that its influence has lasted until today.

In jazz the 'bop' revolution of the mid-forties similarly shaped a style that has lasted twenty years, while the New Orleans revival touched off the trad-modern warfare which bedevilled the music until the 1960s. 'They give us hell, so I give them hell,' said Louis Armstrong. The only point of agreement between the schools was that small groups were economic and big bands were not.

There was a revolution in pop singing too – as well as the first realization that folk singers (like Josh White, with his great success *John Henry*) were viable club and concert soloists. Before the 1940s most 'vocalists' were appendages to bands. Now increasingly they broke away and the era saw the first mass emergence of singers (no longer were they called 'crooners') as solo idols. The women who arrived included Peggy Lee, Lena Horne, Dinah Shore, Doris Day, Jo Stafford, Ella Fitzgerald, Vera Lynn and Anne Shelton: among the men were Dick Haymes, Perry Como, Nat King Cole – and, predominantly, Frank Sinatra. His sexier, more archly sentimental singing superseded the jollier style of Bing Crosby in the crucial vocal battle of the forties. It has been massively imitated ever since.

With Sinatra, hysteria was also scientifically harnessed for the first time to thrust a pop singer forward. At one of his early solo concerts a publicity man planted fifteen girls in the audience and told them to scream. They did; the legend of Swoonatra began; and the maternal instinct – or whatever it was – of women of all ages made him a legend in twelve months. For pop singers the screaming era began while The Beatles were getting born.

We're going to hang out the washing on the
Siegfried Line,
Have you any dirty washing, mother dear?

We'll meet again, don't know where, don't
know when,
But I know we'll meet again one sunny day.

The war dominated the songs of the forties for five years. There were virtually only two kinds of song manufactured by Tin Pan Alley. One was patriotic, ranging from the straight-faced to the comic – often anti-German, often cracking up the Anglo-American alliance. The other was more 'personal', the song of sentimental love; it was escapist, recalling snatched weekends and brief reunions, lamenting absence. It was as romantic as the more serious literature of the time and often as banal as the patriotic songs, though it seemed less so at the time.

The titles of the patriotic songs are almost all self-explanatory: 'Comin' In On A Wing And A Prayer'; 'Till the Lights of London Shine Again'; 'Victory Polka'; 'There'll Always Be An England'; 'Der Fuehrer's Face'; 'The White Cliffs of Dover'; 'This is the Army, Mister Jones'; 'My British Buddy'; 'Got Any Gum, Chum?'; 'Shine On Victory Moon'; 'Run Rabbit Run'; 'Silver Wings in the Moonlight'; 'When The Great New World Is Dawning'; 'Kiss Me Goodnight, Sergeant Major'; 'We Mustn't Miss The Last Bus Home'; 'We Don't Know Where We're Going Till We're There'; 'Goodnight, Good Neighbour'; 'Let The People Sing'.

The history of many of these songs was odd. Two which almost became alternative national anthems in Britain – 'Roll Out The Barrel' and 'White Cliffs of Dover' – were American in origin. 'There'll Always Be An England' was written *before* war broke out, in the phoney-peace spring of 1939, by Ross Parker and Hugh Charles. According to Parker (quoted in *Tin Pan Alley*, the memoirs of a song plugger called Eddie Rogers, which is a rich source book on pop characters) the music publisher Irwin Dash one day threw on to his desk a copy of the American paper *Variety* which showed 'God Bless America' at the top of the US best sellers. 'Listen Ross,' Dash said, 'if the American public will buy this hogwash, why don't you write a tune for Britain?' Parker's response sold two million records.

Some war songs were sung by both sides. The Eighth Army picked up 'Lilli Marlene' from the Germans, but before it finally got its English lyrics at least one writer refused to compose them. It would, he said, be collaborating with the enemy. The song helped to make Anne Shelton a star and it sold over a million sheet-music copies at a time when these, not records, were the vital statistic in pop music charts.

The Germans used 'We're Going To Hang Out the Washing on the Siegfried Line' in a different way. Britons sang it (and the Nazi propagandist Lord Haw Haw attacked it) until Dunkirk, when the BBC abruptly dropped it from their programmes. The Germans now developed a taste for it and it was used by Goebbels in a propaganda film with new words pitched in a mockingly minor key. Not until the victory advance of 1944 did the Allies bring it out of cold storage.

'Der Fuehrer's Face' was a safer kind of patriotic 'novelty' number. Spike Jones and his City Slickers, a comedy band which produced send-up parodies of songs like 'Chloe' and 'Cocktails for Two' and frequently won the 'King of Corn' title in American music polls, did a version of this which included raspberry-blowing, sieg-heiling and a background noise aping German band music. It sold 1½ million records.

The titles of the wartime songs of sentimental love – usually, in pop jargon, 'ballads' – speak just as clearly of the period which produced them; some of the lyrics could have applied equally well to peacetime situations, but the war gave them special overtones: 'That Lovely Weekend'; 'Home-coming Waltz'; 'I'll Be Home for Christmas'; 'I'll Close My Eyes'; 'I Wish That I Could Hide Inside This Letter'; 'No Love, No Nothin''; 'I Left My Heart at the Stage Door Canteen'; 'I'm Gonna Love That Guy'; 'Sunday, Monday and Always'; 'Ice Cold Katy (won't you marry the soldier); 'There's A Ship Rolling Home'; 'Shoo, Shoo Baby (your poppa's off to the seven seas)'; 'Sailor Who Are You Dreaming of Tonight'; 'Long Ago and Far Away'; 'Goodnight, Wherever You Are'; 'You'd Be So Nice to Come Home To'; 'Goodnight Sweetheart'; 'Spring Will Be a Little Late This Year'; 'Coming Home'; 'Try a Little Tenderness'; 'My Sister and I'; 'The Last Time I Saw Paris' (the last two might be called 'refugee' ballads).

Only occasionally did a piece with traces of the dry, brittle wit Rodgers and Hart had injected into songs before the war creep into popularity. 'They're Either Too Young or Too Old' was one example. And even the songs which seemed in the mainstream of the mood of the day often ran into trouble.

The opening lines of 'That Lovely Weekend', written by the bandleader Ted Heath and his wife Moira in 1941, went:

I haven't said thanks for that lovely weekend,
Those two days of heaven you helped me to spend.

It was a hit for both Vera Lynn and Dorothy Carless, but the song was banned in America by the major broadcasting companies. The lyric, they explained, was 'too risqué'. There was no indication anywhere in the song that the couple were married: it therefore implied a weekend of illicit love.

Britain retaliated in early 1944 when 'I Heard You Cried Last Night' was enjoying a huge success in the US. The BBC kept this off the air for a time because – in the words of a report at the time in the magazine *Melody Maker* – it 'suggested a man crying and this was not a good thought at the present time'.

If the introduction of patriotic songs stopped short when peace came, there was no respite in the flood of songs of escapism and aching sentiment. It seems, in retrospect, exactly right that 1944 should have been the year of Irving Berlin's 'White Christmas'. A song which epitomizes the extreme of the idealized romantic fallacy, it remains the biggest seller in pop history.

As the age of austerity succeeded the age of war the big hits retained their yearning, glittery romanticism: 'Now Is The Hour', 'So Tired' (with Russ Morgan's wah-wah trombone obbligato), 'My Foolish Heart' and 'My Mother's Day', written by a Briton, Billy Reid, which at the last count was the record most requested on *Housewives' Choice*.

With few exceptions the many songs I have mentioned are rarely sung now. But the forties did produce a library of quality songs which have become 'standards' – usually because jazz players have taken them up and used their themes as the basis for improvisation. Among them are 'Do Nothing Till You Hear From Me' and 'Don't Get Around Much Any More' (1940); 'Flamingo' and 'I'll Remember April' (1941); 'Paper Doll and 'That Old Black Magic' (1942); 'People Will Say We're in Love' and 'Surrey With The Fringe On Top' (1943); 'I'm Beginning To See the Light', 'Long Ago and Far Away' and 'Sentimental Journey' (1944); 'Laura' (1945); 'Stella by Starlight' and 'Tenderly' (1946); 'Almost Like Being In Love' (1947); and 'Baby, it's Cold Outside' (1948).

A, B, C, D, E, F, G, H, I got a gal in Kalamazoo,
Don't want to boast but I know she's the toast of
Kalamazoo.

Is your band good for dancing?
Definitely not. The greatest dance band in the
country is Lombardo.
(Stan Kenton in *Down Beat*, 1948)

The war was a great time for the meaty sound of big bands, jazz or sweet – and in those days the demarcation line between 'jazz' and 'commercial' bands was far less rigid. America had Ellington, Basie, Goodman, Harry James, the Dorseys, Bob Crosby, Jimmy Lunceford, Guy Lombardo, Artie Shaw, Glenn Miller (the last two abandoned civilian bands to lead Service ones) and dozens more. In Britain there were Service groups like the Squadronaires (based on a tight nucleus of ex-Ambrose musicians and playing a roaring pastiche of Bob Crosby-type dixieland) and the Skyrockets, plus a string of multi-toned civvy or part-civvy bands including Geraldo, Carl Barriteau, Eric Winstone, Joe Loss, Lew Stone, Oscar Rabin, Ambrose, George Elrick and Billy Cotton. A bevy of all-girl bands sprang up too, following the American lead, as the ranks of Archer Street were thinned out by the demands of the Services: Ivy Benson, Gloria Gaye and Blanche Coleman led three of them.

Dance band music was staple BBC fare. Nine broadcasts a week (*Tip Top Tunes* was the best known) were at one stage given to Geraldo, who had the best band outside the official Service orchestras, featuring great musicians like Harry Hayes and Leslie 'Jiver' Hutchinson, and as many as five supporting vocalists (Dorothy Carless, Doreen Villiers, Ruth Howard, Beryl Davis, Benny Lee, Johnny Green, Archie Lewis and Len Camber passed through his ranks).

To be allowed, as a teenager, to stay up late for the American Expeditionary Forces programmes (signature tune: Charlie Barnet's 'Skyliner') was the high point of my week – and in the latter half of 1944, units drawn from Glenn Miller's Services band (The Swing Shift, Strings With Wings) could be heard on the BBC practically every day. The BBC, indeed, had become almost enlightened. It even ran a weekly programme called *Radio Rhythm Club* which for five years featured regular groups led by Harry Parry, Buddy Featherstonehaugh and Duncan Whyte.

London, where I lived, was a good place for live concerts. One of the finest jazz performances I have ever heard was given by George Chisholm one Sunday afternoon playing alone in ill-fitting RAF uniform in front of the curtains at the old Stoll Theatre, Kingsway, while scene shifting went on backstage. There were plenty of tickets going for BBC band broadcasts – usually from an underground studio at the Paris Cinema, Lower Regent Street, where one bandleader appeared for a show during the flying bomb raids wearing carpet slippers. I even managed to get into an American camp near London to hear the full Miller orchestra of around fifty musicians.

Miller towered above his competitors. He best sums up the band sound of the forties. When he launched his civilian group in 1939 it took him only a year to become the world's No. 1 dance band, with his characteristic clarinet-led reed section and muted brass. The Services unit he brought to Europe in 1944 – conventional big-band brass and reeds plus massive string section – carried the formula for a jazz-tinged, but widely appealing, dance orchestra to its peak.

It included some wonderful musicians – Ray McKinley (drums), Mel Powell (piano) and Trigger Alpert (bass) – and his superb arrangements, played with crisp precision and attack by the brass, posed against the sweetness of strings and saxophones, renewed his reputation for perfection.

Miller died on December 15, 1944, when a plane taking him to Paris disappeared, but his influence is stamped on popular music. The tunes he played – 'American Patrol', 'Tuxedo Junction', 'Serenade in Blue', 'In the Mood', 'Chatanooga Choo-Choo', 'Kalamazoo' – were wildly successful in the 1940s (though too many were not then widely available on records) and scarcely sound dated today. His influence on modern leaders like Nelson Riddle and Paul Weston, and on composition and arrangement generally in popular music, is obvious. Ted Heath, who started the most brilliant British big band of the post-war period in 1945, says his ideal at the time was the discipline and power of Miller's orchestra.

Miller's achievement, however, was not enough to prevent the decline of the big bands once the war was over. Apart from the increasing economic problems of keeping large groups of musicians on the road, there was another reason for their demise. In the 1930s and early 1940s the swing bands played *for dancing* and won massive public acceptance: after 1945, with the harmonically revolutionary bop musicians gaining the ascendancy, big bands seemed increasingly not to want to bother with dancers. There were some odd happenings.

In America, Stan Kenton said he did not believe in playing for dancing and proclaimed of his 'progressive' jazz: 'I'll go back to playing red-light piano if my style of music is not accepted by the public.' In Britain, Ted Heath refused to play waltzes when he appeared at the Hammersmith Palais. But finally he had to take on a clutch of singers – Dickie Valentine, Lita Roza, Dennis Lotis – to survive.

Others were not so lucky, and as the dancers (Silvester style or jivers) began to turn to Latin-American and trad, and to limber up for the rock 'n' roll age, the bands crumbled.

For jazz the sound was already becoming, in the late 1940s, that of the 'combo' – the bop-orientated small group. The new style, which stressed more adventurous cross-rhythmic patterns and accents for the drums, and a whole new range of harmonic progressions for the horns, represented the most important and fruitful revolution to seize jazz: yet it was carried through with astonishing rapidity and thoroughness. Charlie Parker, Dizzy Gillespie, Miles Davis and Thelonious Monk replaced the school of Louis Armstrong as the new idols.

Bop changed the British jazz scene irrevocably too. Tito Burns, with Ronnie Scott and Tony Crombie, led one of the first bop-infected units in Britain. In the same year, 1948, I used to wake up in an RAF camp with the sound of Kenton's 'Artistry in Rhythm' on the early morning Tannoy. By the next year I was having to explain to my CO why a group of airmen had been discovered stolidly sitting in berets and dark glasses (the bop uniform made fashionable by the goatee-bearded Gillespie) listening to Parker's 'Cool Blues' in the hut where the station jazz club I was supposed to supervise met.

Traditional jazz, reviving in America quite early in the forties – veteran musicians like Kid Ory and Bunk Johnson, for whom new teeth had to be bought before he could play, were eagerly sought out – had not yet become a commercial proposition in Britain: but the first fruity sounds were coming from George Webb (and his Dixielanders), Humphrey Lyttelton and Freddy Randall.

Keep Betty Grable, Lamour and Turner,
She makes my heart a charcoal burner,

It's heaven when I embrace.
My Nancy with the laughing face.

Why do you whisper green grass,
Why tell the trees what ain't so,
Whispering grass the trees don't have to know.

There had been Bing Crosby, Al Jolson and a few others: but now the desire of singers, especially the women, to get out from under the shadow of the big bands became a stampede. As the forties unwound there emerged an army of competing star singers.

If Sinatra made it the fastest, then he, like the others, had to have some big hits with the band he belonged to before he could go solo. Crucial to him were 'I'll Never Smile Again', which he made with Tommy Dorsey's vocal group, the Pied Pipers, in 1940, 'There Are Such Things' and 'I'll Be Seeing You'. By 1944 he and another member of those 1940 Pied Pipers, Jo Stafford, were established so firmly that they were named top male and female singers by *Down Beat magazine.*

Sinatra's thin, anguished tones became *the* voice of the middle and late forties with a series of songs – 'Nancy', 'Embraceable You', 'I Couldn't Sleep A Wink Last Night', 'I Only Have Eyes For You' – for which the lachrymose string and woodwind backing provided by his musical director, Axel Stordhal, were vital. Rivals like Crosby, Dick Haymes and Tony Martin were left trailing: only Nat King Cole ultimately rose to challenge him.

But the voice of the *early* forties was female, not male – and for obvious reasons. Girl singers were substitute figures for the women the men had left behind. The husky, vibrato-laden voice of Vera Lynn, with her idiosyncratic catch-in-the-throat and her misty-eyed repertoire, dominated Services radios and gramophones. Any word of criticism against her would spring letters in the papers not only from privates but from puzzled lieutenant-colonels who wrote to say that their men dropped everything when 'Miss Lynn' came on the radio.

She learned her art while singing with the Ambrose Orchestra. So did the other big British name of the forties, Anne Shelton, who first sang with Ambrose when she was a schoolgirl of fourteen. She became Lynn's only significant rival for the 'Forces' Sweetheart' title, did the usual tours of Service camps at home and abroad, was asked for as guest singer by Glenn Miller, and sang duets with Bing Crosby at Rainbow Corner, the GI pleasure palace off Piccadilly Circus.

Despite her success with the Services, Vera Lynn was never accepted as was Shelton by the heavy students of pop-and-jazz form. She did not make the first four in the *Melody Maker* poll of 1944, which read: 1 Anne Shelton, 2 Doreen Villiers, 3 Beryl Davis, 4 Dorothy Carless.

In America, too, the girl singers had to make their mark with bands before the solo dash. In the early 1940s Lena Horne was with Charlie Barnet, Peggy Lee with Goodman ('Why Don't You Do Right?' in 1943 was her springboard to the top) and Doris Day with Les Brown (and His Band of Renown). A million-selling version of 'Sentimental Journey' put Day in the near-star category and sent her to join the other solo artists – Dinah Shore, Judy Garland and Ella Fitzgerald.

For the modern pop vocal group, the 1940s were a classic age, dominated by the kind of intense close harmony which went well with the big band sound. The version of 'Sunny Side of the Street' which the Pied Pipers made with Tommy Dorsey still sounds great today – and Miller had a group with his Services band called the Crew Chiefs. There were British imitations of course – including Geraldo's Three Boys and a Girl.

But the biggest groups, again, were those not attached to bands. The Ink Spots ('Whispering Grass', 'Bless You', 'Do I Worry?') were probably the most successful group voice of the 1940s – beating off the Mills Brothers ('Paper Doll') – though not, with their counter-tenor lead and their dark bass recitative, the most typical of its style. This was ingrained in groups like The Merry Macs ('I'm For Ever Blowing Bubbles') and The Andrews Sisters, whose recording of 'Don't Fence Me In' with Bing Crosby in 1943 was not only a million-seller but was said by psychiatrists to represent Service reaction against wartime discipline.

For thousands, though, the forties are probably still most vividly evoked by memories of that sub-fuzz of popular singing in what might be called Palm Court style (not to mention Ivor Novello tunes and shows like 'The Lisbon Story'). Its equivalent instrumentally was the music – vastly popular with elderly age groups – played by Sandy Macpherson on the cinema organ and by Albert Sandler's Palm Court Orchestra. Its typical protagonists were tenors (e.g. Josef Locke), preferably Irish; and its most typical song was the pseudo-operatic or Italian pastiche pop number.

You could see this baleful influence at work in the amateur talent contests of the day (another thumbprint of the forties). Any bellower offering 'Come Back to Sorrento' was certain to decimate the field.

The 1940s did lack one thing conspicuously: easily portable, unbreakable and freely available recording materials to capture its sounds on. But that, too, was remedied before the decade was out. In 1949 the first long-playing records, light and bendable, came out in America. Pop music as a money spinner has never looked back.

'Lilli Marlene': a song for all armies

10 SEPTEMBER 1967

Every three months a plump statement of accounts plops through the door of Norbert Schultze's house in West Berlin. It lists the not insubstantial sums in royalties which still accrue to him from 'Lilli Marlene' ('Lili Marleen' in the original German) for which he wrote the music.

In the first quarter of 1967 recordings of the song were played, according to the account, in Austria, Canada, Australia, Japan, New Zealand, the USA (several hundred dollars' worth of royalties), the United Arab Republic (a mere seventeen pfennigsworth), Holland, Spain, Belgium, Norway, France, Denmark, Greece, Italy, Sweden, Switzerland, Peru, West Germany, Britain and a score of other countries. 'Lilli Marlene' has lasted well. Twenty-five years ago it had a similar world-wide appeal, though Schultze was not at that time collecting the proceeds. Royalties from the song were withheld from him by the Custodians of Enemy Property in various countries for many years after the war, too. Only in the last fifteen years has he received the full rewards. He estimates the song has brought him in around £50,000 – and for this he owes a great deal to the combined offensives of the Afrika Korps and the Eighth Army. Before they stepped in, the odds against 'Lilli Marlene' becoming virtually the only memorable song to emerge from the 1939–45 war were ludicrously long.

The poem which inspired it was written, and half-forgotten, by a German soldier called Hans Leip in 1917. When, twenty years later, the words were set by Norbert Schultze to the tune we know – his was by no means the first version – the song was hawked around thirty German publishers before it was unenthusiastically accepted. The first record of it made in 1939 by Lale Andersen, daughter of a shipwright, born in Bremerhaven, sold seven hundred copies. Then it was forgotten.

Even when it burst out of obscurity, by accident, in 1941 it was nearly buried again. Goebbels hated it so much he ordered one of the two master matrices to be destroyed; the other, fortunately, was in London. The authorities in Britain weren't very keen on the song either. It was, after all, German. And the woman in the song seemed to be – well, some sort of trollop, wasn't she? So they said, anyway, maybe for propaganda reasons. But at least they didn't ban it – certainly not in the nice English version which they soon got written – unlike an American war music committee, which believed it would harm soldier morale.

Equally oddly, this is a song whose sense demands that it be sung by a man. Yet the notable recorded versions among the many dozen made of it have always been by women – from Lale Andersen, through Anne Shelton, Vera Lynn and Marlene Dietrich, to Connie Francis. Nobody associates it with Bing Crosby or Hank Snow or the Band of the Coldstream Guards or a pianist called Honky van Tonk, all of whom also recorded it.

Perhaps the biggest piece of luck for both Schultze and Lale Andersen was that her record of 'Lili Marleen' was lying with a few others in the dust of a cellar in Vienna during the summer of 1941. Radio stations for Axis propaganda were being set up, and in newly-captured Belgrade a studio was prepared to beam programmes to the *Panzerarmee Afrika*. The station had an announcer and a whole wad of news and propaganda – but no records. A soldier was sent to Vienna to find some.

There have been many claimants to the role of the war's most inspired pop-picker. Not even Schultze knows for sure who did him the favour – but he thinks it was a corporal named Kistenmacher. Frankly, Kistenmacher hadn't much choice in that cellar. He brought back to Belgrade the handful of records he found. An officer played them over and liked the bugle-call intro which had been written for Lale Andersen's 'Lili' by her accompanist. He thought it would be great as the station's close-down music. 'Without that bugle call,' says Schultze, 'my song would still be gathering dust.'

Radio Belgrade played it first on August 18, 1941. Within a week there were several thousand requests (demands, rather) from German soldiers in North Africa for it to be played again. Soon it became a fixture on Radio Belgrade at 9.55 p.m. – the last record of the night. (Goebbels might not care for its sentiments or its sentiment, but even he wouldn't push such a potent morale-builder off the air. He attempted to substitute a rousing military band version for the soft and haunting air which Lale Andersen sang, but this was greeted with derision and threats by the troops). Once established, the original recording was played nightly – often twice nightly – on Radio Belgrade, until the last stages of the war. On only three nights did it fail to appear – immediately following the smashing of the German armies at Stalingrad, when Goebbels banned entertainment of any sort. During the three years of its greatest popularity (1941–4) a dozen German radio stations were playing it up to thirty times a day, especially for Nazi 'victory' broadcasts.

But, ironically, the whole world was soon singing it. Within a year it had become the Second World War's classic. The Eighth Army quickly picked it up in the Western Desert, partly from their radios, partly from Axis prisoners. It had become a song for marching to, a song for sitting down to – the property of virtually every nation engaged in the war. From German soldiers, Lale Andersen received an estimated one million fan letters, usually addressed to 'Lili Marleen', during the first year or so after the song crept on to the air. Versions of it were written in many languages.

The first verse in the German version, roughly translated, went: 'In front of the barracks, before the heavy gate, there stood a lamp-post, and it still stands there. Let's hope we meet again there and stand beneath the lamp as we used to do, Lili Marleen.' It went on: 'Our two shadows melted into one. Everyone could see from that how deeply in love we were . . .' and so on.

The message was given an idiosyncratic twist by every nation which provided lyrics. For the Italians, one verse (undiscoverable in the original) began 'Give me a rose, and press it to my heart'. The French ('*Et dans la nuit sombre Nos corps enlacés*') disguised nothing. The English went squarely down the middle:

Underneath the lantern
By the barrack gate,
Darling I remember
The way you used to wait:
'Twas there that you whispered
tenderly,
That you loved me,
You'd always be
My Lilli of the lamplight
My own Lilli Marlene.

The man who wrote those words, Tommie Connor, is a lyricist who has had around three thousand songs published. 'I Saw Mummy Kissing Santa Claus', 'It's My Mother's Birthday Today', 'Who's Taking You Home Tonight?' and 'Under The Spreading Chestnut Tree' were some of them. '"Lilli Marlene" is far from my favourite song,' he said in the summer of 1967. 'Frankly, I took it as a work of propaganda. I prefer songs that come from my own experience – like "The Little Boy That Santa Claus Forgot."

'I was rung up in 1942 and told that the BBC and the Government were desperate for a lyric that would go to the hearts of people. There had been a lot of controversy over the song, which was being sung out in the desert to amateurish lyrics which were, to put it bluntly, dirty and risqué. I knew about the German version, but I couldn't use that. Wasn't it all about a young prostitute who wanted to give as much for her country as the soldiers – so she gave her body. Can you imagine that in English?

'I had to write a song imagining the girl was a daughter, a mother, sister or sweetheart – a song that wouldn't offend the hearts and morals of people. Honestly, I was stumped – so I said a prayer, and the lyric was finished in twenty-five minutes. Anne Shelton made the first record of it in Britain, and it sold a million.'

Parodies of the song abounded in every language, as Tommie Connor, and every soldier in the Western Desert, well knew. These were, of course, the true ballads of the war, usually cynical in tone, and often bawdy. Like most ballads, they were great morale-builders. The official line, which wants slop and sentiment and instant patriotism, rarely hits the true feeling of soldiers at war. One desert version of 'Lili' had a refrain which went 'We're off to bomb Benghazi, we're off to bomb B.G.', but the best known emerged after the Desert War when the Eighth Army, fighting a slow, foul and bitter war in Italy, heard a rumour that a woman politician back in England had referred to them as 'D-Day Dodgers'. The words which expressed their reaction began:

We're the D-Day Dodgers, out in Italy –
Always on the vino, always on the spree.
Eighth Army scroungers and their tanks,
We live in Rome, among the Yanks.
We are the D-Day Dodgers, way out in Italy.

There were far more sombre overtones to other parodies, however. In Denmark and Norway one ran: 'In front of the barracks, beside the heavy gate, there stands the lamp-post, but now it is too late. Who is it I see hanging there? A little man, with wayward hair. You know, Lili Marleen, you know, Lili Marleen.'

In all such parody versions, 'Lilli Marlene' was the undoubted successor to 'Mademoiselle from Armentières'. But it was the straight version which, along with the carol, 'Silent Night', was heard along *both* front lines as the Germans and the men of the Eighth Army wearily faced each other across the mud and snow of Italy at Christmas, 1943. It was the same version which, some time later, WAAFs near London were forbidden to sing within earshot of German POWs, because it might lead to fraternization.

About 250 women like to think they were the original Lili Marleen, according to Hans Leip, who wrote the original poem. He was a fusilier in the Kaiser's army, and while he was on an officers' course in Berlin he got involved with two girls.

One was Lili (real name Betty, the greengrocer's daughter downstairs), the other Marleen, a doctor's daughter whom he picked up in an art gallery. Lili was really a friend's girl, but one night on his way to sentry duty she begged him 'Stay, stay.' With Marleen, a part-time nurse, he was much more involved.

On the night of Lili's invitation, Leip was on guard duty. It was rainy, the street lamp glowed on the wet pavement. Then Marleen passed by, in feather boa. She said 'Bye-bye, so long.' Later, on the hard iron bed of the guardroom, Leip wrote his poem.

'My thoughts clung anxiously to the forms of the two girls, as though one were not enough to engage fate to bring me safely home,' he has said. 'Their names could no longer be coupled together with an "and" – they melted into one, not too shapely, as a pleasure and pain.'

The poem that Leip wrote is a sad, touching piece; 'a private little love-song', he calls it. Why the general idea emerged that the woman was a prostitute (which is the least fantastic of several versions of the genesis of the 'Lili' original) is unclear. Was the notion encouraged by Allied propagandists who instinctively disliked the notion of a German song becoming all the rage?

Leip is mystified that the idea should have taken root. 'They were both very proper girls,' he says. And his verses are a straightforward love story about the sadness of parting in wartime, and the last stanza is metaphysical in tone. The man sees himself dead ('in earthly depths, my dear') and returning to meet the girl under the lamp as a ghost. In 1917 there was no literary mystery. Leip went to the front and never saw the girls again. The poem was, ultimately, published in an anthology of Leip's works. Sales were modest.

Norbert Schultze first heard about 'Lili Marleen' in 1938. He was a young composer of light music making his way in Berlin.

He was working on his first movie score (*Moroccan Romance*). He had recently had his children's opera, *Black Peter*, performed. A tenor in the chorus asked Schultze to turn out some songs for his radio jobs – and handed over the Leip book. Schultze set ten of the poems to music, but the tenor didn't like 'Lili Marleen'. 'Today he is still very angry not to have sung it,' says Schultze, who today is an established composer, well-preserved, looking sixtyish, with a shock of grey hair. So he gave it one day to Lale Andersen, whom he had known around the cabarets of Berlin and Munich for several years. 'In those days she had a dreary, moaning voice. But she looked marvellous. Blonde hair, white sweater, white teeth. I liked her.'

Lale Andersen didn't care much for Schultze's work either. She already had another composer's version of 'Lili Marleen' in her repertoire. But she sang both versions in clubs to see how they went, and when audiences preferred the marching rhythm of Schultze's tune, she stuck to that. She sang it once on Radio Cologne in 1939, then put the song on record – the first she had ever made. But in Hitler's Germany, sentiment demanded much more martial, nationalistic, rabble-rousing airs. 'Lili Marleen' quietly sank out of sight.

But if his tune was quickly forgotten, then Schultze was not. Unknown to him, he had been placed on the Nazi list of creative artists who would be excused military service. They were needed to hymn the achievements of the New Order at war. Towards the end of 1939 he received his first commission: the music for *Baptism of Fire*, a propaganda documentary about the rape of Poland.

'For the first time,' Schultze recalls, 'I saw the horror of war. The bombing of Warsaw, the holes in the houses. I thought, my God, I feel sorry for these people. What can I write? I told the Air Ministry people how I felt and they said they felt the same. But they said there would be a voice coming out of heaven saying "For all this misery, all this horror, you will have to bear responsibility one day, Mr Chamberlain". I thought that only a solemn march like *Eroica* would do. So that's what I wrote.'

Schultze, richer by £150 for his first propaganda score, was now launched on his wartime career. Soon Hitler wanted a song about the new enemy: Schultze turned out 'Bomben auf Engelland'. In the next four years or so he wrote twenty-five war songs to order – 'Songs of the Nation', as the Germans called them – including 'Panzer rollen in Afrika vor'.

In 1941, when the demand was for a song to go with total war on Russia, Schultze turned out 'Fuhrer Befiehl' – with Goebbels' help. He was summoned, along with another composer, Hans Neil, to play over their competing versions in the Air Ministry building, which still stands near the grass-covered bunker where Hitler died in the wasteland of the Potsdamer Platz, hard by the Berlin Wall on the Eastern side. Goebbels preferred Schultze's song, but wanted to improve on it.

'He banged his hands on the piano and shouted "It will *go like this*",' says Schultze. 'He punched out a new ending – much more military. I had to say it was better.'

Beside all this, the sudden success of 'Lili Marleen' in late 1941 seemed to the Nazi bosses, and even to Schultze, almost incidental. But it impressed Rommel enough for him to send over an officer, laden with boxes of coffee brandy, to see Schultze. Could he compose a song for Rommel? 'I could scarcely refuse,' says Schultze. The result, recorded by the Luftwaffe orchestra, was called 'Forward with Rommel'. 'But by the time I'd finished it, Rommel was going backwards, so it was never used.'

Schultze knew nothing about the resurgence of 'Lili Marleen' until friends told him it was being played on Radio Belgrade. The first that Lale Andersen knew about it was when she began to receive letters addressed to Lili Marleen, Radio Belgrade, Berlin, Germany. She had been singing, relatively unsensationally, in German clubs. Suddenly, everyone wanted her – and if the troops couldn't get her, they settled for Schultze and his second wife, Iva Vanya, the Bulgarian-born actress he married in 1941.

'I made some money from the record,' says Lale Andersen, 'but my life didn't change much because of the war. I had the whole world before me, but I couldn't enjoy it.' Her life, in fact, swiftly changed for the worse. Goebbels became very interested in the woman who meant so much to the Afrika Korps and the Eighth Army, who sang a song of which he disapproved strongly. He discovered that before the war she had acted in a play in Zurich directed by Rolf Liebermann, a Jew. She seemed still to be friendly with Liebermann, who was still in Switzerland. So though she sang for troops in Germany and other occupied countries, beady eyes were watching her.

In 1942, she travelled to Italy to sing to wounded German soldiers and was unwise enough to write to Liebermann asking for the addresses of people who might help her get back to Zurich, via Milan. The Gestapo intercepted the letter and she was brought back to Berlin. 'They told me it was the end of my career, that I would be sent away to a camp. The night after that interview there were three air raids and I thought, I'll finish the whole thing. I took all the sleeping pills I had. It was three weeks before I knew anything again, and I expected the Gestapo to kill me. But a British broadcast saved me.

'The BBC put out a report that I'd been taken to a concentration camp and had died. Goebbels saw it as a golden opportunity to prove that the English radio told lies. He needed me alive. He put out a broadcast that I wasn't dead, but that I'd been very ill, that I wouldn't sing again for a long time. So they didn't send me to a camp. Instead I had to report to the Gestapo twice a week.'

Lale Andersen stayed in Berlin until 1944. The Gestapo seemed slowly to lose interest in her. One night she slipped away to Langeroog, a small island in the North Sea where her grandparents lived. There she remained until the war was nearly over.

For Lale Andersen, the end of the war meant the resumption of a career which, though never world-shattering, was underwritten by her wartime fame. In 1945 the British Forces Network in Germany invited her to sing at the Musikhalle in Hamburg. There followed years of tours in Europe, America, Britain; a film based on the song, which featured Lale in 1952; a steady flow of recordings of songs which today sound strangely outdated.

In the spring of 1967 Lale Andersen was back in Hamburg's Musikhalle, still slim and blonde, with pink mink and dark glasses, in her fifties, on her final farewell tour. She sang 'Lili Marleen' of course – in a sad sort of whine introducing it as 'my fateful song' – to an audience of the faithful, very middle-aged, five hundred in a hall that can seat two thousand. The past seemed alive for them. After almost every number, someone rushed on stage to give her flowers.

'Five thousand, ten thousand, twenty thousand times I have sung it,' she said afterwards. 'Who knows! I am never tired of it. The lyric is never routine. It is too strong and too good.'

For the other two people who created the most popular song in German history, peace was rather different. Hans Leip, still a poet and novelist, was living in Switzerland – and was in the Tyrol when Eisenhower visited US troops there in 1945. He asked to see Leip one evening. Leip says he was asleep at the time – according to the locals, he had been going to bed before ten for years to avoid having to listen to 'Lili Marleen' on Radio Belgrade.

Eisenhower, Leip says, ordered that he was not to be disturbed, 'because he's the only German who has given pleasure to the entire world during the war'.

Norbert Schultze and his wife were trapped in Berlin as the Russians blasted their way into it. Sometimes he hid in attics; occasionally he sang with his wife at Russian concerts; twice he was pushed into a detention camp. Finally they managed to move to the American Zone of Berlin, where they began entertaining at officers' clubs. In December, 1945, an officer invited them to come and sing 'Lili' at a dinner which Montgomery was attending. The officer said Montgomery had told them he had never heard 'Lili Marleen' or known that the soldiers sang it. He wanted to hear the song from the composer.

'So Iva and I went. They'd organized a whole floor show. Montgomery said he didn't want the floor show. He was old and wanted to go to bed early. But "Lili Marleen" – that he would hear. So we sang it. In French, German, English. I can still see him sitting there. Perhaps he thought of all that this song meant. But it seemed to make no impression on him. He clapped, got up, and went away.

'Later in the evening a British war correspondent came up and asked me hadn't I written "Bombs on England"? Next day there were newspaper reports about how I had wormed my way in to sing in front of Montgomery. They were very anti, very terrible stories. I was called up to the OSS office and told I was on the black list. I was not to be allowed to perform.'

For two years Schultze worked as a labourer – on building sites, in gardens. In 1948 he managed to get away from Berlin to his home town, Brunswick, and slowly picked up the threads of being a composer again. He was officially 'denazified' though even today Berlin papers call him a 'Nazi composer'. He is now modestly successful, writing operas, film and television music.

'I can't,' said Schultze in 1967, 'regret that I wrote all those songs. It was the time that governed it, not me. Other people shot. I made songs. Our enemy in those days was England. What was I supposed to do? I composed with a clear conscience. I felt obliged to do something for the war. I write counterpoint and I know nothing about politics. I told the court in 1950: either one is a pacifist or one isn't. If not, you have a duty to your country. Didn't other composers do similar things for *their* countries?

'But I can understand how people feel today. They remember they had to sit in shelters and listen to my marches on the radio and now they say "My God, that is the man who composed all those bloody marches".

'They don't sing "Lili Marleen" anywhere much in Germany today . . . When did we last sing it, Iva? Maybe 1951? It's all past. In Germany it's associated with the war, and it's all unpleasant. Maybe a pianist in a bar will play it around one in the morning when a group of old officers full of beer demand it – but he hates it.'

INDEX

Main references are indicated in bold type